'*The Ecological University* really is *the* book of o
It distils and much advances the essence of a
university that's been developing in Ron Bar
powerful effort'.

Søren S.E. Bengtsen, *Associate Professor, Centre for Teaching Development and Digital Media, and Deputy Director, Centre for Higher Education Futures, Aarhus University, Denmark.*

'At a time where higher education everywhere is facing calls for increased social responsibility and change comes Ron Barnett's visionary proposal for the Ecological University. Don't just read this, put it into action!'

Professor Budd Hall, *Co-Chair, UNESCO Chair in Community-Based Research and Social Responsibility in Higher Education and Professor of Community Development, University of Victoria, Canada*

'This is a timely and important new book by one of the world's preeminent scholars in higher education. Ron Barnett does not shy away from some of the most pressing problems we face on this planet. The work of constructing feasible utopias involves, as he puts it, "the forging of new relationships between the university, humanity and the world". To this imposing task, Barnett brings a sharp philosophical eye, an openness to new ideas, and a deep sense of ethical commitment. The result is a robust but readable account of the ecological university, a vision that is both realistic and hopeful.'

Peter Roberts, *Professor of Education, University of Canterbury, New Zealand*

'The position of universities within our society has never been simultaneously more vulnerable nor important. We are under siege from the perfect storm of reduced public finances, the rise of an anti-intellectualist political and populist culture and the dominance of a neoliberal order that requires a financial justification for knowledge advancement rather than the social, environment or cultural benefits that may develop. How should we respond? In this outstanding volume, Ron Barnett presents us with a path forward with the Ecological University. Beyond the traditional use of the term, Barnett outlines how the university is involved in a range of ecologies, from the social and cultural, to the political and environmental. The role of university, Barnett argues, is to apply an ecological philosophy to lead, strengthening and enhance these complex relationships – a message we should be inspired and guided by – before it is too late. The Ecological University may be utopian, but it is certainly feasible.'

James Arvanitakis, *Dean of the Graduate Research School, Western Sydney University, Australia and Academic Fellow at the Australia India Institute and Centre for Policy Development, Australia*

'Ron Barnett's odyssey to understand the core purposes rather than surface features of the university has taken more than a quarter of the century, and the dialogue has been as much with himself as us, his many readers. His latest book *The Ecological University* is much more than the latest adventure in his odyssey. It may read like a culmination, a gathering, but his thesis – now and always – is that the university is necessarily an unfinished project. There can be no homecoming to Ithaca.

'In this book he argues that the university is situated in seven ecosystems, of which the economy is only one (despite the dominant neoliberal discourse that has suborned so many politicians, scholars and even universities themselves). It is from these complex and fluid situations that the Ecological University has emerged, and which free it from imagined constraints and offer it endlessly open possibilities.'

Sir Peter Scott, *Emeritus Professor of Higher Education Studies,*
UCL Institute of Education, UK

'Ron Barnett's latest book is framed within an ecological parlance of inquiry that accounts for the university on the basis of assemblages, engagements, reflections and sightings. Intelligently and passionately, he justifies the ecological university as a curricular space that is professionally and reflexively engaged within the world in relation to striated and smooth encounters.'

Yusef Waghid, *Distinguished Professor of Philosophy of Education*
at Stellenbosch University, South Africa

'This is a deeply thoughtful and surprisingly optimistic celebration of the possibilities inherent within our universities from one of our most important theorists of higher education.

'In this timely book Ron Barnett offers a compelling "eco-philosophy of the university". Countering the narratives in which universities have become unduly wedded to instrumental reason, Barnett offers a utopian vision of the university, one which attends to the more complex ecology of the university – the engaged and critical university with a deep sense of responsibility to foster the open circulation of ideas.

'Barnett reminds us that the university is most needed at a moment when it is in peril. This is essential reading for those who care about the future of our universities.'

Judith Squires, *University of Bristol, UK*

'*The Ecological University: A Feasible Utopia* is a hugely important book. It presents a refreshing and hopeful view of higher education that reminds us of the importance of lifting our heads and looking beyond our own narrow measures of institutional performance to the bigger picture. It encourages us to look to the evolution of our universities whilst recognising the influence and fluidity of the ecosystems around us, and reminds us of our duty to work in harmony with them, to support them, and to nurture them.

'The message of this book is clear – it is time for universities to step up, and it is time for us to come together to redress the imbalance that our focus on the "economic" ecosystem has caused. We must restore faith in experts and in the role that universities play in our society. This book should be compulsory reading for anyone who is reluctant to accept the new "post-truth" reality that we now find ourselves facing.'

Joy Carter, *Vice Chancellor, University of Winchester, UK*

'At a time when higher education's purpose within the wider society is being questioned and in many ways diminished, there is a pressing need for new conceptions of the nature and purpose of the university. Ronald Barnett's highly original proposal that we rethink the university as an ecological university is timely, felicitous, and profound. Conceiving the 21st century university as embedded in a network of ecosystems reflects the increasing complexity of universities and their interconnectedness with multiple aspects of the social, cultural, and material worlds. This is essential reading for understanding the nature and purpose of the 21st century university.'

David S. Owen, *Professor of Philosophy, University of Louisville, USA*

THE ECOLOGICAL UNIVERSITY

Universities continue to expand, bringing considerable debate about their purposes and relationship to the world. In *The Ecological University*, Ronald Barnett argues that universities are falling short of their potential and responsibilities in an ever-changing and challenging environment.

This book centres on the idea that the expansion of higher education has opened new spaces and possibilities. The university is interconnected with a number of ecosystems: knowledge, social institutions, persons, the economy, learning, culture and the natural environment. These seven ecosystems of the university are all fragile and in order to advance and develop them universities need to engage with each one.

By looking at matters such as the challenges of learning, professional life and research and inquiry, this book outlines just what it could mean for higher education institutions to understand and realize themselves as exemplars of the ecological university. With bold and original insights and practical principles for development, this radical and transformative book is essential reading for university leaders and administrators, academics, students and all interested in the future of the university.

Ronald Barnett is Emeritus Professor of Higher Education at University College London Institute of Education, UK. He has spent a lifetime in advancing a philosophy of higher education, and *The Ecological University: A Feasible Utopia* represents the culmination of that project.

For Janey,

With very best wishes
in & for all things,

Ron.

June 2019

THE ECOLOGICAL UNIVERSITY

A Feasible Utopia

Ronald Barnett

Routledge
Taylor & Francis Group
LONDON AND NEW YORK

First published 2018
by Routledge
2 Park Square, Milton Park, Abingdon, Oxon OX14 4RN

and by Routledge
711 Third Avenue, New York, NY 10017

Routledge is an imprint of the Taylor & Francis Group, an informa business

© 2018 Ronald Barnett

The right of Ronald Barnett to be identified as author of this work has been asserted by him in accordance with sections 77 and 78 of the Copyright, Designs and Patents Act 1988.

All rights reserved. No part of this book may be reprinted or reproduced or utilized in any form or by any electronic, mechanical, or other means, now known or hereafter invented, including photocopying and recording, or in any information storage or retrieval system, without permission in writing from the publishers.

Trademark notice: Product or corporate names may be trademarks or registered trademarks, and are used only for identification and explanation without intent to infringe.

British Library Cataloguing in Publication Data
A catalogue record for this book is available from the British Library.

Library of Congress Cataloging-in-Publication Data
A catalog record for this book has been requested

ISBN: 978-1-138-72072-5 (hbk)
ISBN: 978-1-138-72076-3 (pbk)
ISBN: 978-1-315-19489-9 (ebk)

Typeset in Bembo and Stone Sans
by Florence Production Ltd, Stoodleigh, Devon, UK
Printed and bound by CPI Group (UK) Ltd, Croydon, CR0 4YY

To the memory of Roy Bhaskar (1944–2014), a good friend and from whom I learnt so much.

Liberal institutions immediately cease to be liberal as soon as they are attained . . . One knows, indeed, what they bring about: they undermine the will to power . . . Our institutions are no longer fit for anything: everyone is unanimous about that. But the fault lies not in them but in us.

          Friedrich Nietzsche, *Twilight of the Idols*
               (2003/1889: 103–104)

CONTENTS

Acknowledgements — *xii*
    Introduction: The coming of the ecological university — 1

PART I
The idea of the ecological — **15**
1 The idea of ecology — 17
2 Assembling the pieces — 29
3 Beyond sustainability — 42
4 Seven ecosystems — 55
    Interlude: A social ecology of the university — 69

PART II
The ecological university — **72**
5 The eco-university: principles and maxims — 73
6 Ecological inquiry — 86
7 Beyond liquid learning to the ecological learner — 99
8 Sightings of an ecological curriculum — 113
9 Towards an ecological professionalism — 126
10 Engaging the world — 141

PART III
Ecological audit — **155**
11 The idea of the ecological university: an audit — 157
12 A university for the whole Earth — 170
    Coda: A revolution in the offing? — 182

Bibliography — *185*
Subject index — *202*
Name index — *210*

ACKNOWLEDGEMENTS

I would much like to acknowledge the kindness of a number of academic friends who have so generously read and commented on the manuscript of this book, namely Søren Bengtsen, Jan MacArthur, Sharon Rider, Hugh Starkey and Yusef Waghid. I fear I have not done justice to all their wise and shrewd insights, which really deserve a further book, but have acted as an enormous source of energy, support and suggestion. I remain, of course, entirely responsible for any errors and omissions.

Book writing is a strange business and I am certainly among those writers whose efforts are much sustained by the support of colleagues. Among those whose conversations I have enjoyed during the writing of this book are Denise Batchelor, David Beckett, Philip Booth, Peter Boshier, John Brennan, Francis Campbell, Joy Carter, John Charmley, Lorenzo Cini, Brandon Conlon, Ruth Finnegan, Jude Fransman, Amanda Fulford, Dilly Fung, Paul Gibbs, Beena Giridharan, Carolina Guzmán-Valenzuela, Alison James, Norman Jackson, Thomas Karlsohn, Ruth Kelly, Maryann Kernan, Manja Klemenčič, Patricia Leighton, Lorraine Ling, Peter Ling, Bruce Macfarlane, Simon Marginson, Karl Maton, Nick Maxwell, Jon Nixon, Michael Peters, Gerald Pillay, Paul O'Prey, Michael Reiss, Peter Scott, Robert Stratford, Paul Temple, Geoff Whitty and Marilyn Taylor.

I acknowledge the following permissions to draw on two of my academic papers:

- 'The Coming of the Ecological Learner', Chapter 2, pp. 9–20, in P Tynjala, M-L Stenstrom and M Saarnivaara (eds) (2012) *Transitions and Transformations in Learning and Education*. Dordrecht: Springer.
- 'Towards an Ecological Professionalism', Chapter 2, pp. 29–41, in C Sugrue and T Dyrdal Solbrekke (eds) (2011) *Professional Responsibility: New Horizons of Praxis*. London and New York: Routledge.

Acknowledgements **xiii**

I have been fortunate to have been able to road-test some of the thinking here via invited talks at various seminars and conferences, including:

- Selwyn College, University of Cambridge, UK
- University of Winchester, UK
- Durban University of Technology, South Africa
- Higher Education Learning and Teaching Association of Southern Africa (HELTASA) Conference, Stellenbosch, South Africa
- Association for Academic Language and Learning (AALL) Conference, Wollongong, Australia
- Scholarship of Teaching and Learning (SoTL) Conference, Stellenbosch, South Africa
- São Paulo State University, Brazil
- Universidad de Buenos Aires, Argentina
- Kwantlen Polytechnic University, Canada
- Newcastle College and Literary and Philosophical Society, Newcastle upon Tyne, UK
- Philosophy of Education Society of Australasia Annual Conference, Fiji
- Uppsala University, Sweden
- Middlesex University, UK
- Institute of Educational Studies, Kaunas, Lithuania
- Charles Sturt University, Australia
- University of Surrey, UK
- Harper Adams University, UK
- Consortium of Higher Education Researchers (CHER) Conference, Queens' College, University of Cambridge, UK
- Universidad Santiago de Cali, Colombia
- Forum on University Innovation, Vigo, Spain.

I am also very grateful for the support I have received from the publishers, Routledge, since putting forward the idea for this book, especially from Anna Clarkson and Sarah Tuckwell and through the comments of the anonymous reviewers of the proposal that led to this book.

Lastly, I would like to mention and acknowledge the very deep support and encouragement I received from Roy Bhaskar, not only for this particular book (and to whom it is dedicated), but for his support for my book-writing efforts over recent years and for the friendship I was privileged to enjoy. I miss our curry suppers, Roy. Rest in much-deserved peace.

INTRODUCTION

The coming of the ecological university

The ecological university is upon us. It is just ahead of us, and is here even now, having already come among us. But we do not see it, being blind to its presence. Its manifestations are unrecognized, so blinkered are we by the dominant ideologies of our age, in which much of what matters in higher education is that which generates income and secures markets, positioning in world rankings and student satisfaction. But what might be meant here by 'ecological' and by 'the ecological university'? What are and what could be its manifestations? And what are the possibilities of its much fuller realization? I shall try to offer answers to all of these questions in this book.

These matters are dauntingly large. The very term 'ecology' hints at the character of the situation. The concept of ecology points in part to interconnectedness, and this is crucial to our story here, but interconnectedness ultimately has no end. And so it is with the university, it being increasingly interconnected with so many facets of the world, human and non-human. This is a story without end. Further, the concept of ecology has been given extensive examination and across many disciplines and traditions, within the academic world and well beyond. There are considerable challenges ahead simply to find a sure path through and to assemble the material to hand. But we can perhaps make a start.

This book has something of an assertive tone due to the pressing nature of the task in hand. It is not that the university is 'in crisis' or is 'in ruins', but rather that the university is falling woefully short of its responsibilities *and* its possibilities in the world. Urgency attaches to this situation, for the gap between the way the world is and the potential of the university to play its part in and for the world, will continue to widen unless the matter is swiftly addressed.

Spaces – presently closing and possibly opening

In much of the world, universities are on a cusp, with malign forces coming their way. Signs are apparent of their being corralled into limited and mainly economic roles, or of being 'negatively positioned' (Marginson, 2017); or being variously repudiated as harbingers of 'experts' (now sometimes disparaged); or seen as purveyors of noxious frameworks (evolutionary theory, ideas of sustainability, alternative perspectives on economics or even just defenders of the humanities); or their international students being down-valued (or worse); or their being diminished as centres of debate and dissent (and their academics even imprisoned). It may even be felt, so Peter Scott has suggested (as reported in *University World News*, March 2017), that the academy has 'ended up on the "wrong side" of history'.

There is a paradox here: the university is most needed at a moment when it is in peril. This is a situation of reinforcing mutual destruction: the more that the university presents as a source of open debate, and proliferating and contending (and critical) frameworks of understanding, and seeks to intervene in the world, the more it is subject to counter-forces that would bend it to other purposes or curtail its functioning. *But*, except for a very few instances, we are not quite at the end of the university; perhaps even to the contrary. Just possibly, the inner spaces of the university, for inquiry, thought, reflection, debate and reasoned action, provide resources that enable much more than its survival in a troubled – and troubling – world. The public realm may be splitting into divided – and hostile and mutually incomprehending – publics, plural. In this milieu, new opportunities may be opening for the university, to play a part in engaging with, and in helping to enlarge, those public spheres.

There is no certainty that such spaces will be accorded to universities, but it is a possibility. However, realizing that possibility calls for a revolution in universities, to imagine themselves anew and to forge new relationships with the whole world, the whole Earth, indeed. This would amount to a widening of the university, to reconceive its place anew and to help in advancing the public realm. This prospect calls for the ecological university.

Admittedly, there is here – in the idea of the ecological university – a profession of faith in the university, not so much as it is now but as it could be. The idea of the ecological university, indeed, reflects 'the exorbitant demand of infinite responsibility' (Critchley, 2008: 40). And there is much to be done in working out, in imagining feasible possibilities for the university, work that must go on continuously. After all, what is at issue here is the forging of new relationships between the university, humanity and the world (in its fullest sense).

A double undermining – and new hope

As is well enough known, the contemporary university owes much to the formation of universities in mediaeval Europe. Certainly, those universities had predecessors in ancient Egypt, Persia, India and China, but the relevant history here is relatively recent, with the birth of the modern university at the beginning of the eighteenth century. That birth was accompanied by a welter of writings on the very idea of the university, writings that were predominantly philosophical in character. Kant,

Schleiermacher, Fichte and Schelling were among the philosophers who spelt out an idea of the university, an idea that rested on reason (Kweik, 2006). Over the next 150 years, that literature steadily accumulated, with many volumes bearing the title 'the idea of the university' or 'the concept of the university' or, more recently, 'the idea of higher education', or variations on the theme. This literature, through Newman and on through Jaspers and Ortega y Gasset, to more recent writers such as Derrida and MacIntyre, has come – we can fairly say – to constitute a Great Tradition that demands to be consulted by anyone interested in the idea of the university.[1]

Recently, however, voices have been raised suggesting, in effect, that that whole lineage cannot be continued, at least not straightforwardly. Two texts stand out in this regard, by Lyotard and Readings. For Lyotard (1984), the condition of 'knowledge' was that the large concepts of modernity – knowledge itself, but we may add others such as truth, reason and critique – had crumbled. The new 'postmodernism' was characterized by an 'incredulity towards metanarratives' (p. xxiv) and such large concepts had dissolved in the wake of contending perspectives. In turn, the university had no alternative but to adopt a stance of 'performativity' (p. 48). All that counted was what worked, very narrowly construed. For Readings (1997), the university was 'a ruined institution' (p. 19), having lost its connections with reason, the nation state and culture. It could dress itself up only in vapid categories of 'excellence' (ch. 4) and (we may add) being 'world-class'. All that was left was the university as a space of 'dissensus' (ch. 12) in which contending voices might have their say.

Together, these two views constitute extreme readings of a *double undermining* that the university has faced over the last half-century or more:[2] on the one hand, an elaboration of its *epistemological undermining*, with the loss of a secure account of knowledge and reason (Lyotard); and on the other, of its *social undermining*, the university having lost a clear legitimacy as a valued institution in society (Readings). Together, these two readings amount to a dismal account of the university, both as an idea and as an institution.

The question that those texts – and many others of the same ilk – have bequeathed is stark: can an account of the university in the twentieth century be provided that doesn't succumb to such hopelessness? 'Hopelessness' is meant literally here, as being devoid of hope. Is it possible, in other words, to come forward with an idea of the university that has a measure of feasibility, anchored in the real world, and yet is expressive of some hope and a due – if limited – measure of optimism? To corral a phrasing from Habermas (2010a:18), is it possible – in relation to the university at least – 'to mobilize modern reason against the defeatism lurking within it'? These are questions that drive this book. I seek to offer an idea of the university that is at once critical of the way the university has become across much of the world, and yet is positive, has some substance to it and could – in the best of all possible worlds – just be brought off, at least to some extent. I believe that the idea of the ecological university, as proposed here, may fit the bill.

4 Introduction

A personal quest

I started on this quest more than 30 years ago, with my first book – *The Idea of Higher Education* – appearing in 1990. Then, there was no serious literature that was concerned with the key concepts in and around the idea of the university. Yes, as remarked, there was a Great Tradition of writings on the idea of the university stretching back (then) more than 150 years, but there was no scholarship of any substance that examined that literature and still less that sought to build on it, offering new concepts which might refresh that genre. Short of work in England in the 1960s and 1970s by Roy Niblett and a small US textbook (Brubacher, 1977), the philosophy of higher education as a field was bare. Since then, however, matters have changed considerably and now there are the makings of a philosophy of higher education movement that spans certainly the United States, the UK, continental Europe, parts of Africa and east Asia, and Australasia. As this is being written, a new academic grouping is being formed in Europe under just this banner (The Philosophy of Higher Education) with a book series underway and a conference being planned. Separately, a new journal, *Philosophy and Theory in Higher Education* is being orchestrated in the United States.[3]

Over these past decades, I have tried to play a part in establishing this field of the philosophy of higher education. The present book, indeed, draws on some of the ideas of mine over that time, but *markedly* extends them, and in two ways. *First*, it reaches into the (vast and complex) territory of the ecological. Here, it makes a particular move, by offering a radical interpretation of the concept of ecology, distinguishing *seven* ecosystems in which the university is implicated. *Second*, it offers for the first time in my work – and perhaps surprisingly for some – a *definite idea of the university*, and a positive idea at that. I have written rather extensively on the idea of higher education and various matters connected with it – learning, being a student, quality, curriculum – as well as more theoretical matters, such as ideology and complexity and – in a recent trilogy – on the very matter of what it is, in broad terms, to understand the university. However, while some of my books have focused on the conceptual underpinnings of the university, I have shrunk from advancing a particular idea of the university. To do so might seem pretentious, given the great tradition of writings on the idea of the university and the weight of its luminaries. But the time has come to enter the lists. If not now, then when?

Resources and bookishness

There are four sets of resources that have helped to energize this book and its ideas.

First, this work takes its bearings from that great tradition of work on the idea of the university, especially but not only in its German and English lines of thought, and several of its contributors are to be seen here (including Kant, Newman, Ortega y Gasset, Leavis and MacIntyre). However immodest it may be to say so, I see this book as in conversation with that genre.

Second, I have been stimulated by some of the contemporary literature on ecology, especially that with a philosophical flavouring. Here, the key figures – for this book –

have been Guattari (especially) and his collaboration with Deleuze, and also Naess, Mackey and Plumwood. In this context, the book entitled *The Three Ecologies* by Félix Guattari (2005/1989) has a particular poignancy. I shall draw upon it several times, but we may note that it is an extremely short book; in fact, the actual text runs to just 43 pages, and yet it is a powerful book. Length is no indicator of substance or of profundity.

Third, I have been energized by modern (and mostly European) philosophers, onwards from the first generation of Critical Theory, but more widely too. Here, Habermas especially, but also Deleuze and Guattari (again), but others include Heidegger, DeLanda and Charles Taylor. Roy Bhaskar is a double source of energy here, through his philosophy of Critical Realism and his engagement with the ecological movement.[4]

Fourth, this book draws inspiration from practices in universities around the world. Part of the argument is that if we look carefully into the interstices of universities, embryonic examples of the ecological university can be spotted. And so there are countless references in this book to such indications. The idea of the ecological university has evidential warrant.[5]

But just what is a book these days, in an era not only of tablets in which a reading may be a hurried scan of a screen between or even *within* other commitments, but more particularly in which chapters can be downloaded and purchased individually? Under such circumstances, the book as a unified and unfolding narrative, with an argument developed across its many chapters, is a problematic entity. With characteristic mischief – including the semi-colon – Umberto Eco co-wrote a book with the declarative title *This is* not *the end of the book;* (Eco and Carriere, 2012), the point being that there are real questions as to the fate of the book. Assuredly, the book *is* changing and the would-be book writer has to heed this new state of literary affairs. This book has been written, accordingly, to ride both horses. It has a narrative that is developed and sustained across its chapters, but each chapter – to a large extent – has also been crafted to stand by itself and is an exemplar of the general argument. There is, inevitably, therefore, a little overlap, just sufficient both to provide that self-sufficiency of each chapter and to enable the narrative to keep going.

An eco-philosophy for the university

I aim, in this book, towards two goals: to advance an 'eco-philosophy' of the university; that is, to place the university in *an ecological perspective* and to identify and articulate certain concepts that arise thereby (including 'ecology' itself, and 'ecosystem'); *and* to advance a *conception of the ecological university*; that is, in a broad-brush way, to indicate the kind of university it might be. There is, therefore, a strategic goal, that of laying out the ground of the university in an ecological perspective; and a more operational goal of illustrating just what it might be to be an ecological university. (Broadly, these two goals constitute Part I and Part II of this book respectively, while Part III steps back and reflects upon the very idea of the ecological university.)

The term 'eco-philosophy' is to be found especially in two literatures. On the one hand, it is to be found in a volume that brought together the Critical Realism of Roy Bhaskar with scholars in Nordic countries, namely *Ecophilosophy in a World of Crisis: Critical Realism and the Nordic Contributions* (Bhaskar, Hoyer and Naess, 2012). Ecology as such had not been much part of Bhaskar's oeuvre, but there were sympathetic connections between his philosophy and this group of Nordic scholars for whom the concept of ecology loomed large (perhaps especially for Naess).[6] On the other hand, the concept of eco-philosophy is also to be found in the work of Gilles Deleuze and Félix Guattari, both in their separate works and in their collaboration, especially in their (2013/1991) book, *What Is Philosophy?*.

Both of these sets of scholarly work – Bhaskar/the Nordic scholars and Deleuze/Guattari – contain a realist element, with a marked sense of the world existing independently of human beings, but also are passionately concerned to underscore the possibilities and indeed responsibilities of humanity towards the world in its entirety. Both philosophies are *Earth* philosophies, conveying a sense of the embeddedness of humanity in all the systems of the world, human and non-human, and urging a concernedness towards that total world.[7] There is both realism and an ethical dimension to the two philosophies.

The two philosophies differ in their realism and in the degree to which they see the world as complex, but of much more interest are their similarities. They demonstrate a concern with the total ecosphere and seek to understand matters against that horizon. They also exhibit – to draw on another contemporary commentator – an 'ecological wisdom' (Mickey, 2016). This wisdom is 'a grounded, terrestrial wisdom' which Mickey opposes to any 'abstract form of wisdom'. It is 'a practice of engaging in one's ecological community. It is a practice of place-making.' (pp. 70–71). Mickey also suggests that 'in our time of crisis, roots and shoots of ecological wisdom are growing around the planet' (p. 80).

All this is significant for the ecological university. In its best moments, for 200 years and more, the university has stood for a double openness, an openness of mind and an open society. *Both* aspects of what it is to be a university have been and continue to be undermined across the world, not only in authoritarian regimes that limit democracy and are nervous about having sources of openness in their midst (and which close universities and imprison academics), but also in countries that have encouraged the formation of higher education markets. More generally, phenomena such as globalization, the digital revolution and the increase and refinement of management systems and surveillance techniques add to this closing of the spaces of the university. But a number of provisos should be acknowledged.

Pessimism and creating hope

First, too much gloom and doom abound. The university is not ruined, as Readings (1997) alleged. Several of its present features imperil it but some are also opening possibilities for a new kind of university. The digital revolution, for instance, is opening possibilities for the university to communicate with society anew and so significantly develop the public sphere, even as it presents issues about screen-based reasoning and thoughtfulness. *Second*, the university has come to be unduly connected with the economy, indeed has become a force of economic production in its own right. But there is no reason to believe that this form of the university – the 'entrepreneurial university'[8] – is the end-point of the university. To the contrary, and this is a *third* point, it may well be that the world will turn to the university to help it address wider problems of social, personal and planetary wellbeing that go beyond the economic realm. *Fourth*, while there has been a narrowing of the ways in which the university is characteristically being understood, large themes such as those of reason, truth, openness, freedom and communication – all of which have rather become hidden from view – may yet help us to understand the university, albeit in new guises.

Yes, the news is disconcerting. For different reasons, the university is in a precarious state. Across the world, academics are incarcerated simply for being academics (and not even for having spoken publicly about political and societal matters); performance management techniques exact a terrible toll;[9] students are infantilized and connive in the process (Ecclestone and Hayes, 2009; Macfarlane, 2017); the world rankings have pernicious effects as governments – quite unrealistically – determine that they must have a number of their universities in the top 100 (Bekhradnia, 2016); there is degree inflation; universities are increasingly required to seek their own funding, so resulting in 'academic capitalism' (Slaughter and Rhoades, 2010; Slaughter and Cantwell, 2018); research and teaching stand in tension with each other; audit regimes tighten their grip as they measure the more trivial aspects of university life; learning analytics are imposing behaviourist thinking on students and threaten to deepen a 'performative' culture that has grown over past decades; and truth has become a hotly disputed category (such that 'post-truth' was the Oxford Dictionaries word of the year, 2016).

In such a context, pessimism is readily understandable, but it is a not entirely attractive response. It may even be self-fulfilling. Hans-Georg Gadamer (2001: 83), indeed, was 'very sceptical of every kind of pessimism'. Why? 'Because no one can live without hope'. Accordingly, an appropriate philosophical quest has to lie quite elsewhere.

The essence of philosophy has often been considered to be that of an interest in concepts. In that just-mentioned book on *What Is Philosophy?*, Deleuze and Guattari advance a view of philosophy not just as a matter of concepts, for that can lead to mere, and even a sterile, conceptual analysis. Rather, they see philosophy as having an interest in the formation of new concepts that may help to reorient the object of attention. 'A concept is . . . valued for its . . . own creation' (p. 31) and 'the task is always to set up [a] new event from things and beings' (p. 33). Indeed, 'every concept shapes and reshapes the event in its own way' (p. 34). Here, our 'event' is that of the university and it is a social institution that cries out for a re-shaping. This is not to turn it around, and to attempt to return it from whence it came, but to redirect it. It is going in one direction (global, economic, managed, marketized) and now the challenge is to tilt the rudder so that it might veer and so take on a new routing.[10] Our imaginative concepts may help to create hope.

I shall argue that the idea of the ecological university provides us with just such a concept. It is a very large concept. An advantage is that the concept can bear much weight. It can bear considerations of the university in the twenty-first century and perhaps even beyond. The university's inquiries – its 'research' – and its teaching, its curricula, its students and their learning, its connections with the wider world and other matters can be informed by the university being seen as becoming ecological; and it can take different forms across both universities and disciplines. A disadvantage of such a large concept as ecology is that it opens to so many considerations that they can barely be done justice in a single book.

A note on ecology

In alighting on the term 'ecology' and in developing it into a concept capable of bearing the weight of this inquiry, I use it so as to do justice to two considerations. First, the university is an institution that is interconnected with several zones of the world. Its interconnections with the economic zone have taken the high ground for half a century or so, overshadowing other zones, and those other zones – knowledge, learning, culture, persons, and society itself, as well as the natural world – have been largely neglected. The concept of ecology helps us in pointing to regions that have some systematicity, but yet are open to the rest of the world. It hints at a diversity that is being imperilled, both within and across different zones. It also suggests some fragility and even impairment, potential or actual. The ecological perspective, therefore, opens horizons for the university.

Moreover, the university does not simply interact with those zones, but is implicated in them willy-nilly. Those zones – I have mentioned seven such zones – act upon the university whether it realizes it or not. Again, the concept of ecology is helpful here, for it harbours a sense of a presence in which one is implicated, come what may. There is a firm *realism* that attaches, therefore, to the ecological outlook.

These are considerations of the way the university *is*. To summon up the concept of ecology here is to call in aid some general empirical warrant for our inquiry.[11] It reminds us that the university is a real institution, with its place in the world, with all that that might entail. But there is a second set of considerations here. The concept of ecology has a subtle *ought-ness*. If an ecosystem is found to be impaired, then one has a responsibility to help to restore it to good health. And so it is with the university. The university has responsibilities in attending to the (seven) ecosystems in which it is especially implicated and play its part – whether modest or profound – in advancing the wellbeing of those ecosystems. There is, therefore, an element of due *concern* that enters the ecological outlook, as the university contemplates its worldly interactions.

Argument

In a nutshell, my central intention is to advance an idea of the university for the twenty-first century as an institution that has an *active* concern for the whole Earth; even the universe. (The clue is in the name – '*univer*sity' – with its connotations of universality and universe.) More fully, the argument of my book amounts to the following 15 theses:

1. The university has grown to become an institution that is complex such that it interconnects with many aspects of the world. (To put it formally, the university has acquired a social ontology.)
2. Certain of these aspects of the world possess a loose coherence, such that we may term them ecosystems. Each may be fragile, and may be impaired in some way.
3. The university – especially through its orientation around knowledge – has come to acquire resources and power, and the university therefore has a capability in attending to the ecosystems in which it is especially implicated.
4. Seven ecosystems are especially significant so far as the university is concerned – knowledge, social institutions, persons, the economy, learning, culture and the natural environment. Of late – the last 50 years or so – attention has focused overwhelmingly on the economy, neglecting other aspects of the university's worldly connections.
5. In the twenty-first century, these ecosystems do not stand outside the university, but rather, they and the university flow into each other. Through this interconnectedness, these ecosystems have come to constitute a 'deep ecology' of the university.
6. Universities are each placed differently in their relationships to these seven ecosystems. Nevertheless, since the seven ecosystems are inherently within the university, there arise immanent ecological opportunities for each university.
7. The ecological university fully emerges when the university – any university – does not merely engage with its ecological hinterland (for all universities do that whether they realize it or not), but when it engages *intently* and with an *ecological spirit*.
8. While the general considerations are universal, being an ecological university is particular to each university, which has a responsibility to work out its *own* possibilities in promoting the wellbeing of the seven ecosystems. The ecological university is, thereby, an ethical university. (A university's 'corporate strategy' would consist of imaginative possibilities, in living out its ethos of *ecological concern*.)
9. This working out of each university's ecological possibilities calls for imagination and for institutional fearlessness. (A university's ecological possibilities are not simply to be read off an ecological scan of its situation, but have to be *imaginatively* created and vigilantly pursued. Realism is not enough.)
10. There is no end-point to this process, either in time or space. *Temporally*, the task of being an ecological university has to go on continuously being revisited

and reinterpreted. *Spatially*, especially with modern technologies, universities can reach out further across the world. The ecological university is in a continual state of *emergence*, as it develops its *ecological profile* across the seven ecosystems (the distribution of itself across those ecosystems always changing).

11 The idea of the ecological university both acknowledges that the university is a real institution in the world and *is* an idea (and these two moments – the university as institution and as idea – stand on the *same* plane, intersecting with each other). The idea of the ecological university is both realist and idealist.

12 The idea of the ecological university is both critical and radical. It offers a critique of the way in which universities have become unduly wedded to instrumental reason and have failed to consider the world as being of inherent worth and interest. But it is content neither with projects of resistance nor of subversion, but advances *ecological reason*, seeking spaces to redirect and re-energize the university in a new direction.

13 The idea of the ecological university is utopian. Perhaps it will never be *fully* realized.

14 However, there is good reason to believe that the ecological university *could* well materialize in significant measure. The world may yet come to realize what the university has to offer it and to seek a wide interpretation of its place in the world.

15 We can point already to embryonic instances of the ecological university in front of us. The ecological university is utopian, but it is *a feasible* utopia.

Structure

This book has three parts. In *Part I* – the first four chapters – I lay the foundations for this book by explaining how I interpret the idea of ecology and I show, in broad terms, how it is that the university can be illuminated by an ecological perspective – both our understandings of the university and its possibilities. In *Part II* – the following five chapters – I take up in turn one particular ecosystem in which the university is especially implicated and I sketch those relationships and offer indications of ways in which the university can better realize its ecological possibilities therein. *Part III* – the final two chapters – reflects on the whole idea of the ecological university in the light of the journey of this book and further draws out the value of this way of thinking about the university. Readers with a more practical interest might wish to start with Part II, while those with a more conceptual and theoretical bent might prefer to start with Part I.

By way of an outline, *Chapter 1* plunges immediately into the very idea of ecology and draws out aspects significant for this inquiry. Central are the ideas of an ecosophy – an ecological approach to understanding complex phenomena, such as the university – and the idea of an ecosystem, with its sense of a configuration that hangs together and yet is subject to dispersal, loss of diversity and impairment. An ecosophy for the university, accordingly, seeks to understand the university as interconnected with fragile ecosystems to which it then has responsibilities.

Chapter 2 takes on board the idea of assemblage and considers the university precisely as a loose assemblage of different kinds of entity but which may be influenced by ideas. Universities have both material and expressive elements, with possibilities of emergence and engagement. The ecological university understands all this, and takes on an 'ecosophical ethics' (Guattari, cited in Mickey, 2016: 58). 'Ecology' can help to supply a unifying narrative to an institution faced with paths of possibility.

Chapter 3 attacks two concepts much in vogue in the work of ecologists, those of sustainability and autopoiesis (the tendency of complex systems to reproduce themselves). Both concepts would confine the university to its present or past self when what is needed is a concept that will enable the university *continuously* to emerge, to reorganize itself and to go on expanding its horizons. Ecology is such a concept and, when brought into contact with the university, it is a radical concept.

Chapter 4 identifies and briefly examines seven ecosystems across which the university moves (whether knowingly or not) *and* which flow into the university, those of knowledge, social institutions, persons, the economy, learning, culture and the natural environment. Collectively, this seven-fold understanding amounts to a social ecology for the university. Together, these ecosystems constitute an *ecosphere* in which the university is now ineradicably implicated.

Part II, as stated, builds on these conceptual foundations by looking to identify ways of realizing the ecological university. It offers sightings of the ecological university from different angles and examines ways in which the university already does and could interact more with its wide ecological environment.

Chapter 5 explores head-on what it is to be an eco-university. Part of that calling lies in the university possessing an ecological ethos and part of it, too, lies in its living out certain principles, and seven such principles are identified, along with their associated maxims. But the eco-university, too, possesses certain qualities, of fearlessness, and of thought as such. *Chapter 6* considers the matter of research or, as termed here, of ecological inquiry. The knowledge ecosystem has to lie at the centre of the ecological university, but knowledge has to be reconstrued: an *ecological epistemology* is required. And that requires a spelling out of its knowledge interests which lie ultimately in an *epistemological otherness*. *Chapter 7* considers the matter of learning, starting from the phenomenon of liquid learning in an overly fluid world. While it also tarries with the idea of the liquid learner, it does not rest there, but goes on to advance the idea of the *ecological learner*.[12]

Chapter 8 offers sightings of an *ecological curriculum*. The curriculum is self-evidently an assemblage, but an ecological curriculum would exemplify certain principles. It would offer the student nomadic spaces and a form of freedom, namely a right to roam such that the student becomes a voyager in a space that is both *universal* and infinite and yet also full of *particular* and personal challenges.

Chapter 9 engages with the matter of professionalism and advances an idea of what it is to be an *ecological professional*. Concepts that it brings into view include those of authentic professionalism, professional responsibility, and professional dispositions and qualities. It concludes by drawing out implications for professional education.

The final chapter in this part, *Chapter 10*, teases out what it is for the ecological university to engage with the world. Entanglement, the public sphere and worldly being are key matters. The idea of the university having *ecological agency* is advanced. But for such agency to be realized, imagination is necessary, not least for the university to discern possibilities for transformation, both in the world and in itself.

In *Part III*, I evaluate the idea of the ecological university.

Chapter 11 subjects the idea of the ecological university to an audit, bringing it up against no less than *nine criteria of adequacy*. These criteria include those of scope and range, timefulness, particularity and universality, emergence, wellbeing, feasibility and criticality. These constitute severe tests which help to bring out the resilience and the potential, and enduring, but also continually unfolding, character of the idea of the ecological university.

Chapter 12 draws out the idea of the ecological university even further, displaying its capacity to work on three planes, its status as a feasible utopia, its powers of criticality, its deep ecological stance and its sensuousness. Ultimately, to speak of the ecological university is to speak of concerns in relation to the whole Earth.

I conclude with a short *Coda*, a skirmish with the thought that the 25,000 or so universities worldwide just could come to constitute a unitary ecosystem in themselves, at once interconnected as a world community of universities and working together for the good of the world. The whole Earth, I suggest, is ready for just such a coming.

Notes

1 See Peters and Barnett (eds) (2018) *The Idea of the University: A Reader*: the volume collects readings from that great tradition, with its various lines – the German (Bildung) Tradition, the English and Scottish (Liberal) Tradition, the American (Pragmatist) Tradition as well as 'other contributions to the discourse'.
2 I advanced this 'double undermining' thesis in my book, *The Idea of Higher Education* (1990). Since then, I would judge that that dual situation has deepened but, paradoxically, as I suggest here, I believe that the possibilities for surmounting it are now real.
3 The book series is *Debating Higher Education: Philosophical Perspectives*, published by Springer, the editors of which are Paul Gibbs, Amanda Fulford and Ronald Barnett. The journal, *Philosophy and Theory in Higher Education*, is being led by John Petrovic at the University of Alabama and is to be published by Peter Lang.
4 Roy Bhaskar also both encouraged this book and wanted to see it published within his Routledge series on *Critical Realism and Education* but, sadly, with his death, it was not to be. (In some ways, this book could be considered to constitute an exemplar of 'applied critical realism' [Bhaskar, 2013: 18], although in wanting to restore an ontological perspective to philosophy, it seems to me that Bhaskar sometimes underplayed the potential of ideas.)
5 In saying that the idea of the ecological university has empirical warrant, I am not suggesting that this form of the university is readily present before us. Rather, to use another phrase from the philosophy of Deleuze and Guattari (2013/1991: 47), I have in mind a 'radical empiricism'. The present form of the university bears within itself the

seeds of ecological possibilities, despite its counter-factual character. The ecological university *could* flower and we can just see the first shoots.

6 The contributors to the book, *Ecophilosophy in a World of Crisis: Critical Realism and the Nordic Contributions*, are almost all Scandinavian. Bhaskar is the only contributor from outside continental Europe. The volume includes a reprinting of an important essay by Arne Naess, in which he distinguishes deep and shallow ecology. In addition to the Preface by Roy Bhaskar and an introductory essay by the other two editors, Karl Georg Hoyer and Petter Naess, I found the chapter by Trond Gansmo Jakobsen – 'Nordic Ecophilosophy and Critical Realism' – particularly helpful.

7 There are evident connections here with the concerns over the separation of humanity from Nature, which Western 'rationality' has arguably exacerbated, in its underwriting of 'reason . . . hostile toward nature . . . subjugating nature' (Habermas, 2010b: 195).

8 The concept of 'the entrepreneurial university' was perhaps first advanced by Burton R Clark (1998) on the basis of a substantial cross-national research study, although it has since entered the wider higher education lexicon.

9 The most egregious example here is that of the suicide of Professor Stefan Grimm, an academic at one of London's universities. There is a mass of material available on the internet that reports, from various perspectives, on Professor Grimm's suicide. Whatever the full truth of the matter may be, it appears that at least a contributory factor was the 'performance management' regime within his institution; for example: www.dcscience.net/2014/12/01/publish-and-perish-at-imperial-college-london-the-death-of-stefan-grimm/; www.timeshighereducation.com/news/stefan-grimm-inquest-new-policies-may-not-have-prevented-suicide/2019563.article; https://en.wikipedia.org/wiki/Stefan_Grimm

10 This view of philosophy as the creation of radical concepts is to be found also in a dialogue between Badiou and Žižek (2009), so as 'to keep one's distance from power' (p. 13), to create an 'exception' (pp. 12–13) and 'change the concepts of the debate' (p. 54).

11 Cf. 'There is something wild and powerful in this transcendental empiricism' (Deleuze, 2012: 25).

12 The idea of tarrying I take from Žižek (1993) in his 'tarrying with the negative'. To tarry with Žižek for a moment, I use the idea of 'dialectic' only rarely in this book and on that idea, Žižek notes that Hegel 'declines' the possibility of a 'dialectical synthesis' (p. 141). Rather (p. 142), 'the potentiality of the object must also be present in its external actuality, under the form of heteronomous coercion'. This position is four-square with the argument here: the ecological university is only to be realized, and then only partially, within the counter forms that the university has become over the last half-century or so – and 'under the . . . heteronomous coercion' exercised by it.

PART I
The idea of the ecological

1
THE IDEA OF ECOLOGY

Introduction

The idea of ecology points to the interconnectedness of all things in the world (and even beyond). It gains its power from a sense of impairment, especially a sense that systems – ecosystems – have been corrupted in some way: their inner diversity has been weakened or some other misfortune has befallen them. It also contains an inner commentary that humanity bears some responsibility for such disturbances and an urging that humanity has a responsibility to help in restoring the integrity of its environment. These five dimensions of ecology – interconnectedness, potential diversity, impairment, responsibility and restoration – are testimony to the idea of ecology being (in the language of Bernard Williams [2008/1995]) a thick concept, containing several components. 'Ecology' is fact and values together. But more, it looks to the past, present and future. It is critical but also hopeful. It is visionary, having a sense of unfulfilled potential, yet to be fully realized. It leaps out from our present condition, and holds up a sense of a better world that can at least be striven for.[1]

And so it is, too, for the university. The university lives among its worldly ecosystems which are not as they might be. Of course, the university cannot be held solely responsible for any impairment that its associated ecosystems might exhibit, but it is implicated in any such impairment, even if just through any disinclination to act where it could so intervene. The university is not merely interconnected with the world but its work has influence in the world. To use a modish word of our time, the university has 'impact' in and on the world. And so the components of ecology already discerned – interconnectedness, diversity, impairment, responsibility and restoration – emerge as components of the university of the twenty-first century and its total ecosphere. The university cannot stand idly by: it now has responsibilities in furthering the wellbeing of the many ecologies with which it intersects.

18 The idea of the ecological

The university is an active variable in the ecological character of the world. This is a universal feature of the modern university – and yet this presence, with its universality, has rarely been recognized. There is something of an ecological void attendant on the university.

These assertions will, of course, have to be fleshed out in what follows. But they already indicate much of the roughness of the terrain ahead.[2] Matters abound as to what might be meant by ecology, ecosystems, universities being implicated in ecosystems, diversity, impairment, responsibility and restoration. And there is dispute over each matter. For example, in relation to the knowledge ecology, is diversity *across* disciplines more – or less – important than a diversity of frameworks *within* a discipline? The ground, therefore, is uneven. It is a terrain, however, that must be trod, for nothing less than the intersecting futures of the world and the university are at stake. The world is not as it could be. Its ecosystems are impaired and the university, too, is falling short of its potential in the world. These two situations are not coincidental, for the university has yet fully to acknowledge its worldly character and its possibilities in and responsibilities towards the world.

Terminology

'Ecology' is a double-barrelled term. It both refers to systems *in themselves* that have an internal unity, the coherence of which could be threatened in some way, and also refers to a *study* of such systems in the world. An ecology is both out there, as a real presence in the world, *and* is a form of thought, understanding and knowledge generated by humanity. (It is at once an ontological and an epistemological term.) This dual-headedness applies also to the university, for the university lives amid ecologies (they have real substance in the world) *and* also has helped to bequeath the formation of ecology as an academic field of study. To aid discussion, for the most part, I shall use the term 'ecosystem' to refer to systems in which the university is implicated, and I shall reserve the term 'ecology' to understandings of such systems.

The ecologists refer to the idea of deep ecology, although its definition varies. Here, what is important in the idea is that ecology is not merely beyond humanity, but rather that humanity is deeply implicated in ecology. The idea that ecology is simply 'out there', something to which humanity might or might not respond (even if it feels some pang of responsibility in the matter), is redolent of instrumental reason. And it was in part through the dominance of instrumental reason that the world has taken on its present character and is now faced with an ecological crisis. This point is cardinal to our present purposes. For the situation that lies before us is not just one of an ecological crisis in front of and outside the university, to which it may or may not respond. Rather, the university is *already* implicated ecologically. Ecological dimensions are already deep within the university.

Opening here is nothing less than an ecological study of the university or, rather, to be more precise, an *eco-philosophy* of the university – or even, to use a term of Félix Guattari (2005/1989), an 'ecosophy' of the university. To my knowledge, this has not so far been attempted and perhaps for good reason. The terrain before us widens and opens pathways going in multiple directions. To adapt a phrase, there are less 'lines of flight' (Deleuze and Guattari, 2007/1980) than there are paths of possible journeying – and even blockages – aplenty before us.

Two features of the situation before us stand out at this early stage. First, the university is intertwined not with a single ecology; and nor, therefore, is there a single ecological crisis in front of the university. Rather, the university is intertwined in multiple ecologies or, as I wish to term them, multiple ecosystems. These ecosystems have already been intimated but we may list them again now, before coming onto them more fully in what follows. They are seven in number, being the ecosystems of:

1   knowledge
2   social institutions
3   persons
4   the economy
5   learning
6   culture
7   the natural environment.

Simply to list these ecosystems is to indicate that to speak of the ecological university is to invoke much more than the ecosystems of the natural world. Moreover, to speak of the ecological world is to imply an interconnectedness of the university with the whole world, in all of its epistemological, symbolic, social and psychological aspects. And it is – through the term 'ecological' – to suggest that the university should have a care for all of these ecosystems. This care now becomes a responsibility that the university cannot evade, except by putting itself at peril and those ecosystems too.

To put it mildly, this is a situation of some complexity. Not only is the university intermeshing with the seven ecosystems, but those ecosystems are interacting with each other. The knowledge ecosystem affects the economic ecosystem which affects the social ecosystem which in turn affects the psychological ecosystems of individual persons.[3] But there is also – as it may be said – *super*complexity present too (Barnett, 2000). For each ecosystem, not to mention the university's intermeshings with it, poses conceptual problems. Is 'sustainability' a helpful or inadequate concept here? To what extent can humanity – and thereto universities – be said to have 'responsibilities' in addressing any shortcomings that an ecosystem might exhibit? If the very concept of responsibility can hold sway here, what might be a proper balance between the social and the personal levels? And just why should the concept of ecology claim the high ground, even if broadly interpreted, in deriving an idea of the university for the twenty-first century and even beyond? These are supercomplex questions in that responses to them could never be susceptible to a consensus, and yet they are significant questions, gnawing at what it is to *be* a university in the twenty-first century.

20 The idea of the ecological

To put the concepts of university and ecological together, then – as in 'the ecological university' – is not only to point to the university being oriented in several directions, but it is also to point to the university acting with intent on different levels, having regard to persons and institutions, to the private and public spheres, and to the local and the universal domains.

Second, the idea of the ecological university has a *real* aspect. It speaks to systems that stand in the world separately from and independently of the university, even if the university has powers to have an impact on those systems. The idea of the ecological university is a hybrid concept, with one foot in the realm of the 'real', and one foot in the realm of ideas; and the two realms play against each other. Its real ontological character keeps one foot on the ground, even if it harbours tendencies to soar into the starry firmament of ideas.

For example, the idea of academic freedom may reasonably be part of the conceptual filling out of the ecological university and opens to a multitude of interpretations, but it would also take a bearing from the way in which academic freedom is playing out in the twenty-first century, not least in the ways in which academics are being imprisoned by some governments and so denied the space to fulfil their academic responsibilities. But work on that topic would also take note of the surreptitious ways in which more democratic states subtly steer academic life – through sanctions only marginally less intimidating than incarceration – to pursue this kind of research, to generate income, to attend to students in a particular way, to leave behind old-fashioned thoughts about academic collegiality, and doggedly to follow bureaucratic protocols. Ideas of academic freedom – however abstract they may be – need, if they are to be appropriate to their age, to be rooted in the relevant aspects of the world.

Always on the move

To speak of the ecological is to imply a world of movement and change. Ecosystems are never static and so it is with the ecosystems of the university. They are turbulent pools and, like the canoeist in the slalom competition, the university has to find ways of working in that motion so as to maintain some kind of course.

Following the work of the philosophers Deleuze and Guattari (in their extraordinary book, *A Thousand Plateaus*, 2007/1980),[4] many like to speak of rhizomatic settings, the metaphor alluding to a directionless entanglement of growing and spreading matter characteristic of rhizomes. There is much in the metaphor but it is far too static. Metaphors of fluidity and liquidity are more to the point here. The university is much more like a squid moving in the multiple currents of the ocean. The university has a shell – it exists as a real phenomenon in the world, with physical, legal, financial and institutional properties – but it has long tentacles that can reach out, and even into small crevices. And it has to keep on the move amid waters that are never quiescent. On occasions, it can even move quite fast.

Time, space, movement and geography all play out here amid these 'global fluids' (Urry, 2003: 60). The ecosystems of the university draw the university in, each university having its own time–space signature. Some of those ecosystems – such as those of the economy, knowledge and even learning – are more digitized than others, and so present with added freneticism. Some – again such as knowledge, the economy and learning – are more global than others. And some – such as social institutions, persons and culture – are more characterized by expressive as against material components (DeLanda, 2013/2006). In these latter ecosystems, language, meaning and intersubjective understandings remain stubbornly important.

As a result, the university finds itself moving in ecosystems that have their own pace and rhythm.[5] The financial systems of the world have become part of a global algorithmic machine that works at the speed of light, whereas culture characteristically still moves at a slower pace. Universities, for all their high-powered computerized resources, struggle to keep fully in touch with a cybernetic world (Peters, 2015). But they also opt to develop their physical grounds as public art galleries in which members of the public are *expected* to move at a slow pace (Hards, Vaughan and Williams, 2014), and they employ resident artists and quartets (with their own time–space signatures).

Another set of concepts deployed by Deleuze and Guattari (in that same work) are those of territorialization and de-territorialization. These concepts go further than matters of geography and speak to the matter of integrity, with 'territorialization' referring to a process in which an entity secures a greater integrity and 'de-territorialization' to a loss of such integrity. We see these processes in university internationalization. Establishing branches in other countries, perhaps even on the other side of the world, can self-evidently bring in its wake processes of de-territorialization. This is less a matter of geographical dispersal but is more a matter of pedagogical integrity, as the university is presented with students' varying 'cultural scripts' (Welikala and Watkins, 2008) in its different locations across the world. Perhaps – *pace* Wittgenstein (1978/1953) – we should rather talk of a 'family' of student experiences within such a university, there being no unifying essence that runs across it.

Significant in this example of internationalization is that six of our seven ecosystems – knowledge, social institutions, persons, learning, culture and the natural environment – are immediately implicated here, while the remaining one – the economy considered as an ecology – also plays its part. And in being active in such a surfeit of ecosystems, a university – in acting in this way – undergoes (to continue with the Deleuze/Guattari lexicon) a process of '*re*-territorialization' (emphasis added). The university moves within its ecological fields and establishes a new ecological *configuration*. It re-territorializes *itself* across its ecological spaces.

To speak, then, of the university and the ecological in one breath is doubly to speak of motion. The ecosystems of the university are each in motion and the university moves in, through and across those ecosystems. But these ecological movements are far from even.

Among the ecosystems themselves, just one ecosystem takes the palm in policy design and in public debate, that of the economy. And much attention is given to the sustainability of this particular ecosystem: will the economy grow? Will it go into a recession? Will it even suffer a major crisis and collapse? Is it in fair shape – or is it distorted, working largely in the interests of the already powerful?[6] Is it sufficiently diverse? In turn, so far as the university is concerned, it is the work that the university can perform in furthering the economy that is all-important. And the worth of the university is calculated accordingly.

(Over-)strong and weaker attachments

This is a debilitating state of affairs. The university's movements within and contributions to the six other ecosystems are underplayed and even downright neglected. And the university often connives in this occlusion of its workings, happy to play up its contribution to the wellbeing of the economy. There it secures its place in the world. Wittingly or unwittingly, it even promotes a certain kind of economy. 'The entrepreneurial university' is a university that is both itself entrepreneurial and works to boost an entrepreneurial economy, characteristically a market economy coloured by self-interest, competition, inequality and power.[7] Its academics, subject to performance management disciplines, may be expected to generate income for their university worth three times their salaries. The university may be being steered to favour the economic ecosystem – but it is tacitly acceding to this state of affairs by constructing both external and internal understandings of itself in this way. This is less a 'line of flight' (Deleuze and Guattari, 2007/1980) and more a projection of a cloak for public consumption.

In these processes, the university strengthens its connections with some ecosystems and loosens them with others and distorts its relationships with yet others. For instance, in allowing itself excessively to be steered towards and within the economy, the university neglects its possibilities in relation to culture, which is weakened in the process.

Readings – in his (1997) book on *The University in Ruins* – claimed that the university had severed its links with culture, but surely went too far. What it did was to abandon its *intentional* links with culture. It eschewed any public proclamations of its having a care towards the maintenance, let alone the furthering, of culture. In which university websites across the world do we see references to culture? But, of course, the university is interlinked with culture in myriad ways, conflictual as they may be – in language, in modes of interpretation, in forms of communication, in pedagogic practices and, in more material aspects of culture, in its technologies and its aesthetic leanings (perhaps, as noted, even with a resident artist or musical quartet). The point here is that the associations that the university is forming now with the economy as an ecosystem are being developed in such a way that the university's possibilities with regard to others of its ecosystems are being unduly limited.

In this unevenness of the university's ecological movements, the university forms overly close attachments in certain of its ecological zones and weak attachments elsewhere. Those weak attachments never recede into *de*tachments; they are never severed. That, after all, is part of the earlier meaning of ecology. From the Greek, *oikos*, it speaks to a home, a household, that is always with us. It can be ignored, but it will still be present, perhaps in a malign state. Accordingly, responsibilities befall the university. To what extent will it self-consciously work out its possibilities within its (seven) ecosystems? Will it seek to plunder its ecosystems for its own ends? Will it seek to engage with each of them? And will it seek to play its part in disinterestedly strengthening each of those ecosystems?

An ecosophy for the university

Opening here is nothing short of an ecological philosophy of and for the university. Or, to draw again on Guattari's term, it is an *ecosophy* of and for the university that is emerging. For what is at issue here is the university in its total set of planet-Earth connections, in all of its natural and human manifestations. Quite some time ago, Ortega y Gasset (1946: 76) put the point well: 'The university must be open to the whole reality of its time. It must be in the midst of real life, and saturated by it.'

Such a perspective opens the way for all manner of investigations (in developing such a philosophy of the university), empirical certainly, but also ethical in character. And it is to open a space for different kinds of tradition to play their parts, traditions across philosophy but other traditions as well. The ecological literature is vast, and we cannot do it justice in a single volume. What is striking, though, is how so many parallel and even rival perspectives are to be found and even rival positions *within* particular perspectives. Feminism, critical theory, religions, faiths of a non-religious character (such as Buddhism), complexity theory and philosophy and many other perspectives have made their contributions. And to say just this is to place the university in the midst of an unending ocean of settings and inquiries, but also of possible voyages and ventures. There is opening here a total eco-philosophy for and of the university.

The term 'ecophilosophy' is posited by Deleuze and Guattari, as noted, in their book *What Is Philosophy?* (2013/1991). Perhaps deceptively simple, that book espies a very large role for philosophy. They seek to encourage the creation of concepts that are attuned to the Earth, in its fullness, and so facilitate planetary renewal (Mickey, 2016: 13). This amounts to nothing short of an 'ecology of life', to draw on a phrase from the anthropologist Tim Ingold (2000: 16).

This canvas contains, as it must do, space for different disciplines, and seeks to encourage fruitful interconnections. Might this not be a philosophy, too, of the university, which acknowledges its manifold relationships with the world, and observes their intricateness, but sees too that those relationships are often impaired, if not actually corrupted? Perhaps a philosophy of this kind can help the university to build networks of 'mutually enhancing relationships . . . which resist the systems that are currently turning the whole world into a pile of property and resources which are worth nothing more than their monetary value' (Mickey, 2016: 43). Perhaps a philosophy of this kind can help the university to glimpse *new* possibilities that at once help to realize the potential that lies with the extraordinary institution that has come – across the world – to be termed 'university'.

To utter the phrase 'the ecological university', then, is at once to work on different levels and move in multiple directions. It is to displace the university so that instead of it being felt to have a position separate from the world – which it then either suffers from *or* imposes upon, perhaps 'entrepreneurially' or with 'impact' – the university is now positioned as immersed in (its) various ecosystems, which both influence it *and* open to the university's own influences. It is to bring into view a new and very large conspectus for understanding the university and for discerning its possibilities that might well be energized by a whole range of ecological, philosophical and even anthropological and theological perspectives. It is to reveal to the university – and to the wider world – responsibilities that now befall the university, in playing its part towards the greater wellbeing of the world's most important ecosystems (for the university cannot but be implicated in those ecosystems).

Some modesty may be desirable here. In speaking of the university and the planet, and the wellbeing of ecosystems, it is not being claimed that the university can save the world, whatever that might mean. Far from it. But the ecological university would be a university that understands its place in the world, and neither with undue humility nor with arrogance. It would be a university that recognizes that it is situated amid ecosystems of vital significance to the planet's wellbeing and that, accordingly, it behoves the university to dwell on its resources and its possibilities for advancing those ecosystems. No more, but certainly, too, no less. It becomes fully an ecological university when it takes this understanding unto itself, and so works to discern and to try to realize its (ecological) possibilities. That is all; but, of course, this is to say much. It is to urge a *continuing* revolution in the way in which universities are understood and in which they characteristically understand themselves.

It has been remarked that, in the twenty-first century, we are faced with a 'new world order' (Porpora, 2013: 184).[8] I agree, but it was always thus. Planet Earth is continually in movement, and its ecospheres with it. In such a world, there can be no repetition. Guattari puts the point in characteristically pungent fashion: 'everything . . . has to be continually reinvented, started again from scratch, otherwise the processes become trapped in a cycle of deathly repetition' (Guattari, 2005/1989: 39). And each university is changing all the time, with its possibilities opening out in new ways. The ecological university is *always* in a process of perpetual becoming. It has no end state. To draw on a key concept of Roy Bhaskar's philosophy of Critical Realism, the ecological university has qualities of *emergence* (Bhaskar, 2008a), in which the university may become other than it is, as it plays out, in successive waves, its ecological responsibilities. And these responsibilities, to reiterate, go well beyond the university's responsibilities towards the natural environment. What is in question here – in the form of its seven ecosystems – are the university's relationships with and responsibilities towards its total environment; indeed, towards the whole planet.

A singular achievement

A key concept in Guattari's (2005/1989) short book (*The Three Ecologies*) is that of singularization. By this term, Guattari wishes not only to insist on the individuality of entities in the world but on their growing individuality, especially in an ecological context. For under ecological conditions, in which entities are caught in swirls of forces, currents and eddies, their individuality must perforce become more marked. Entities acquire ever-greater singularity. And so Guattari speaks both of singularity and singularization. We are directed both to the individuality of entities in the world and to their individuality being progressively increased. In this way, Guattari is urging 'an ecology of resingularization' (p. 65).

Crucial is it to recognize that individual entities are not thereby torn ever-further apart, pitted in a widening separation from — still less competition with — each other. To the contrary, 'Individuals must become both more united *and* increasingly different' (emphasis added). And Guattari adds that, 'The same is true for the resingularization of schools, town councils, urban planning, etc.' (p. 69). (We may assume universities can comfortably be included in the 'etc.' here.) It follows that 'the question becomes one of how to encourage the organization of individual *and* collective ventures' (p. 65; emphasis added).

We see all this playing out in perverse ways in higher education. Amid the competitiveness brought on by the marketization of higher education, universities attempt in their branding (Pringle and Naidoo, 2016) to distance themselves from each other. Each university pumps up its individuality as it stridently competes with others, both for research funds and for student enrolments and, in the process, emphasizes the particular characteristics and resources that it has to offer. But, contrariwise, we see also references in state policy documents to students as if they constituted a single entity and we see universities forming themselves into collective associations, both nationally and internationally.

Superficially, then, it might appear at first glance that Guattari's conceptualizations of singularization and 'collective ventures' are being played out very nicely in the higher education arena. But, of course, this is not at all what Guattari's ideas might look like, if taken seriously. Just what they might look like in the best of all possible worlds is precisely the matter before us in this book. Here, though, we may make some quick observations and suggestions. Being prompted by marketization, the individuality — of institutions, of academics, of (digitized) students — reinforces a strident set of differences that proclaims 'You are nothing to do with me' and 'I am nothing to do with you'. On the contrary, we will emphasize further our separateness by competing against each other.

A trivial example: several elite universities (such as Princeton [United States], Warwick, University College London, and Durham [all in England]) have each set up an Institute for Advanced Studies. These centres are characteristically initiatives to encourage disciplines *within* each university to talk to each other and so produce collective cross-disciplinary resources to grapple with cross-disciplinary themes. Such centres might also enable the harnessing of cross-disciplinary efforts more ready to bid for research project funding directly focused on the large issues of the age, which typically straddle disciplines.[9] There lies in such initiatives a most worthwhile element and one that speaks directly to Guattari's ideas, that of cross-disciplinary conversation out of which might form new kinds of academic 'collective', and 'transversality'. *But* the potential value of these laudable efforts is limited while they are pursued in the context of the global competition between universities (prompted by world rankings and so forth), for what are being generated here are largely conversations *within* each university so as to project further its intellectual fire-power, rather than conversations that are directly intended to reach out across universities and to wider publics.

But what, then, of our other observations, as to the unifying character of much higher education discourse? After all, the very phrase 'higher education' (and its translated form in other languages) presupposes a unified system, characteristically at a national level. But again, this is not the kind of collectivity that Guattari could have had in mind. To use the term 'students' insensitively to massify students, and to objectify them into a single entity, is to destroy the individuality of each student. And that universities are coming together in groups across countries, regions and the world is, again, not what Guattari could have envisaged, had he turned to higher education. In these groupings, birds of a feather flock together: universities signal their perceptions of themselves and of other universities. Far from signifying collectivity, these 'gangs' (as David Watson, a former UK Vice-Chancellor used critically to refer to them [Temple, 2016]) signify their difference and their distance from other – and typically inferior – universities.[10]

Trivially, then, in the spirit of Guattari, we can glimpse that singularity and collectivity need not delimit the other; both can ride together. But we can say more. For instance, that singularization, understood in a context of ecology, should lead to a *re*-singularization, in which each university comes to an understanding and works hard at discerning its own ecological possibilities; a discernment that calls for an institutional imagination. And, *this* singularization should go forward in the company of collectivities of universities, traversing the seven ecosystems of the university. This singularization, in turn, should be a matter of heeding the total other – here, that each university should understand that, with its own individuality, it is present in and part of a large set of ecosystems.

Conclusions

The time of the ecological university has come. However, 'ecology' here must include but go far further than the natural environment. To place the concepts of university and ecology together is to do no less than open perspectives on the relationships between the university and its total environment, at once personal, social, epistemological, cultural and economic, and its natural environment and its pedagogical situation.[11] Each of these (seven) aspects constitutes its own ecosystem and, together, they form the ecosphere of the university.

But then a revolution is called for in our thinking about the university. No longer set off against the world – which it either exploits for its own end (with 'impact') *or* falls victim to, overpowered by a tsunami of malign forces *or* which it even vainly attempts to ignore as it continues to pursue knowledge as 'its own end' – the university can be seen as lying deeply within its ecological setting. The university can understand itself to be surrounded by and interpenetrated by its ecosystems, but also understand that it can act purposively in this setting and *vice versa*. To put the concept of ecology in the company of the university is, then, to open an *ecosophy* of the university.

To speak of the ecological university, therefore, is to assert that the university has spaces for agency; indeed, its own ecological agency. In the wake of the work of Deleuze and Guattari (Deleuze and Guattari, 2007/1980; Guattari, 2016), it is fashionable to speak these days of 'lines of flight' but perhaps a more apposite way of putting matters is to suggest that there lie before the university *paths of possibilities* or even paths of *imagination*. (Actually, Guattari seems to point in this direction in his assertion that 'no-one is exempt from playing the game of the ecology of the imaginary!' [Guattari, 2005/1989: 57]). And the ecological paths will have to be discerned or imagined for each university, for each university will possess its own *ecological capital*, resources and 'equipment' (Guattari, 2016; emphasis in original), and will of course enjoy its own position in each of the seven ecosystems identified here.

To juxtapose university and ecology is also – and the point must not be shirked – to usher into our deliberations an ethical component. It is to pose the question: 'What, if any, is the responsibility of the university in the world today?'. And it supplies an answer of forbidding proportions, namely: 'to strive to do all it can to further the wellbeing of each and all of the seven ecosystems'. This is a formidable response on two levels. First, the ecosystems are themselves ecological. They are all interconnected, so that major challenges arise for the university in working out impossibly steady paths, amid the intricate interweavings of its ecosystems. If the university has a care towards expanding the public sphere, placing its activities in the open, to what extent does it give spaces to voices that would seek closures of some kind (whether in the economy or in society)?

But, and second, to speak of ecology and ecosystems is a shorthand for opening to the interconnectedness of the world and the cosmos. Many in the ecological movements are pointing to a need for humanity to become 'anthropocosmic' (Mickey, 2016: 90–92). To speak, therefore, of the ecological university turns out to conjure the largest possible vistas, and to seek to understand both the university's place and its possibilities against such an unending spaciousness. This is an eco-philosophy of and for the university of the fullest kind and it is a quest that must be opened.

Notes

1 It follows that '[e]cological thinking is to do with art, philosophy, literature, music and culture. Ecological thinking has as much to do with the humanities wing of modern universities as with the sciences . . .' (Morton, 2010: 4).

28 The idea of the ecological

2 Mention of roughness here brings aptly into view Joseph Dunne's (1993) magnum opus *Back to the Rough Ground*. As an aphorism at the start of the book, Dunne has a quotation from Wittgenstein: 'We have got onto slippery ice where there is no friction . . . We want to walk: so we need friction. Back to the rough ground!' Roughness for Dunne, I take it, refers to difficulties ('friction'?) in thinking through and struggling through such problems ('aporias') in bringing theory and practice into a proper balance, in forming a satisfactory alternative to 'technical reason', and in working out the relationships between experience, deliberation, action and communication. All of these matters are directly relevant to working through the concept of the ecological university more fully than is possible here. There are, of course, too, some nice connections between the metaphors of slipperiness and friction on the one hand, and the smooth and striated surfaces of which Deleuze and Guattari (2007/1980) have spoken – to which I refer in this book. And there are significant overlaps between the authors examined by Dunne and those energizing this inquiry (notably Newman and Habermas).

3 We have here, therefore, a 'human ecology' that exhibits 'qualitative complexity' (Smith and Jenks, 2007). However, as my paragraph runs on, it is evident that I wish to elevate the complexity of thoughts and ideas above that implied by talk of the cognitive dimension. Ideas can affect ontologies, not least the massive structures and systems that universities collectively constitute, even though they may be mutually opposed.

4 A volume that Roger Scruton, an English philosopher, has (*Spiked Review*, December 2015: n.p.) called 'a totally unreadable tome'.

5 The university's ecosystems, accordingly, could justifiably be subjected to a 'rhythm-analysis' (Lefebvre, 2004/1992).

6 The very many critical and informed commentators here include Piketty (2014) and Stiglitz (2013). Neither wish – so far as I can judge – to supplant markets, but seek to find a way of taming their worst excesses, which include distortions in the public flow of information (Stiglitz, 2013: 232).

7 On the connections between the university and the market economy (and the pernicious impact of the latter), see, for instance, in an expanding literature, Bok (2003) and Brown (2011).

8 Porpora's essay connects at several points with the argument here, especially in his claim that (Bhaskar's) Critical Realism offers a meta-theory and a meta-philosophy under which other philosophies, concepts and theories might be placed, *and* offers us a horizon for facing the unfolding new world order.

9 These initiatives could be construed as an institutional attempt to foster 'transgressivity', as depicted by Nowotny, Scott and Gibbons (2001: 223–225). This transgressivity 'can never be reduced to the simply scientific and the purely technical' (p. 224). Of course, it is then 'open to contestation because . . . experts speak to matters that transcend their competence' (p. 225). This is a danger that the ecological university has to risk.

10 In his book, *Lines of Flight*, Guattari hoped to see the emergence of universities as 'collective assemblages of enunciation' (2016: 67–68). That he glimpsed it in the American universities 'during the 1960s' suggests its possibility, if also its slender likelihood. Just such an assessment is part of the present argument.

11 The term 'ecology' is being used here in a doubly metaphorical way. First, in understanding the university, it brings into view a term that has its natural home in the natural sciences; and, second, it profoundly radicalizes its usage by putting it to work in observing relationships that go far beyond the natural world. The tests of such metaphorical stretching are straightforward: is this metaphorical gambit helpful? Does it illuminate the issue before us (the idea of and the future of the university)? Do its associated concepts – here, for instance, complexity and emergence – readily extend to the object before us? Does it lend itself to policy and practical implications? These are matters for the reader to judge, but my answer would be 'yes', on all counts. On 'ecology' as metaphor, see Proctor and Larson (2005) and Weaver-Hightower (2008).

2
ASSEMBLING THE PIECES

Introduction

Recently, Manual DeLanda (2013/2006) has advanced a systematic philosophy of the social sciences built around – as he terms it – assemblage theory. It is an impressive attempt to develop a realist account of society which builds on the fragmentary ideas of assemblages to be found in the philosophical work of Deleuze and Guattari (in both their separate and their joint writings). There are several elements to the theory, some of which we have already glimpsed, such as the idea of territorialization (and de-territorialization), which refers to the integrity of an entity (or loss of its integrity); and the distinction between expressive and material elements of an entity. In this chapter, we shall bring those ideas more into view plus others in examining the interconnectedness of the ecological university.

The questions in front of us are these: just what kind of 'assemblage' *is* the university? How do the different elements of the university hang together, if at all? How do they interconnect with the university's various ecosystems? How static or dynamic are these elements and systems? We have already made a start on these questions – in observing that the economy considered as an ecosystem commands the largest attention, but that the university is connected with a number of other ecosystems, *the hierarchy of which, so we may note, has altered over time* – but clearly there is more ground to be trod here.

Forming attachments

Assemblage theory – at least in the hands of DeLanda – posits two large ideas. The first is that there is a world independent of our thoughts and ideas about it. It is, after all, an avowedly realist social theory. The theory has immediate application here. We may have *ideas* of the university – there is a long tradition, going back nearly 200 years, of books on the idea of the university, and the idea being projected here (of the ecological university) is precisely *an* idea of the university – but the university has an institutional independence that is separate from our ideas of it. Since the mid-twentieth century or so, as higher education has been incorporated into the equipment of the state and the economy, it has taken on legal, financial, physical and environmental presences in ways that are significantly new. Certainly, each of these presences is informed by our ideas of the university but, in each domain, the university has an ontological aspect that is independent of our ideas of it.[1] If a university makes a disastrous investment – whether on the stock market or, say, in gaining a loan to build a new student residence block – its financial consequences are real; and if a university engages in some kind of corruption – for instance, if it tries to bribe a national audit agency[2] – a legal situation arises that has a real presence in the world (irrespective of any views that might be entertained about the audit agency's methodology).[3]

The second large aspect of assemblage theory that I wish to pick out is the idea of 'unpluggability'. As DeLanda sees it, in assemblage theory, the elements of an entity – say, a university – hang together in a contingent way. Each of its elements could be unplugged and still we would be in the presence of (say) a university. Again, we see this in the university setting. University x might lose a major research centre – it might have been poached by a neighbouring rival university – and yet we would still want to say that university x still existed. Contrariwise, that university might decide, say, to develop a presence for itself in policy studies and do so by adding, establishing and developing a new department of policy studies. Still, we would want to say that it was the same university, even though it now possessed an additional element. There is no essence that attaches to a *particular* university.

These two aspects of universities – their 'real' character and the contingency of their elements – are important for two and almost opposed reasons. *On the one hand*, to point to these characteristics is to emphasize that universities are having to make their way in the world, with all of the contingency that it places upon universities. And universities have options as to how they respond to the exigencies that successively face them. Do they just add on units (whether administrative or academic) as new situations present themselves or do they infuse the work envisaged in a more organic way? There is, therefore, an *ontological openness* to universities. In the words of another contemporary advocate of realism, there is at work here 'a principle of unreason. There is no reason for anything to be or to remain the way it is; everything must . . . be able to be and/or be able to be other than it is' (Meillasoux, 2008: 60). Moreover, as complex entities in the world, universities are liable to collide with many other entities in the world, sometimes of their making and sometimes not.

On the other hand, contemporary realism tends severely – and unfortunately – to downplay the power of ideas.[4] Universities are what they are *partly* in virtue of ideas held of them, both at their outset and as any such ideas have changed over time. In the United Kingdom, to cull examples from nearly 200 years, University

College London, Birkbeck College, Keele University, the Open University and University of Sussex owed much to the particular ideas of their founders. Universities, accordingly, do not have just an ontological set of presences and they are not just contingent blobs on the landscape of higher education. They are so called because of their hinterland of a set of ideas, both with which the term 'university' has universally been associated over many hundreds, if not thousands, of years; *and* often with which they were additionally associated in their founding moments.

Even now, it is not implausible to suggest that there is a large imaginary (to draw on Charles Taylor's [2007] term) about the university that derives especially from German philosophers in the early nineteenth century, although certainly inflected by sentiments associated with other cultures, notably in the United States and in England and in Scotland (Peters and Barnett, 2018). This imaginary is constituted by a constellation of ideas to do with reason, truthfulness, contestability, openness, established forms of inquiry – with their own if changing and contestable rules of method, disinterestedness, public utterance and examinability.

Assuredly, ideas are not all-powerful in the face of the university's ontological presences in the world. The university is beset by political, ideological and economic forces that forcibly steer it. Ideas of the university may still, however, gain a purchase. To spell out the point, at a macro-level, the ideas of Kant and other leading German philosophers were formative in the re-development of the German universities in the early eighteenth century (notably in von Humboldt's vision and founding of the University of Berlin). To pick up some of the other examples just mentioned, in the mid-twentieth century, the birth of Keele University in England was much influenced by the thinking of its Christian first Vice-Chancellor, A D Lindsay (Gallie, 1960). Two decades later, the ideas of Michael Young, the social reformer, were influential in the establishment of the UK's Open University (which in turn acted as an emblem for many other open universities across the world). Several of the 'new' universities of the 1960s – notably Sussex, Essex and York – were moulded in part by the *educational* ideas of their inaugural Vice-Chancellors.[5] And at local levels, individuals are influential within universities in establishing new kinds of programmes of study or research units, bringing into play ideas that they have been nurturing perhaps for many years.

A matter before universities, therefore, is that of forming attachments, both to the world *and* to ideas that might help to give it new momentum. There is a question here of stickiness: what might cause or enable a university to stick to the world in some way? And what might cause ideas to stick to a university?

Two kinds of glue are required, one to enable a university to adhere to entities in the world (say, a business enterprise, another university or a particular community); and another to enable ideas (say, about its possibilities in the world) to stick to the university. Different surfaces call for different glues in order to produce the necessary stickiness. Of course, these two adhesives will often be found together. A university will characteristically find a way of adhering to – forming a close relationship with – another institution via a set of ideas that both parties find congenial. Universities can and do stick simultaneously both to other institutions and organizations *and* to sets of ideas. Indeed, the two kinds of *viscosity* gain support from each other (cf. Urry, 2003: 60). And so a measure of adhesion – call it a *stickability quotient* – could in principle be identified for different kinds of surfaces to which a university might attach itself.

A moving kaleidoscope

Universities are complex institutions moving in a complex set of spaces and this total environment is both moving and unstable. The university moves somewhat uneasily across its seven ecosystems and each ecosystem is dynamic, constantly moving and changing. And a single university is a complex entity, with its elements having different levels of propensity and capability in forming attachments within its ecosystems. To take just one example, that of the knowledge ecosystem, the different departments of a university will each form their own configuration within it. Some departments will have more of a global reach; others will be orienting themselves, say, to professional fields where embodied knowledge or knowledge-in-action are important; and yet others will be intent on exploring possibilities for income generation by putting their knowledge to work in the economic sphere. To use a modish term, there is here an *intersectionality*, in which multiple fields and interests may well be interacting, so as to produce an incoherent picture.

The picture is rather like one of those child's kaleidoscopes, in which – through the viewfinder – the pieces are liable to comport themselves into a random pattern, with the different pieces overlapping each other in haphazard ways, their varied colours adding to the spectacle. This is an unstable situation, with the slightest shake causing the pieces to be juxtaposed into a quite new arrangement. A question for us here is this, therefore: might there just be a way of imparting *some* semblance of order to the arrangement of the pieces or is the place of the university, together with its myriad elements, destined to be subject merely to the forces acting haphazardly on it?

There is an important difference between the fragments. A university might so set up its systems, for example, that it succeeds in attracting a high number of international students. It might reach out to prospective students in international fairs overseas, it might meet and greet new international students at airports, it might ensure that they have good accommodation and it might ensure that each new international student has a 'buddy', a more experienced international student to act as a mentor. It might, in other words, do what it can to set up its university-wide *systems*. But the teaching approach and the pedagogical relationship might go largely unchanged across its departments. There might be very little attention paid to the 'cultural scripts' and personal meanings with which international students present. To draw again on a distinction from DeLanda's assemblage theory, both material and expressive components are important, but they are separate in the development of universities.

There is a dual contingency present, then, in the university's intersections with the wider world, contingency being present in both its material and its expressive components. And to this consideration we should add the twin concepts of complexity and supercomplexity.

Complexity speaks more to the systems in and around universities, and that a university is implicated in many systems simultaneously only adds to the complexity facing universities. A decision to set up an accommodation block for students in a poor part of a city may in turn generate an upturn in the local housing market and a heightened level of opprobrium from local residents, now being priced out (and so emerges a twenty-first-century return to the town-and-gown disputes of the Middle Ages). This is formally a situation of complexity in that it exemplifies a non-linear set of interactions within and across systems, the outcomes of which cannot readily be computed.

On the other hand, the very question as to what it is to be a student in the twenty-first century is an example of *supercomplexity*. Once a pupil in an advanced finishing school, now we are told variously that a student is a 'customer', a 'global citizen', an initiate in the 'conversation' of humanity (Oakeshott, 1989), a 'professionalist' (Lyotard, 1984), a researcher, a 'producer',[6] a surfer and a self-educator, with much rivalry between these and yet other perceptions. While the entanglements of complexity could be mitigated, to some extent (given more resources, more time, more money), the entanglements of supercomplexity can *never* be dissolved. To the contrary, the more that there is reflection and debate, the more entangled will such dispute become, as new concepts, insights and evidence tumble over themselves.

For the most part, universities try to slide over the surfaces on which they find themselves but so often collide with forces and ideologies that are circulating in the ecosystems that they inhabit. There is now an inevitable *intertextuality* to the university's situation, assailed as it is from so many quarters, and open to innumerable readings and discernments of its possibilities. Understandably, the university appears to be fragmenting, in being faced with these challenges, so many of them hostile as it may seem, and angled in from all directions. Not infrequently, too, the university adds to its own fragmenting. Rather than attempt to percolate its whole offerings with a new policy or idea, it will often resort simply to adding a new unit here (say, in leadership studies) or a new centre there (say, in complexity studies). The university grows disjointedly in response to the heterogeneous openings that come its way. It is a moving kaleidoscope in which the patterns are haphazard, even if they are somewhat colourful.

Emergence and engagement

The ecological university is a university that takes its networking seriously, and even imparts an ethical flavour into those connections. It is a university that not only understands that it is interconnected with the world in manifold ways, but actively seeks to do what it can, through those interconnections, to advance the wellbeing of the world. More specifically, this kind of university recognizes that it is caught within certain ecosystems – seven are especially evident – and that the university is well positioned to assist *their* advancement.

However, the main story of these past few paragraphs has been one of fragmentation, destabilization, pluggability, detachment and distance. Certainly, there was mention of stickiness, of finding glues that enabled the university more securely to attach itself to entities – organizations, institutions and even other universities – in the world and to ideas. But it was left open as to the substance of those glues. Just how might the university attach itself to the world – in both its institutional and ideational aspects – such that the university can play out its ecological possibilities?

There are, at this point, three sets of considerations that bear on the argument, all of which we see in the separate philosophies of Roy Bhaskar's Critical Realism (especially his later [2010] 'East–West' philosophy) and the 'rhizomatic' philosophy of Deleuze and Guattari. Briefly, and rather crudely, these three considerations are, *first*, that we live in the world, not apart from the world, but in it. And, here, 'world' means the whole Earth in its human and non-human aspects. *Second*, this is a world of material entanglements, and deep structures, with its fissures, splits, collisions and chaotic situations. But – and *third* – spaces can be discerned precisely as a result of the massive movements occurring at subterranean levels. There is a paradox here. The very presence of massive and interlaced steering mechanisms – globalization, cognitive capitalism, the knowledge society, the digital revolution, and inquiring desires generated by mass higher education itself – is opening spaces for new actions, paths of possibility and imagination. This is the world in which the university finds itself. As it reaches across the globe in so many ways, it is buffeted by huge forces largely outside its control, but it is not simply a victim of those forces. Gaps open for it to make its own sorties into even hostile lands.

Here, we should juxtapose two further concepts, those of emergence and engagement. Both are to be found but reside in different literatures and are rarely brought together; and both suffer from or enjoy – depending on one's disposition – multiple interpretations. By 'emergence', I wish to point to the capacities of situations to bring forward potentials that were not originally evident and could not have been foreseen.[7] The energies in situations, with the presence of multiple forces and open systems, both cause new movements and release new energies. By 'engagement', I refer to the possibility of an entity – such as a university – taking serious account of *some* thing, be it another institution, an idea, or a material entity and yielding to it in some way. The two concepts come together in this way.

The university is always in *emergent* situations. Opportunities present themselves as the exigencies of the moment break open the world surrounding the university, both material and expressive; and these opportunities could not have been glimpsed earlier. A government decides to become active in nanotechnology, or sustainable technologies, or social integration and so invests in appropriate research programmes, so opening new opportunities for its universities; or that government may seek to attract international students from a particular region of the world.

Opportunities open all the time for universities to engage with the world, which then have options in determining priorities and the purposes that might be followed.

Less obviously, ideologies clash, offering an opening for a university to cloak itself with a new language that appeals to the warring parties. It takes on a discourse of 'impact' or 'student satisfaction', but inflects them with its own values and stance in the world. Less prosaically, institutions move and financial situations change, all the time opening new possibilities for action on the part of the university, placed – as it is – in open systems.

Certainly, the university has to be careful in any action that is taken in its name. A false move could bring the might of, say, a dictatorial state down upon it (with its key researchers and intellectuals being put on trial where the verdict can be foretold in advance); or, as noted, could plunge a university into a financial crisis; or could act to discourage potential students from applying for entry. But to note these possible elephant traps is to confirm that the university is a 'corporate agent' (List and Pettit, 2011), with at least some room for manoeuvre in a total situation of continuing emergence.

Engagement is part of this university world. The university has *some* room not just to discern paths of possibility for itself, but also to determine the causes, the institutions, the ideas and the locations to which it wishes to attach itself; in other words, to choose where and how it engages. And engagement includes inner possibilities. For example, a university might determine that there would be value in it engaging seriously with a university-wide initiative aimed at improving the relationship between its research and teaching (Fung, 2017). But, then, different departments *within* that university, and different groups *within its departments*, may pursue that possibility in quite different ways, with varying balances and relationships between, and contrasting priorities accorded to, research and teaching (depending partly on the autonomy and power granted to heads of department).

It is notable that a university cannot nowadays take all that it might discern as possible directions of travel for itself. Here arises the matter on which we touched earlier, that of stickability. Engagement and stickability are reciprocals: the more of one, the more of the other. But stickability takes the palm. Engagement will be secure only where there is stickability. Unless ideas and institution stick together, engagement will be a flimsy affair.

Stickiness is liable to be found where there is a mutuality between a university's being in both its material and its value aspects, and the entity or path of action that is opening for it. One university chooses to establish scores of 'spin-out' companies, generating considerable new sources of income; and another university, even in the same city, chooses to reach out to African universities, to host its scholars and to establish mutually helpful links and research activities aimed at social and rural development. They follow quite different paths of possibility that reflect their quite different stances towards the world. In each case, there arise contrasting patterns of mutuality between a university, its values and stance and its discernment of its possibilities in the world.

But, then, if there are such differences across universities, why might it be felt that the ecological university might have a *universal* presence? Because the university is naturally fitted to its having an ecological orientation. This is not to say that the concepts of ecology and university are identical. Rather, they fit together, like two pieces of a jigsaw puzzle (each of the two pieces, intrinsically, may be quite different, but together they form a unity). The fit lies in some of the themes that are especially associated with the university. They include those of a concern for understanding, a sense of the unity of the world (for all knowledge is ultimately interconnected), an openness to the world, a sense of equity in that all can in principle participate in a conversation, an interest in a diversity of ideas and perspectives, and a sense that progress cannot be achieved through power. All of these value orientations fit with an ecological disposition, a disposition – in other words – to have a concern for the whole world and to see the whole world as comprising partners with an interest in the world as such.

As a matter of description, the ecological university – in a thin sense – is already with us. The university is unavoidably embedded in ecosystems, whether or not it takes up an intentional stance towards them. Some universities are, even if hesitantly, treading the path of that possibility. They are beginning to exhibit 'ecologies of practice' (Kemmis et al., 2012), showing a concern towards the world and wanting to improve it in some ways; and the world is often on their side. Exigencies of the moment provide openings that, with a suitable will, can be discerned and even entered. The ecological university has to be created, with the imagination being brought to bear *in situ*. And once openings have been espied, expressive and material resources have to be harnessed. Points of stickiness have to be found, if such engagement is to solidify. The ecological university is always-emergent and has always-to-be-engaged.

Trans-engagement

Coming into view here, as we may put it, is the idea of *trans-engagement*. The ecological university is trans-engaged in four dimensions.

First, the ecological university is *trans-disciplinary*. It not merely speaks about the benefits of interdisciplinarity, but also works at encouraging disciplines to engage with each other.[8] It identifies large themes and practical projects on which disciplines can work together and bring their contrasting perspectives to bear. In so doing, it opens spaces for meta-levels of communication and joint working to evolve. It brings into play wide and open epistemological horizons, in which inner disciplinary values and ways of comprehending the world might just be made visible and even subject to gentle interrogation. In this milieu, the engineers and sociologists – let alone the philosophers and the theologians – no longer talk past each other, for they understand themselves to be travellers in a common venture, that of comprehending a world in flux.

Second, the ecological university is a *worldly* institution, sensitive to its having possibilities in and across the world. It understands itself as a member of the family of universities worldwide and seeks to establish connections with some other universities in other parts of the world and so help to develop conversations across nations. It sees itself as part of a global ecology of universities (cf. Temple, 2014a: 65). Even if unevenly, this kind of university develops its own institutional 'ecological wisdom' (Mickey, 2016: 80), having a care towards the total world and, all the time, exploring possibilities that open thereto.

Third, the ecological university *engages* with the world, across all seven of its ecosystems. It reaches out to the world in ways congenial to its own trajectory. It sees which communities in the wider world it might orient itself towards and how it might advance human understanding in those communities – perhaps in particular professional communities, in developing countries, in urban situations closer to home. It considers how it might put different kinds of understanding into the fray. It works with communities in developing its research projects and it brings the challenges of the world into its curricula – in sports studies, medicine, legal studies, philosophy and so on. And, as indicated, the wider world and the relevant communities include itself and its own internal communities. Each university will, accordingly, develop its own *zones of engagement* and, thence, its own *ecological profile*.

Last, the ecological university works within and across *itself*, transforming itself so far as is practicable, encouraging an 'ecological' orientation deep in its own heartlands, at the levels of its courses, the experiences of its students and the individual research and scholarly projects of its academic staff. An ecological spirit reveals itself in the openness of the university's conversations, internally and with the wider world. In this way, the ecological university becomes a form of continuing co-production, with the whole university engaged on the project, working out – at all of its levels, and across individuals and departments – its possibilities for and with the world.

For each university, then, there will develop a characteristic set of 'regimes of engagement' (Thevenot, 2013), as it plunges deliberately into the seven ecosystems. Over time, it will come to possess its own *ecological signature*. Some universities will be hard at work in developing countries, and perhaps – whisper it softly – depending on a past colonial background, will be more heavily predisposed to working in some regions than others. Some universities will be energetic in working in explicitly cultural settings, widening – for instance – public understanding of ethno-musical traditions. Others will come to be understood for the ways in which they are interacting with the political sphere across countries and are helping to construct open and critical public debates about large worldly issues; and often sensitive issues at that – they will run risks in so doing. Others will experiment with ways of doing justice to the idea of students as global citizens, with all that that entails in promoting understanding of and an empathy towards peoples in other lands. Yet others will take seriously their interest in the student experience and seek to outflank contemporary forms of closure – in learning outcomes, and student satisfaction – and develop pedagogies that disclose a wide world to students. And yet others will find ways of breaking through the boundaries that disciplines present

38 The idea of the ecological

and seek ways of bringing colleagues together in collaborative ventures with trans-disciplinary themes and projects.

The ecological university, then, is a *stretched university*. It is also a liminal institution, on the brink of difficulties as it opens itself to the world. It plays on the edge of political and social problematics. It exposes its students to challenging issues, not least of the limitations of disciplines and of the challenges of seeing beyond one's own discipline. It is a *transgressive institution*,[9] engaging across disciplines, ecosystems, institutions, practices, persons – and the world. It forms the knack of taking itself to the world and bringing the world into itself; and so it brings the distant into proximity with itself. It becomes a spacious world in itself.

A unifying narrative

The ecological university cannot hope to bring all of its elements into a single pattern. Any university is too complex for that. It can, though, seek in ecology a unifying narrative, albeit one that has continuing limitations. The ecological university will remain caught up in markets of the national and global learning economy, and in many other hugely powerful forces. And its sub-systems – departments, research centres, programmes of study, enterprise units – may have degrees of independence to forge their own ventures and worldly connections. So, any university narrative can carry the day only to a limited fashion. But, still, a narrative of ecology can help to impart some direction and can serve as a discursive symbol to indicate abroad its intended positioning.

The ecological university takes itself seriously *as* an ecological university. It embraces the idea of ecology and seeks to understand itself and its possibilities across the seven ecosystems of higher education. Its disciplines will exhibit their own epistemological values but, still, the ecological university can develop over-arching themes that will help to advance the wider knowledge ecology. The theme of global citizenship can open hitherto unglimpsed paths of possibilities for its programmes of study. Perhaps some courses can link with comparable courses in institutions in another country (aided by suitable memoranda of understanding signed with those other institutions). The theme of co-production can prompt researchers to consider ways in which interest groups in relevant communities can be enlisted to develop research programmes. The theme of the 'university beyond walls' (Finnegan, 2005) can prompt thinking about how academics can project their work to, and even work with, wide audiences and so advance the public sphere.

If a mark of modernity, and the competitive environments associated with it, has been the emergence of homelessness – not merely individual but even institutional – an eco-philosophy for the university can give it a *homefulness* that is fitting for the twenty-first century. This is not, it should be clear, to invent a space for the university that separates it from the world or offer a space in which all of its endeavours can find a home. The world, the university and the university's interconnections with the world are too chaotic for that. Indeed, many of the university's possibilities and its actual endeavours will fall outside of an ecological disposition. The university will doubtless continue to sustain unequal life chances, to keep an eye out for itself in global rankings, and to look to defend and advance its own interests. But, as intimated, the ecological university will, over time, come to take on an *ecological spirit*,[10] which provides energies and inner steering capacities.

This ecological spirit will find its way into the interstices of the university. Individual students, individual academics, and particular research units and centres would come to exhibit ecological movements. The ecological spirit works in intimate spaces. The twentieth-century French philosopher, Gaston Bachelard, developed a philosophy of just this kind, giving prominence to a sensitivity to the minutest elements in the environment, natural and man-made, human and non-human (Bachelard, 1994). It would reflect an 'inner immensity' (Mickey, 2016: 92). The ecological point of view cannot refer to a world beyond, but has to come into being, into (here) the ecological university. All that the ecological university touches would be susceptible, in principle, to an ecological feeling. It would be a particular kind of acute attention-giving, always on the look-out for ways of seeing and advancing the interconnectedness within the university *and* of the university with the world.

The ecological university has 'an ecosophical ethics adapted to this terrifying and fascinating situation' (Guattari, quoted in Mickey, 2016: 58). It is, in consequence, extraordinarily open. It opens itself to the world, of thought, of perspectives, of being. More, it traverses its seven ecosystems, always sensitive to its unintended consequences in an unpredictable world (whether negative *or* positive). It attaches itself to ecology as an over-arching narrative which does not bind it, but frees it to glimpse possibilities anew. It lives beyond itself, in the world, creatively espying ventures that might help the world. '[T]he future of humanity and of life on Earth depends on our engagement in the diversity and complexity of beings' (Mickey, 2016: 58), and the ecological university understands itself in precisely this way. Certainly, it does not immodestly pretend that the future of humanity and of life on Earth depends upon it, but it grasps that it has a part to play, and that playing its part depends upon its 'engagement in the diversity and complexity of beings' (Mickey, 2016: 58).

For the university, ecology becomes a universal cause and a universal narrative and ethic. The ecological university accepts that it is already ecological, albeit in a weak sense. Willy-nilly, the university is implicated in seven ecosystems. It can choose to ignore those ecosystems, it can act malevolently – even if unwittingly – towards them, or it can choose to explore its ecological possibilities. With this last stance, ecology becomes a unifying and strong narrative for the university. This is a university that displaces itself, becoming aware of its embeddedness in the world. But in taking on ecology as a self-sustaining narrative, it does not lose sight of the individual features of its being in the world. It actually becomes more sensitive to them, having a care towards the individual – the student, the family in a neighbourhood in which it is active, the individual member of staff, as well as the individual entities in its total environment. Ecology *is* a totalizing narrative in that it is difficult to see that any feature of the world could be potentially beyond the territory of the ecological university. Singularity and universality are held together in the space of this university.

Conclusions

In the twenty-first century, the university has its being in a demonic world, at once chaotic and replete with lines of power that strike into it, to which it has to respond. Being a complex entity, its constitutive elements respond in different and rivalrous ways. The department of sociology responds in ways quite different from the department of engineering or pharmacy. In this mayhem, the university evinces splintering tendencies, both instrumental and humanistic. But still, a single university retains some unity and ventures forth, cloaking itself with grand over-arching themes – of 'research-led teaching', of 'service' to the wider world, and of 'excellence' and of 'world-classness'. These are thin legitimations, with little sensitivity to the complexity of the world.

In front of the university is the challenge of alighting on a theme both that does justice to the situation of the university and that can open a sense of its responsibilities to the world. The university touches this Earth, through seven ecosystems, but this glimpsing of an ecological university only confers further challenges. The ecosystems, at once epistemological, social, personal, economic, learning, cultural and environmental, fan out, providing potential zones of engagement. Against such a vista, 'assembling the pieces' – the title of this chapter – turns out to be but a metaphor. The pieces cannot be assembled to form a coherent picture. The ecological university is no simple assemblage. But 'ecology' may just play a part in imparting some direction to its paths of possibilities and so energizing the university, while hinting at an ethical stance of a certain kind towards the world. Instances of the ecological university can already be glimpsed in the micro-engagements of its units. The narrative of ecology can yet play a fuller part in redirecting the university.

Notes

1 It follows, therefore, that I am in sympathy with the view that 'ontology cannot be assimilated under epistemology' (Smith and Jenks, 2007: 258). However, as I suggest in this chapter, in rightly wanting to bring ontology into view, the new realists often overlook the power of ideas and thereby underplay the relationship between ontology and ideas.
2 There is some suggestion that in some regions of the world, higher education quality assurance agencies can be subject to undue influence by interested parties (see Guzmán-Valenzuela, 2016a).
3 For a robust articulation of an independent social world that constitutes a 'real world', see the work of John Searle, especially over the past two decades or so (Searle, 1995; 1999; 2010, ch. 5). Significant in Searle's position, and relevant here, is a distinction he makes between social facts and institutional facts. See his exchange with Barry Smith (Smith and Searle, 2003).
4 I would consider both Bhaskar (at least in his early philosophy) and DeLanda to be guilty as charged, whereas my sense is that – for example – neither Meillassoux nor Harman could so readily be charged.

We may note that Harman (2010: 183), too, links both Bhaskar and DeLanda, but in a much more positive spirit (and in a way with which I concur) as philosophers of 'the much maligned "deep and hidden"', in which assemblages are 'never fully actualized'.
5 See Sloman (1964); Briggs (1964). For a lively account of those new English 'plateglass' universities, see Beloff (1968).
6 The idea of the student as 'producer' has been promulgated at the University of Lincoln, England, especially through the work of Mike Neary. The project 'emphasised the role of the student as collaborators in the production of knowledge': http://studentasproducer.lincoln.ac.uk/
7 See Maccarini (2013), who advances a stratified conception of 'social emergence', the features of which include 'structural aspects', 'external conditions', 'internal dynamics' and 'agency, with its creative . . . potential' (p. 34). All of these elements are part of the story here.
8 There is a growing literature on interdisciplinarity that goes back at least half a century, but rather little on the linkages between ecology and interdisciplinarity. Guattari's book on *The Three Ecologies* is cited in the text. Otherwise, a key text here is that of Bhaskar et al. (2012) on *Interdisciplinarity and Climate Change*. Several of the chapters resonate with the idea of the ecological university as explicated here, especially those by Bhaskar (2012), Naess (2012), Cornell and (to a lesser extent) those by Parker, and Rommetveit, Funtowicz and Strand.
9 On 'transgressivity', see Nowotny, Scott and Gibbons (2001).
10 There are, in these reflections on spirit, and an active sensitivity to the world, links to the 'spiritual life' as understood in some religious traditions. '[The Buddha] never advocates indifference or detachment from life, but instead he urges us to care for others in a non-detached way, without desire or personal interests clouding the issue' (White, 2013: 40). There is much here that chimes with several components of the present argument.

3
BEYOND SUSTAINABILITY

Introduction

A favoured concept within much ecologically oriented thought is that of sustainability but, for our purposes here, it must be put to one side. The ecological university is not concerned with *sustaining* life or systems or institutions or persons or technologies or cultures or learning or knowledge or even the natural environment, but is rather concerned with advancing or strengthening or positively *developing* life in all of its forms. The ecological university is not even concerned with change, but is concerned to play its part in change so as to bring about ever-enhanced wellbeing in the world. It is far more than 'the sustainable university' (Sterling, Maxey and Luna, 2013).[1]

To say this at once raises profound issues. What is so limiting about the idea of sustainability? What might be meant by improving or strengthening aspects of the world? Do the seven ecosystems of the university stand differently here? These and other related matters are in front of us in this chapter.

On not sustaining the world

The idea of sustainability is bequeathed to us primarily from biological studies of systems and organisms in the natural environment. There, tendencies are found such that systems and organisms have degrees of resilience and powers of endurance. They are able to weather the vicissitudes that normally beset them under natural environmental conditions. However, under unnatural conditions, of the kind that humanity has unleashed upon the world through its technologies and ways of life, those powers of resilience in biological systems are impaired and the very existence of those systems is placed in jeopardy.[2] Consequently, and quite justifiably, the ecological movement brings forward concerns to restore those systems such that they are continuingly sustainable.

Already, it is apparent that the idea of sustainability is a hybrid. It looks to systems in the natural environment being sustainable and, indeed, self-sustaining. *And* it also looks to humanity to acknowledge its part, both in bringing about the present impairments in systems and in changing much of humanity's forms of life so as to re-establish those sustainable systems in the natural world. Sustainability, therefore, looks in two directions at once, to the natural world and to humanity itself. And in this bifurcation, the concept of sustainability both embraces descriptions about the world and opens ethical spaces that prompt more normative matters about humanity's responsibilities in the world.

But the concept of sustainability takes on yet other complexities. As its ethical component has been taken up, so – not unnaturally – many of its adherents have sought to identify ways of improving the world. The United Nations (2015) has adopted no fewer than 17 '*Sustainable* Development Goals' (emphasis added). They include:

1   *Poverty* – End poverty in all its forms everywhere
2   *Food* – End hunger, achieve food security and improved nutrition and promote sustainable agriculture
3   *Healthy lives* – Ensure healthy lives and promote wellbeing for all at all ages
4   *Education* – Ensure inclusive and equitable quality education and promote lifelong opportunities for all
5   *Women* – Achieve gender equality and empower all women and girls . . .
8   *Economy* – Promote sustained, inclusive and sustainable economic growth . . .
16 *Institutions* – Promote peaceful and inclusive societies for sustainable development
17 *Sustainability* – Strengthen the means of implementation and revitalize the global partnership for sustainable development.

Two features of this (truncated) list stand out. First, several items include the term 'sustainable'. They are, therefore, somewhat tautological: sustainable goals sustain sustainability! (I shall return to this point, pedantic as it may seem.) Second, each of these goals looks to bring about some form of improvement in the world, whether in the economy, in life chances, in health and education or in societies more broadly. Together, these Development Goals do not just presage a huge transformation of life on this Earth but intentionally seek to improve the lives of people and societies. So, as it has developed in practice, the idea of sustainability has been stretched to include efforts and encouragements *to improve* world systems of various kinds, both natural and human.

The term 'sustainability', therefore, is now being asked to do much work, and rather too much work. It is being brought into play in relation both to human and to non-human environments. It has come into play in scientific fields with descriptive, analytical and causal aspects, but it has also come to have ethical goals, intended to reorient human activities, both at the personal and societal levels.

44 The idea of the ecological

And, most notably for our purposes, it is deployed both to urge change in human affairs so as to bring about a more sustainable world *and* it is drawn upon to critique the world and open vistas of quite different orderings of society and so even take on a revolutionary aspect. No term can achieve coherently all of these ends and so its uses are liable to be ambiguous and opaque with unacknowledged resonances. We see just this in practice, not least in those UN Sustainable Development Goals which, on interrogation, turn out to be something of a mish-mash of tautologies, myths (for instance, that health or that the ending of poverty could be achieved as an 'end' state – for both of these are relative concepts, always moving), pious hopes and implied descriptive accounts of the world. This incoherence is precisely a result of the idea of sustainability being required to carry too much weight.

There is, however, an even more fundamental point here. It is that the world can *never*, in any straightforward sense, be sustained; and so the term 'sustainability' is liable to be misleading. As philosophers have observed for two millennia, from Heraclitus to Deleuze, the world, with its gamut of ecosystems – both human and non-human – is always in flux.[3] The concept of 'sustainability' – and its associated language of 'sustain' and 'sustaining' – speak to a situation of repetition, of a set of circumstances being sustained over time. Witnessed against the backcloth of a vibrant, changing and even chaotic world, the idea of sustainability is out of place. It is also dangerous, for it implies something of a steady-state; and *that* circumstance is neither possible nor desirable.[4]

This situation is especially the case, for example, in the matter of thought, ideas and understandings; in other words, in relation to knowledge considered as an ecology. To pick up just one ecosystem, the knowledge ecology, its sustainability is not at issue. Rather, the issue is one of its ever-fuller flourishing: does it exhibit a due diversity with, say, non-scientific forms of thought being accorded legitimacy? Is there an ever-greater circulation of ideas in a polity? Is there a continuing creativity in those ideas? Do the dominant knowledge frameworks include those of peoples across the world, including the South (Connell, 2007) and indigenous traditions (de Sousa Santos, 2016)? Does the knowledge in a society reach out so as to form ever-wider publics? Is there a healthy degree of continuing scepticism, debate and even rivalry, with groups pitted against each other in critical dialogue? If the answer to questions such as these is 'yes', then we are not in the presence of a knowledge ecology that is being *sustained*, but rather one that is being strengthened and developed. And, of course, *it is a further matter as to the extent to which universities are assisting this development in ways that the questions imply*.

Autopoiesis – another cul-de-sac

Another concept that not infrequently looms into view in the ecologically oriented literature is that of autopoiesis. Some, indeed, have even tried to draw a tight relationship between the two concepts of ecology and autopoiesis (Naruse and Iba, 2008) and offer an understanding of an 'ecosystem as an autopoietic system'.

The theory of autopoiesis was developed by two Chilean cognitive biologists, Humberto Maturana and Francisco Varela, in the 1960s and early 1970s (Seidl, 2004: 4). The central idea is that a living system reproduces itself through its own elements – which they referred to as 'autopoiesis' (from the Greek: autos – self; poiein – to produce). For example, a cell reproduces itself from its own properties. Crucially, for our purposes, this concept of autopoiesis was taken up by Niklas Luhmann (2013: II: 4), and generalized so as to be applicable to non-biological systems, including the social domain (Bakken and Hernes, 2003; Luhmann, 2003). Luhmann's work, itself voluminous, has spawned a huge literature and much debate, notably a long-standing dialogue with Jurgen Habermas (Kjaer, 2006) – which is relevant to our purposes here.

The attractiveness of linking the ecological perspective to the idea of autopoiesis is readily apparent. The ecological perspective, after all, points up the inner unity of systems – ecosystems – and raises a concern about their impairment. The idea of autopoiesis offers a way of developing that approach, for the ecologists can now add that ecosystems have natural autopoietic tendencies. Left to their own devices, ecosystems would go on reproducing themselves. It is just that, largely due to human actions, they have become impaired in some way. Perhaps their natural diversity has been severely diminished. So there is an affinity between the concepts of ecology and autopoiesis.

The theory of autopoiesis also contains within itself an important distinction, on the one hand, between the *reproduction* of a system – and *this* capability is strictly the autopoiesis of the system – and, on the other hand, the self-determination of its structures, referred to as *self-organization*. As Seidl (2004) remarks, for autopoiesis to be present,

> it is irrelevant what concrete cells are produced; whether the plant [say] produces a new leaf, extends its roots, or grows a blossom does not matter. . . . The fact of the reproduction . . . is . . . the *autopoiesis* of the system.
> (Seidl, 2004: 4)

On the other hand, as well as having powers of self-reproduction, systems also have powers of self-organization; that is, the powers of determining which new shapes they may take. This important distinction we shall need to bear in mind.

There are, however, three limitations of autopoiesis theory, especially as it has been extended to social systems. That it underplays the interactions between systems and the wider world; that it does not contain an adequate conception of human communication; and that it does not allow for considerable change in the nature of social systems. Much of this set of critiques formed the substance of a long-lasting dialogue between Jurgen Habermas and Luhmann (Kjaer, 2006);[5] and all three critiques are crucial in understanding the university and its possibilities – and responsibilities – in the world.

The university is not and now cannot be a self-reproducing island, cut off from the world, but is integrally a part of the world. Moreover, it engages with the world to a large extent through – though by no means only through – its powers of communication, and in many modes. Last, and most important of all, in stretching towards its full self, the university – especially the ecological university – contains within itself a sense of its working to change the world, not least to advance the wellbeing of the (seven) ecosystems in which it is particularly implicated. The ecological university and worldly transformation are *pari passu*: they go step by step with each other.

What is it for the ecological university itself to be ecological?

There is one further observation to be made on the ideas of autopoiesis and sustainability, and one much in their favour. It is that these two ideas of sustainability and autopoiesis prompt the question: is the ecological university itself ecological? While the ideas of sustainability and autopoiesis turn out to be something of a cul-de-sac for this inquiry, still they suggest the following line of thought.

So far, the ecological university has been construed as a university that not merely circulates among the (seven) ecosystems in which it is implicated – and *they in it* – but dwells upon, and works on, those interconnections, so as to impart greater wellbeing to each ecosystem. The ecological university is ecologically wise. It is not of-the-world nor merely in-the-world, but *from*-the-world,[6] drawing its inspiration from its understandings of the world. And it is also *for*-the-world, playing its part, however modest, in assisting the world, through its interweavings with several of its major ecosystems (of knowledge, social institutions, persons, economy, learning, culture and the natural environment).

The ideas of sustainability and autopoiesis may have initial attractions here, but we have found both of them wanting. Sustainability underplays the capacities of the university to help advance the ecosystems in which it is implicated. Autopoiesis underplays the interaction of systems and their powers to transform each other. *But* perhaps there are insights here for the ecological university. Perhaps the ecological university not only has a concern about and a care for the ecosystems in which it moves, but has a concern towards sustaining and reproducing *itself*?[7] This is a prospect worth contemplating.

If the ecological university is minded to play its part in advancing key ecosystems in the world (and no fewer than seven have been identified), the ecological university will also understand that such a view imparts responsibilities upon the university to maintain its own wellbeing; its own *ecological health*, indeed. If the ecological university is to sustain and develop its capacities to advance the world's knowledge ecologies, it will need its own internal epistemological capacities to be vibrant. Its academics need to have space to be creative in their own ways, and they need the encouragement to engage with each other across their disciplines. Each department and each institution tends to have its own epistemological footprint, with its favoured theoretical frameworks and hallowed luminaries (dead and alive), and thereby a characteristic epistemological habitus. These rather fixed knowledge dispositions need to be weakened and the strong 'classification' characteristic of higher education (see Bernstein, 1996) and associated boundary maintenance need to be at least partly dissolved. After all, if the ecological university is to engage with the wider ecology of social institutions, it will need to be socially and epistemologically adept in the wider world and to have an internal *epistemological buoyancy*, not weighed down by set knowledge dispositions, but ever-ready to take up surprising epistemological alliances, and – so to speak – be light on its epistemological feet.

This epistemological adeptness is one way in which the ecological university needs to become ecological. The ecological university will need to go on developing itself so that it is continually re-shaping itself to maximize its ecological possibilities in the world. It will need its own self-reflexive powers. Here, the distinction made earlier (but rather left hanging), that between self-reproduction and self-organization, is helpful. The university has to attend to its powers of self-reproduction *and* give thought to its self-organization, both its *powers* of self-reorganization and its possible *forms* of reorganization.

If the university is fully to realize its possibilities in advancing the ecosystems of the world, its self-reproduction *as such* will actually be anathema to it. Rather, it will be concerned to go on reorganizing itself so as to be evermore free, creative and transgressive, as it attends to its possibilities for the whole Earth. And it will need to give attention to the forms of its organization that best enable it in any period of time to be fully ecological in the world. Its powers of self-reorganization will be orchestrated in the ecological interests of the world. Of course, there is a legitimate self-interest here: the ecological university's powers of self-organization – which will enable it to be fully ecological – will at the same time assist its own survival in a challenging world. But now, its self-reproduction will be a by-product – though an important by-product – of its central interest in advancing the wellbeing of the whole Earth, especially of the seven major ecosystems in which it is particularly implicated.

These can only be schematic points at this stage of the argument, but they do double duty here. *First*, these reflections on the university being itself ecological help extend the idea of the ecological university to *itself*. Of course, the ecological university will be concerned about itself in relation to the natural environment: is it unduly using fossil fuels? Is it polluting the local atmosphere? Are its new buildings designed and built in a sustainable fashion? Is it recycling much of its waste? Has the management of its backroom services taken on an orientation in favour of a 'greening of the campus'? (This last example can now be seen in universities across the world, including in developing countries, and it presents large challenges of organizational culture [Marques Pereira et al., 2014].) But the ecological university goes much further.

The ecological university – above all – cannot be a university solely turned in upon itself. If it is to be fully ecological, the university has to work through the implications for itself, in its internal organization, its dispositions towards the world (is it simply for-itself, attempting to advance its competitive position in the world and extract what it can from the world and so impoverish the world *or* does it

48 The idea of the ecological

have a care and concern for the world, wishing to deepen wellbeing in facets of the world?) and, thereby, its range of engagements with the world. It would make for a nice empirical study to compare two universities, say in the same city, for their ecological footprint (understood to include the entire university environment).

Second, these reflections point up again the limitations of the concepts of autopoiesis and sustainability. The ecological university will have a care for itself, but it will seek neither merely to sustain itself nor to reproduce itself. Simply to reproduce and to sustain itself will leave it ill-equipped to maximize its ecological

TABLE 3.1 Sustainability, autopoiesis and ecology compared

	Sustainability	*Autopoiesis*	*Ecology*
Open/closed systems	open systems	closed systems	open systems
Connectivity	open connections with natural world	restricted connections	open conversations with wider world
State of being	restoration to former organic state	confirmation of former state	transformative improvement towards new state of the world
Emergent properties	systems' emergence	stasis	doubly emergent – natural and facilitated
Change character	corruption and amelioration	natural self-reproduction	agentic/intentional change (re-organization)
Ethical situation	concern for natural environment	ethically neutral	total openness (concern for the whole world)
Imaginative potential	relatively fixed conception of rightness (steady stade)	given conception of rightness	highly imaginative – discerning and creating hitherto unforeseen possibilities
Focus/pitch	focus on natural environment	focus on social institutions and social organizations	all-encompassing (boundary crossing across multiple ecosystems)
Worldly situation	of-the-world	in-the-world	from-the-world and for-the-world
Horizon	immanent within a system	given by the social institution or organization in question	ever-expanding

possibilities in a changing world. An undue interest in reproducing itself will condemn it to a world wryly observed by Bourdieu, in which the academic community turns in on itself, satisfied with its own 'scholasticism' and academic capital (Bourdieu, 2000). Its pedagogies would be those of 'reproduction', in which students are consigned to take on the identities of their tutors rather than being encouraged to open themselves to the challenges of the world.

An interest in sustaining itself will, in contrast, certainly offer the university possibilities for internal *change*, for in its subsequent incarnations, the earlier forms of a university will be successively modified (as in the evolution of animals). But these will still amount to limited changes. The concepts of autopoeisis and sustainability are limiting concepts and, if taken up, would leave a university falling continually short of its responsibilities and potential, as it seeks to discern possibilities to realize its full ecological situation in the world. The ecological university is continually in a state not even only of self-becoming, but rather of self-transformation; and quite radical transformation at that.

Drawing on the analysis offered so far, and anticipating the discussion still to come in this chapter, we may summarize the differences between the ideas of sustainability, autopoiesis and ecology as set out in table 3.1.

Beyond sustainability

A key issue before us at this juncture is this: just what is the stance of the university to be in a world of continuing change, in which the concept of sustainability has little to offer? What is it to go beyond sustainability – and autopoiesis for that matter? Two sets of considerations are important. I shall deal with positive considerations here and, in the next section, will embrace what *prima facie* may seem to be somewhat negative considerations.

An ecological philosophy for the university – an eco-philosophy – brings a sense of its being caught up in the world. The very term 'world' is difficult, for it has taken on connotations of particular geographies and global socio-economic and political formations. It has taken on hues of being a rather human-centred concept when this is precisely what is in question for the ecological university. The ecologists like to speak rather of the 'Earth' and that term has attractions. It displaces humanity such that it is part of a much larger whole, but even this term ('Earth') has its difficulties.

We may note that the so-called Anthropocene is a critical concept, calling attention to the way in which humanity – not just in its technologies, but in its epistemologies, culture and economic arrangements – has placed itself in the centre of understandings of the world. In turn, the idea of the Anthropocene opens to the possibility of humanity turning its attention to possible new relationships between itself and the Earth, of which it now understands itself to be a part.[8] The ecological university takes these considerations on board. It embraces a geophilosophy that 'de-territorializes' thinking and goes beyond humanity's immediate concerns and projects, connecting thinking to the whole Earth. This geophilosophy of the university, in other words, will 'facilitate a renewal of human–Earth relations' and so orient the university to 'summon forth a new earth, a new people' (Deleuze and Guattari, 2013/1991: 99).[9]

Several ideas flow from these schematic remarks. First, and as stated, the ecological university is not concerned merely to sustain the world but has a constitutive interest in its improvement. But what might be said so as to begin to fill out the idea of improvement? Little can be said here of a universal character. Each ecosystem will exhibit improvement in different ways. What it is for the university to improve the knowledge ecology is different from improving the natural environment or the ecology of social institutions or the learning ecology. Each ecosystem will be susceptible of improvement in its own way. And each university, depending on its ecological stance and ecological profile, will rightly discern particular ways of aiding any such improvement. Some general principles may, however, be identified.

First, *a principle of openness*: an ecosystem will often be strengthened when it is open, both within itself and to the wider world (cf. Peters, 2009). Of course, care needs to be taken here. Some external interests or presences, once allowed inside, may act to corrupt or further impair an ecosystem in some way, especially where those influences themselves would herald closure. In the *knowledge ecology*, a university biochemistry or pharmacy department that allows in the petro-chemical or pharmaceutical industry may find that its research, publications and curricula efforts are unduly curbed. So openness may be deleterious but, in principle, it is necessary in advancing ecosystems.

The university advances the *learning ecology* by encouraging students to open themselves so as to reflect in the fullest way on their learning and so develop new powers of self-understanding; a 'self-hermeneutic' reflectiveness, indeed. The university advances the *ecology of social institutions* in the world when, for example, its departments of planning and architecture – perhaps with its students – work on a community estate with residents and awaken possibilities for urban development and so develop an openness in social institutions of planning, architecture, regional politics and so forth.

A second principle is that of an *expansion of horizons*. The university is in a position to expand horizons in positive ways. In putting its activities into the public domain, perhaps through the judicious use of the internet but also by physically opening itself as a space for public conversations *in situ*, the university can help in expanding public understanding of matters. This at once expands the boundaries of the knowledge ecology, the ecology of social institutions (for example, in bringing the political sphere into wider contact with the polity), and the learning ecology. This principle is key for the ecological university in acting to widen consciousness across the world and across ecosystems.

For Jurgen Habermas, a feature of modernity is precisely its differentiation of segments of society – of religion, science and the lifeworld – such that they are increasingly unable to engage productively with each other. That insight can be radicalized, for we can observe that the seven ecosystems of the university have tendencies to split apart, not least as the economy comes to acquire particularly marked forms of separateness. The horizon typically associated with each ecosystem is, as a result, unduly limited. The ecological university understands that it has a part to play in expanding the horizons of its ecosystems *and* their interconnections and, as just indicated, is well placed to do so.

A third principle lies in the *advancement of a world community* (Bartelson, 2009).[10] The ecological university works in the interests not of itself, nor of any particular ecosystem (such as the economy), but of the whole world. To draw on and extend the terminology here, the ecological university becomes one of the 'creative participants in the emerging Earth community instead of [one of its] dominators . . . a matter of becoming anthropocosmic instead of anthropocentric' (Mickey, 2016: 98). This is a university that sees itself as playing its part in the development of the whole Earth, across all of its ecosystems. It understands itself as held within and as having a care towards the Earth and its precarious setting in the universe.

The ecological university cannot be a university that simply advances itself amid 'cognitive capitalism' (Boutang, 2011), that works in its own interests and in the interests of a certain kind of economy, fraught with inequality, power and competition. It is rather a university that seeks to help the world understand itself as a community, even amid difference. For example, it will take seriously the idea of the student as global citizen, but impart to it an ecological orientation. Any tendency to orient students to become worldly entrepreneurs (Peters, 2018), able to traverse the world with apparent ease to gain economic and personal advantage, will be eschewed. Rather, students would be encouraged to form empathy for the world, for its cultures and languages, for its indigenous and also for its impoverished peoples and to feel a one-ness with those peoples. And some universities are doing just this, incorporating such experiential aspects within the curriculum.

Openness, an expansion of horizons, boundary crossing and a world community: these are four sets of ideas to help form principles to enable the ecological university to realize its potential in improving the world. They are, as it were, positive principles, strengthening and enhancing existent ecosystems of the university. But there are also some negative aspects of the world to which the ecological university will be sensitive.

Absenting absence

The idea of absenting absence is part of Roy Bhaskar's philosophy of Critical Realism. It is one way in which that philosophy gains its 'critical' spurs. In the concept of absence, Bhaskar wished to open the prospect that, at least in the social world, real features may be critiqued not only for their malign aspects but also for their deficiencies and, thereby, their absences. Absences may be real and 'real absence, according to Bhaskar, can have causal effects' (Assiter, 2004: 63).

The identification of poverty is also, *ipso facto*, to point to an *absence* of acceptable living conditions *and* of a proper distribution of resources, often for the many in a society. The identification of unnecessary waste is to point to an *absence* of proper means of waste recycling. The identification of gross inequalities in gaining access to higher education is to suggest an *absence* of acceptable levels of social and educational provision, and of a proper institutionalization of a due equity, for the young across the whole of society. So the real features of society – as they really are in the world – can be fairly critiqued for their absences. And, in turn, the pointers towards social and political policies that such critiques trail in their wake amount to a plea to 'absent absences' – and so, for example, to urge forward a more equitable, socially just and ecological society.

> Absenting absences, which act as constraints on wants, needs or . . . wellbeing, is essential to dialectics interpreted as the logic of freedom. And the whole point of argument, on which dialectic has been most traditionally modelled, [is] to absent mistakes.
>
> (Bhaskar, 2008a: 42)

If the ecological university takes seriously its inner intentions of advancing or strengthening its (seven) ecosystems, it will therefore strive to do what it can to address the absences, the gaps and the insufficiencies in those ecosystems.[11] It would, for instance, work against any disappearance of an interest in the university as a space for critical thought. One looks almost in vain now for mention of criticality in the statements on higher education emanating from governments and state agencies.[12] It will have a concern for the woefully limited public understanding of the relevant background to large issues of the day, and will seek to play its part in injecting just such a public understanding; and, in the process, help to build a substantial public sphere, at once rational and informed, even if disputatious. It will scrutinize public policy documents across all fields to see not only what they say, but what important matters are left out of the reckoning. It will look inwards and review its curricula and, for example, where it observes absences, it will inject pedagogical spaces such that (for instance) students on professional courses can be enabled critically to reflect on a profession as such (as well as acquiring the appropriate knowledge and skills and ways of being associated with practitioners *within* the field).

It is evident then that the ecological university is an *in*tolerant university. It is intolerant of narrowness in thought, of communicative and symbolic closure, of injustice, of un-freedom, of gross inequality, and of social and political arrangements that diminish wellbeing. In all these ways, and as they fan out across the major ecosystems, these malformations represent absences that will, sooner or later, come within the ambit of the ecological university's activities. Of course, such a university, in explicitly putting itself into the fray, will find itself in choppy waters and will have to play matters carefully if it is to maximize its ecological potential.

Conclusions

Emerging here is nothing less than a radical orientation for the university. Far from confining itself to *sustaining* its ecosystems, the ecological university will be on the look-out for large deficiencies, both in the wider world and where they present within itself (in the conduct of its research, the formation of its students and its inner intellectual life). The ecological university will be playing its part in re-shaping those ecosystems, such that their deformations are removed and thereby take on a more satisfactory shape. The ecological university turns out to be a revolutionary university.[13]

The ecological university represents an assault on such contemporary university formations as the entrepreneurial university or 'the corporate university' or even 'the digital university'. After all, at least in their most excessive incarnations, those university forms go with the flow of the global knowledge economy and, indeed, seek to wrest what they can from those particular spaces of flows (Castells, 1996) so as to advance their own interests. Far from combatting absences in ecosystems, these university formations compound the inequalities and serve the dominant interests of the age. The ecological university, then, would be not merely another university formation among the many with us today, but rather a counter-university form, self-consciously addressing precisely the deformations that both contemporary universities and society more widely are exhibiting.

In turn, the ecological university would have an eye to its own possible deformations and its continuing reorganization; and not merely to sustain its ecological effectiveness but to enhance that effectiveness. There will always be more that the ecological university can do in developing the conversations between its disciplines, in stretching its students into strange places, in opening dialogues with the wider society, in listening attentively to the world and attending to demonstrable large issues, and in imagining new possibilities for itself and for the world.

All this calls for continuing attention to the university as an institution, in its internal communication flows horizontally and vertically, in the spaces available to its academics and students, and in its pedagogical relationships. But it calls also for a certain kind of ethos, characterized by such virtues as service, integrity, institutional trust[14] and mutual respect. Explicit attention to the ethical character of universities has long been in short supply (in an age of arithmetical performance indicators and targets and covert surveillance), but there is surely a sufficient bedrock of such institutional virtue (Nixon, 2008; Higton, 2013) on which to build anew.

Notes

1 I want to open clear water between the ideas of the ecological university and the sustainable university for two reasons: (i) the full idea of ecology goes beyond sustainability to include programmes of advancing the world and continually improving its stage of wellbeing; (ii) the concept of sustainability has particular traction in relation to the natural world. Certainly, the volume referred to here (Sterling, Maxey and Luna, 2013) contains chapters that are in tune with this doubly broad approach to ecology that I am suggesting, especially those by Sterling (2013) (who urges 'a transformative' redesign process [p. 36]), Taylor (2013), Tilbury (2013), White (2013), and Sayce et al. (2013). See also the volume edited by Bartlett and Chase (2013) which, again, while tilted in the direction of the natural environment and green university policies and the 'campus ecosystem' (chapter by Christian Wells: 133), still contains resources for the project being proposed here, not least those concerned with university leadership.

2 Often, in ecologically-oriented texts, the term of the 'Anthropocene' is wheeled out, referring to the supposed way in which humanity has so imprinted itself upon the Earth that it has significantly displaced natural forces as a source of energy. However, this is a hotly disputed notion. On the one hand, it is disputed within the natural sciences, since the evidence of a human stratum of entities and materials that would correspond to geological strata is not fully recognized. On the other hand, within philosophy and social theory, the idea is internally inconsistent. It is offered as a critical concept, critical of the way in which humanity has harnessed the resources of the Earth to its own interests, but its all-encompassing character would seem to exclude any kind of alternative course of action, which – at least in some hands – is part of the motivating source of the concept.

3 The key text of Deleuze here is that of his (1994) *Difference and Repetition*. For Deleuze, repetition is associated with blockage, with repression, with non-comprehension. However, it can 'heal us' (p. 19). There is 'dynamic' repetition, as in 'rhyme' (pp. 20–21), or 'learning' (p. 23). This repetition 'involves the Other – involves difference' (p. 23).

> That is why it is so difficult to say how someone learns . . . We learn nothing from those who say 'Do as I do' . . . Our only teachers are those who are able to emit signs to be developed in heterogeneity rather than propose gestures for us to reproduce.
>
> (1994: 23)

4 After all this time, Donald Schön's 1970 Reith Lectures, published as *Beyond the Stable State* (1971), form a crucial text.

5 Efforts have certainly been made to reconcile Luhmann's theory of autopoiesis with critical theory. See Fuchs and Hofkirchner (2009) as well as Kjaer (2006).

6 I am most grateful to Søren Bengtsen for suggesting to me this last dimension ('from-the-world'), which fits exactly with my argument here.

7 Notably, Kenneth Minogue advanced a 'concept of the university' that constituted a two-world view of the university, as he termed it. It was a university concerned only with knowledge, having no concern with the world, neither the external world nor (by extension) even its own sustainability. The latter view, that there is a 'single continuum' across these worlds, Minogue castigated as 'monism', 'the belief that there is a single world of facts for man to use' so as to 'control' the world (1973: 76–77).

8 See note 2 above.

9 This phrase of Deleuze and Guattari – 'summon forth a new earth, a new people' (2013/1991: 99) – is matched in that same volume by 'a new earth and people that do not yet exist' (p. 108) and 'the people to come and the new earth' (p. 109). All of these phrases are close to the sub-title to a volume of significance to the argument here, *Deleuze and Guattari, Politics and Education: For a People-Yet-to-Come* (Carlin and Wallin, 2016). Perhaps the chapters by Hroch (2016), by Cole (2016) and by Carlin (2016) are especially pertinent.

10 See also Naidoo (2015) on 'global well-being': https://srheblog.com/2015/10/14/transnational-perspectives-on-higher-education-and-global-well-being/

11 I am not suggesting that any such 'absences' could ever be entirely overcome. Bhaskar is clear on this point: 'you can coherently imagine or conceive of a world without presence, but not without absence' (Bhaskar with Hartwig, 2010: 124).

12 The Texas Republican Party (2012, Election 'Platform') was minded to outlaw 'critical thinking': 'We oppose the teaching of Higher Order Thinking Skills (HOTS) (values clarification), critical thinking skills and similar programs.'

13 See Guzmán-Valenzuela, C. (2016b) for a discussion of the possibility of both the transformative and the revolutionary universities.

14 See Gibbs (2004) whose book on *Trusting in the University* advances an idea of 'existential trust' in the university against the much more technological 'competence of trust'. Bruce Macfarlane has written several books on the 'moral compass' (2012) of universities, playing up the virtues of integrity (2004) and service (2007).

4
SEVEN ECOSYSTEMS

Introduction

I have suggested (Chapters 1 and 2) that the university is implicated in seven ecosystems. I want now to fill out that suggestion by looking in turn at those ecosystems, so as to form an overview of the relationship between each ecosystem and the university.

The overall thesis of this chapter is fourfold: (i) there is real substance that attaches to the seven ecosystems. They are not mere constructions in the mind but have a real presence, and one that is independent of the university. (ii) Those ecosystems influence the university but not in a hands-off fashion, as it were. The university is implicated in those seven ecosystems because each ecosystem is now present *in the university itself*. (iii) The ecological university has responsibilities in responding to and in working out its relationship towards those seven ecosystems. (iv) Moreover, the immanent presence of those ecosystems opens possibilities for the ecological university, starting with itself. Trojan horses can be neutralized and even put to work.

The idea of ecosystem

The term 'ecosystem' is rather honorific. The term 'system', after all, betokens robustness in the world and definite boundaries and even some manipulability. Ecosystems, however, are precisely not like this; they are always inchoate. They have little, if anything, in the way of definite boundaries. They are more like clouds, always changing their formations and irrevocably permeable. However, even while being outwardly inchoate and formless, they still retain some degree of inner cohesion, with their elements clinging together. They have, as we may put it, a thin ontology, but they have a presence nevertheless.

56 The idea of the ecological

Given all these limitations of the term 'ecosystem', a happier term would be that of ecological *zones*. Zones denote spaces and allow for movement in and out. Zones can overlap, fade from view (while still being present). They can be sites of power and even intimidation (think of the zones into which Berlin was divided during the Cold War in Europe). Zones can also be liberated.

Seven ecological zones

I have suggested that the university is implicated in seven ecological zones. They are:

1   the knowledge ecology
2   the ecology of social institutions
3   persons
4   the economy (considered as an ecology)
5   learning (both learning as a societal ecological zone *and* personal 'learning ecologies')
6   culture
7   the natural environment.

These are not in any particular order, save for two qualifications. First, the list starts with 'the knowledge ecology' because knowledge is a necessary concept in filling out the idea of the university. It has more of an internal relationship with the university than the others, even though it is also independent of the university and now pervades the wider world. Second, the list ends with 'the natural environment', if only to point up that to bring together the ideas of university and ecology is by no means to privilege the natural environment, which is just one of the university's ecosystems.

These points made, we may now venture into each of the (seven) ecological zones.

1. The knowledge ecology

Knowledge swims in and across the knowledge society, the university becoming but one source of knowledge production. However, the university remains a crucial node not only in the production but also in the circulation of knowledge. We await an adequate set of integrated concepts and theories to describe this matter – how knowledge circulates, what counts as knowledge in the contemporary world, where its levers of power lie, the interests it represents and the parts played by the university.[1]

Currently, terms denoting open-endedness are much in vogue – chaos, rhizomatic structures, 'ethno-epistemic assemblages' (Irwin and Michael, 2003), complexes, emergence, hybrids, bricolages and so forth: let us say, at least, that we are faced here – to coin another phrase – with an *epistemic mélange*. **But** such terminology serves only as a cover for our ignorance and for a current antipathy towards firm structures.

In his early work, Jurgen Habermas (1978) offered us a powerful set of insights pivoted on 'knowledge interests'. Habermas posited three forms of knowledge backed by separate sets of interests: scientific knowledge was backed by technical –instrumental interests in control; hermeneutic knowledge (that is, knowledge governed essentially by a focus on meaning) was oriented towards an interest in reaching collective understandings in the lifeworld; and critical forms of knowledge were sustained by an interest in influencing social change and even emancipation.

Stealing a concept from his later work, we can say too that Habermas (1989: 355) evinced a concern that technical–instrumental knowledge had 'colonized' the other forms of knowledge. Perhaps even this is too gentle: one could be forgiven for believing that technical–instrumental reason is now suffocating other forms of reason. And if so, the university must surely accept some responsibility in the matter. The near-global marginalization of the humanities in universities is a pointer here.[2]

This schema now needs to be developed. *First*, the digital age has brought with it 'multimodality', with its implicit sense that at least the media of knowing efforts are widening, and also the sighting – through the presence of the internet – of a more democratic and even 'socialist' form of knowledge, as individuals can now very easily speak to the whole world (Hassan, 2003; Kress, 2010; Virilio, 2010; Peters, Gietzen and Ondercin, 2012). *Second*, Habermas himself rather neglected the ways in which professionals come literally to embody their professionalism. They may have acquired a formal education in universities and extended it in postgraduate studies, but their professionalism comes to reside in their *embodiment* of their understandings of their particular worlds (Dall'Alba and Barnacle, 2005; cf. Merleau-Ponty, 1994). *Third*, knowledge production has been influenced by large state – and international – agencies as well as mega-corporations, which steer knowledge in their corporate, financial and even military interests (reflected vividly in the 'triple helix' thesis [Etxkowitz and Leysdesdoff, 2000; Langley, 2009]). The university has come even to partner with such powerful agencies. *Fourth*, there is a global interest – and by no means confined to affluent societies – in cultural knowledge. The performing arts become not only cultural adornments, but even take on significant revenue-generating dimensions. The techno-rational world spreads into the cultural sphere, and again the university is implicated.

But how does the idea of ecology gain a bearing here? In this way: *ecological* health entails *epistemological* health – a thesis that warrants some elucidation.

We are in the presence of a number of knowledge ecosystems, in different fields of effort and of interest, characterized by varying degrees of power and openness. Of any epistemic region, we can inquire into its health. Is it vibrant? Is it open to new ideas? Is it easy to contribute to its development or is it a closed shop? To what extent are the epistemologies of the North subjugating those of the South and those of indigenous traditions? (de Sousa Santos, 2016) To what degree is one field open to another? And to what extent is a field connecting to the wider society and working to advance public understanding of significant issues? Through questions of this kind, we may perceive the *ecological potential* of a knowledge field.

Knowledge takes on ecological characteristics through its powers to extend the wellbeing of the world. This power has increased significantly over the past 200 years, with the coming of the knowledge society and with faster and more open forms of communication. Now, more or less the whole planet is interconnected. I am not sure that this rather elementary point about these new *knowledge possibilities* has yet been fully explored.[3] But it has this dual consequence: spaces are opening for universities in relation to the knowledge ecologies of society and, thereby, the ecological potential of universities is now considerably expanded.

2. The ecology of social institutions

Social institutions exhibit contrasting tendencies, and so too universities. Generally, social institutions are exemplified by powerful market-oriented corporations *and* by public-sector institutions; by face-to-face organizations *and* those that are also based on digital forms of communication; by organizations that are worldly conglomerates with large degrees of independence *and* by others that are small and specialized and are much more subject to local regulatory regimes.

Less apparently, the knowledge systems attaching to organizations exhibit a parallel inchoateness. There is a dominant shift not just towards science, technology, engineering and mathematics (STEM) but towards a complex of advanced science, computerization and computer science, and high-end technologies – of which bioengineering is a characteristic example. For some, it is tempting to see in this onward march of STEM disciplines a cognitive ratcheting up of neoliberalism and instrumental reason. Whatever the validity of such a thesis, of interest here is – *for example* – that bioengineering can be directed towards surveillance systems of the most instrumental, inhumane and financially motivated kind *and* it can be directed towards the development of flexible carbon prosthetics for young people with disabilities, so as to enable them more fully to engage in society. This latter development is imbued with a *hermeneutically loaded* form of cognitive interest, being inspired by an empathic care towards individuals. In short, even though there are dominant forms of cognition, they are accompanied by markedly open, differing and even rival value systems.

Universities exhibit much of this organizational disparateness in the wider world. They may be so large as to be the largest employer in a city and they may straddle the world, and may have become in effect a holding company for a number of quite separate enterprises; *or* they may be quite small in size, with specialized functions. They may sit largely in the private sector *or* in the public sector. They may function primarily as face-to-face institutions *or* work largely through digital forms of interaction. And, too, some will be heavily involved in the creation of knowledge while others – 'teaching universities' – will pursue their activities largely by reproducing the knowledge and systems that already exist (perhaps generated by a separate private company).

Again in keeping with organizations in the wider world, universities will exhibit a multitude of value positions, not only across themselves but also within themselves. Characteristically, different value positions will be adopted as between the sciences and the humanities, but the situation – as we have observed – is quite messy. We have just noted an example within bioengineering, but even within a field such as nursing studies, both instrumental *and* caring values may be observed.

So there is something of an isomorphism between universities and organizations in the wider world. *Both* sets of organizations present with considerable variation and accompanying epistemological orientations and value positions. This *mirroring of profound differentiation* – across universities *and* across organizations in the wider world – is explicable. *Both* sets of organizations – in the wider world *and* universities – are now placed in globalized systems, of commerce and of the academic world respectively. And in such globalized systems, there is bound to be extreme variation.[4]

This variation, in the university world as in the wider world of organizations, is exhibited both in financial and cognitive power *and* in value orientations. Furthermore, far from exhibiting a bell-curve of power and financial might, both sets of institutions – in the wider world and universities – show a near 'L' shape, with a very few institutions possessing the lion's share of the spoils. In the university world, perhaps only 500 universities at the most can take a serious interest in the university world rankings, but this is less than 2% of the 25,000 plus universities to be found across the world.[5]

Three implications of this story stand out for the ecological university. First, the wider organizational world indicates that *rival* value systems may be found there, even if there is a dominant value set (buttressed by neoliberal forces). Universities can exhibit a range of value orientations and perhaps this heterogeneity will even widen. There is succour here for the ecological university. Its values may find a ready reception *somewhere* in the wider organizational world, even if the ferreting out of those receptive spaces takes time and effort.

Second, universities are being encouraged to trade with organizations in the wider world. It follows that universities have an extraordinarily wide array of organizations with which to associate. Some organizations or institutions will turn out to be more attractive than others, either on account of their own ecological leanings ('ecology' understood in the broad way being advanced here) or on account of their exhibiting a state of disrepair that the resources of the ecological university can address (perhaps in the local community or even, say, in the developing world).

Third, that wider hinterland of societal institutions, in all its heterogeneity, is already engaging with universities. Governments, corporations in the private sector, professional bodies, local and regional authorities, and many others have beaten a path to engage universities; and not, we may presume, always in the interests of universities. In other words, there is an ecology of institutions attendant on the university and it has crept increasingly into universities, such that universities have to a large extent become machines of those institutions and their interests. But the university often retains powers to energize itself as a machine for its own interests.[6]

From all of this, it follows that the ecological university will be alert to the total ecology of social institutions that encircle it. It will develop an astute *institutional grasp*, in working out its options for advancing wellbeing in the world.

3. Persons

Human subjectivity has attracted the attention of philosophers and social theorists for more than 200 years. A major concern has been that of the relationship between persons and the wider world (whether in the form of the state, or society or, more recently, postmodernity and globalization). Some commentaries have taken rather dismal tacks, seeing only the disintegration of the individual as a coherent entity. Others have been more optimistic, seeing the possibility of individuals advancing their own agency in their own – if unfolding – life projects (aided not least by their own 'internal conversations' [Archer, 2003]).

Both of these options have taken extreme variants. On the one hand, the pessimists have seen only nihilism, with human subjectivity torn apart or, alternatively, manufactured by large state and corporate interests. This was the position of Adorno and Horkheimer, whose (1989/1944) thesis of the collapse of the Enlightenment project had only the most pessimistic reading of human subjectivity, manufactured – as they saw it – by the increasingly global corporate world with its interests, backed by the state, in 'mass deception'. Others, notably Sartre and Marcuse, at least searched for the possibility of bringing together the emancipation of the individual psyche with that of society itself: Marx and Freud could be united.

These concerns have continued to the present day and assuredly can only intensify, not least with the onset of the digital world. In this new order, we witness both a speeding up of time into instantaneous or even future-oriented time (Nowotny, 1996; Hassan, 2003) and a compression of spaces, such that private spaces are diminished. Now, to exaggerate only a little, most people on the planet are more or less immediately contactable by most other people (the so-called peer–peer communication situation). The emergence of the surveillance society (Hier and Greenberg, 2007) is but a particularly egregious source of contemporary disruptions to human subjectivity. In its wake has flowered interest in life coaches, personal counsellors, complementary therapies, community self-help groups and so forth. It is no longer just the high middle classes of Vienna or Los Angeles that turn to psycho-therapeutic support. The therapeutic society (Rieff, 1987) is now ubiquitous.

There is, therefore, an ecology of persons before us. As with all ecosystems, it is loose, without anything of a tight formation, and yet it is present; and at both the individual and societal (and even global) levels. As, too, with other ecosystems, we can inquire into its wellbeing: does it hang together? Does it have any boundaries? Is there anything in the way of a coherent 'project'? Is it deformed? Or has it dissolved irredeemably? If so, does it matter? Is it now just to be seen as the individual's marshalling of a heterogeneity of personal 'identities'? Might some overarching theme – God? Hedonism? Adventure? Money? Complexity? – be found to bring a semblance of unity to human subjectivity? Or are we all expanded Jekyll and Hydes, with multiple identities and personalities?

This, then, is something of the ecosystem of persons before the university, and in which the university is doubly implicated. First, it contains individuals who are bound to be subject to the challenges just intimated in managing their own subjectivity. How, in the university of the twenty-first century, might 'academic identity' be construed and what might be the university's responsibility to it, *if anything*? (Barnett and Di Napoli, 2009). Second, the university has a responsibility in the formation of its students. Certainly, across time and geography, there is dispute as to the extent of that responsibility: *is* it the responsibility of the university to have a care for its students' psyche and their personal wellbeing?

There is a contemporary paradox here. In the old days, there was a particular cleavage between those, on the one hand, who espoused a rather English cause – following Newman in the mid-nineteenth century – of liberal education, prized for its concern with the development of the student as a whole person and so were interested in breadth; *and* the utilitarians, on the other hand, who were interested in the utility of higher education, especially in its contribution to economic growth. Now, the tables are somewhat turned. For many utilitarians are now seeing in higher education its capacities in helping to develop the whole person and even – whisper it softly – students' critical thinking (which just may assist productivity in the world of work). On the other hand, those who see students as at the 'heart of higher education' and who are keen on student satisfaction and on providing a multitude of student counselling and psychological services could be suspected of tacitly *narrowing* the maturation of students, so prompting their becoming much less able to withstand the challenges of the contemporary world and – for some – their forming into a 'snowflake generation' (cf. Fox, 2016; Furedi, 2016).

Whatever a fair reading of this course of events may be, it is surely clear that the wider ecosystem of persons has found its way into the university and that there lie here large matters with which the ecological university should wrestle.

4. The economy

The modern economy is really a set of interrelated economies, public and private, and large-scale and micro-scale with all manner of exchange systems; and concerned with the manufacture and exchange of products, whether tangible objects or services or even, as in education, persons. Questions can be asked about its own health: is it in robust health or is it impaired? Universities are doubly implicated here, directly and indirectly.

Directly, universities have come to constitute a significant portion of any economy (characteristically around 3%), are evaluated in those terms (with suitable economic metrics) and have been steered by their host state so as to maximize their efficiency. Issues arise about their own financial health and their economic adeptness – especially in regimes where they enjoy (as 'private' institutions) some financial autonomy. *Indirectly*, universities have become points of investment on account of the financial returns they are expected to make, whether for the state, or for private backers. In the knowledge society, universities not only have become a big business but are expected directly to contribute to the growth of business. And so what was quaintly sometimes called the university's 'service' function (alongside teaching and research) has morphed into a 'third mission', in which universities can demonstrate their measurable impact – and preferably economic impact at that. 'Academic capitalism' is now entrenched in universities, worldwide (Slaughter and Rhoades, 2010; Slaughter and Cantwell, 2018).

This is an extraordinary turn of events for a reason not often noticed. It is, on reflection, sheer chance that a marginal institution with origins in mediaeval manuscripts open only to a small clerisy in a society prior to universal literacy (cf. Gellner, 1991; Rothblatt, 1997; Mullins and Jacobs, 2006), and having a strange interest in a collective inquiry for a disinterested understanding of concepts and arcane scholarship, could morph, with a little tweaking, into a massive institution that, several centuries later, could come to mirror and help to sustain an ultra-capitalist world, with its mixture of global and applied cognitive interests.

We witness here what has been labelled the 'financialisation' of the academic world (Peters, 2013: 197–199). Universities have come to be understood as financial entities – their gross income, their income from research, their wider income streams, their annual surplus, their working capital, endowment funds and gearing, and their financial autonomy – *and* they have come to be valued largely through the contribution that they make to the wider societal economy. It is perhaps difficult to realize just how significant and sudden is this shift. Much like those graphs that show the emergence on Earth of *homo sapiens* as occupying the last few moments of a very long trajectory, so too this economizing of the university. Against the *longue durée* of its history – which stretches back well *before* the mediaeval age – this contemporary framing of the university is but the present page in a long and continuing saga.

The issue is whether – in relation to the economy as an ecosystem – further episodes await the university. The ecological university does not shun considerations of itself in economic terms – it understands that university activities are cost-heavy, especially when conducted seriously – but rather works to widen a sense of economy. It seeks to embrace a panoply of resources beyond the financial realm. It seeks to maximize its discretionary income so that it possesses resources that can promote the wellbeing of the wider society. It will seek not merely to critique the dominant sets of assumptions that largely constitute the field of economics,[7] but also to instantiate alternative approaches around 'commons' models, and seek to develop instruments for the evaluation of public goods (Deneulin and Townsend, 2007; Ostrom, 2012), not least in developing research instruments for understanding the economics of higher education itself (Dill, 2016).

The ecological university will seek in its engagements with the world to be both economic *and* beneficent, rather than seeing these dispositions as mutually inconsistent. It will ensure that its investments have an ethical dimension and avoid armaments and tobacco industries. While being economically adept, it will understand its economic interests as but one set of interests, in its movements across its seven ecosystems, in which the economy is accorded its due measure but no more than its due measure.

5. Learning

The idea of the learning ecology is potent for the university, for the idea fills out at two levels. The university is implicated in the total learning ecology of the wider society *and* is implicated in the learning ecology of each individual.

'The learning society' has waxed and waned as a theme in public (not to mention academic) debate. Perhaps it had its zenith in the 1990s – which saw, in the UK, a major national inquiry taking the idea as its core theme (NCIHE, 1997). Indeed, fleetingly, the idea acquired some momentum. All organizations, both in the private and public sectors, were expected to become 'learning organizations'. The theme even found its way to higher education, with a call for learning universities (Duke, 1992) and, separately, an interest in universities' role in continuing education (Schuller and Watson, 2009). Parallels were to be seen in philosophy in the idea of the public sphere, vaunted – for example – by both MacIntyre and Habermas in their different ways. The public sphere, after all, was a space not just for open and even critical dialogue but also for mutual learning.

Pleas for those planes of collaborative learning – in learning organizations and as part of the public sphere – have, however, surely weakened.[8] And this dissolution is understandable against a background that has seen a strengthening of so-called 'knowledge capitalism' (Peters, 2013), which encourages an environment that is increasingly competitive, individualized and oriented to economic gain. In this milieu, what matters is less learning as such (and still less, knowledge and understanding), but economically valuable skills and resources, albeit with a cognitive flavouring and the capacities for self-monitoring and preferable self-transformation throughout life.

However, the social world seems strangely unwilling to accept this economically loaded script and at both the societal and the individual levels. At the societal level, there seems to be an unfulfilled appetite for social learning, both via modern media and via continuing traditions (witness, in the UK, the University of the Third Age, a self-sustaining learning community mainly for 'retired' people). Spaces open anew for the university to continue to pursue its role in assisting societal 'learning processes', as Habermas (1987) depicted them.[9]

Multiple learning ecologies at societal levels can be glimpsed in which the university can be active – in the mass media and social media and in working with galleries and museums – in helping to advance the public understanding of matters (through documentaries, investigations and in the sheer provision of disinterested information). Increasingly, universities, too, are directly engaging with wider publics – for instance, with citizen scientists – so developing learning communities in the wider world.

At the individual level, the idea of a learning ecology takes on a particularly challenging aspect for the university. For each individual has her and his own learning ecology (Peters and Araya, 2009; Jackson, 2016). The idea connects with that of life*wide* learning (Barnett, 2010), the sense that learning takes place not just chronologically, as a series of learning endeavours through the lifespan but also horizontally, as it were. At any one time, an individual will be learning in various spaces – and places – both in formal and non-formal settings. Beyond their formal studies, and often unbeknown to their tutors, students may be placed in a very wide variety of learning situations, both intentionally and unintentionally.

It is apparent, then, that the learning ecologies of the wider world are on the move, becoming more dense, both at the individual and societal levels, and the university is not immune from these processes. As with other ecosystems, they have seeped into the university, and again at both the individual and societal levels. But this interweaving of the learning ecosphere with the university brings new possibilities for the university in helping to advance the learning ecologies both of individuals and of the wider society.

6. Culture

For Ortega y Gasset (1946: 44), culture was at the heart of the university: 'culture is what saves human life from being a mere disaster ... Culture is the vital system of ideas of a period ... [but] the contemporary university ... has abandoned almost entirely the teaching or transmission of culture'. It has to be admitted, however, in the twenty-first century at least, the very idea of culture has become troublesome.

Opening here is what might be termed the Scruton–Eagleton debate: can one any longer speak without embarrassment about Culture, with a capital 'C' as it were, to refer to, and even endorse, what might commonly be taken to form the most significant – and liberating – symbolic achievements of a society (cf. Habermas, 2001), *or* can one only seriously critique – or even deconstruct – any such profferings and search for their ideological underpinnings? Can cultural symbols stand up to scrutiny or must they always collapse under the weight of interrogation? Culture, for many at least, is not only inchoate but lacks any framework that would provide it with some generally accepted legitimacy. On the other hand, even if there can be said to be some substance to the idea of culture, it is surely far too disparate and rivalrous a set of entities, movements and themes to constitute an eco*system*.

There is another provocative line of thought here. Advanced societies for the most part pride themselves on their rationality, a rationality in which culture is outré. The emergence of rationality was, in many ways, a story of a society freeing itself from culture: reason came to be understood as a culture-free zone. And this whole story had been given explicit justification by philosophers, notably Descartes: the nostrum of *'cogito ergo sum'* depicted reason as secure in-itself, and not requiring any support or succour from cultural institutions. One just got on in being a supremely rational and independent being (Gellner, 1992).

Here, in this inquiry, that story takes on additional force. Over the last 200 years or so, the university has come to understand itself as a search for and an upholding of reason *per se*. Accordingly, culture produces a frisson of nervousness within the university. Whose culture? Which culture? How, if at all, might it be legitimated? Could the idea of a 'common culture' really hold water in the context of higher education?[10] Such difficult questions lead to a defence of value-freedom, of disinterestedness, of 'pure reason'. If the university were to embrace 'culture', it could only do so as an object of critique, not as an endorser. And just such a reading was given added backing by Bill Readings (1997), who saw in the rise and fall of the nation state a falling away of culture as an underpinning for the university. All that might be envisaged here perhaps were 'culture wars', with the radicals and conservatives noisily engaged in their mutually destructive warfare. At least, it has to be said that the university is no spectator but is heavily implicated here.

These reflections encourage some caution. Even so, in advancing the idea of the university, a sense of culture as an ecosystem may still hold water. A first step is to acknowledge that the university might pretend to be above and beyond culture, but that it is inherently a *culture-laden* zone. Some time ago, Gouldner (1979) intimated that academic life was to be understood as sustaining a 'culture of critical discourse'. Admittedly, this idea is itself in jeopardy in a customer-focused, not to mention a post-truth, age. Students increasingly want their universities to be safe spaces, in which they can avoid being discomfited (Furedi, 2016; Hillman, 2017). It is understandable if academics fall in with such a wish for they are increasingly being judged on the basis of their students' satisfaction scores. And judgemental regimes, within *and* beyond the university, may be prompting a situation in which academics pull in their horns. This reluctance to disturb those on whom the academics' livings depend can be seen elsewhere, whether in not writing a research report that might offend an (external) sponsor or in not inviting a controversial speaker who just may raise some (internal) hackles. As an abiding ethos for the university, then, the culture of critical discourse may be wearing rather thin. Is there another culture that might be entertained?

Here lies a challenge. The ecological university seeks to welcome others into a conversation in a quest to advance itself as a space of reasoning (cf. Bakhurst, 2011). The ecological university takes it as an axiom that events and entities in the world are interconnected and seeks to bring disciplines together, and so has a generosity towards rivalrous perspectives. It has a sense, too, that such interconnectedness is accompanied by ineradicable complexity and so a disposition of carefulness and patience is called for. Last, the ecological university is motivated by a belief that knowledge and understanding can be placed in the service of a greater flourishing in the world. The ecological university, then, cannot be culture-free but, to the contrary, possesses a culture that turns on dispositions of care, openness and generosity. To use a Heideggerian term, it is a culture of *concern*.

Such a culture of concern spills out into culture in the wider society. There are the makings of empirical evidence, at least, to suggest that the presence of a university may have a dramatic effect in enhancing its city's cultural sphere. In ways not yet fully understood, it appears that through a complex set of connections within the social capital in a region – its 'social fabric' – a 'varied and thriving cultural life, thanks to the presence of a university' may emerge, such that the cultural sphere can 'become the largest economic sector after health care and education' (Sorlin, 2002).

The university is, therefore, heavily implicated in the cultural ecosystem, both in its innermost culture and in its connections with the wider cultural sphere. It is an ecosystem towards which the ecological university, accordingly, cannot remain indifferent.

7. The natural environment

The ecological university's concerns far transcend the natural environment and matters of 'sustainability'; but it cannot ignore this ecological zone. It will have a care towards its use of natural resources and will seek to ensure that it is carbon-neutral so far as practicable. It will develop its curricula so that students are alerted to and think through environmental dimensions of issues under discussion. It will advance research into environmental matters. And it will be sensitive to its impact on the physical and natural environments, whether in the immediate locality of its campuses or further afield, in its various national and global activities. It would strive to become a 'sustainable university' (Sterling, Maxey and Luna, 2013)

Put like that, however, we would simply be in the realm of a 'shallow ecology' (Naess, 2012), a set of ecological approaches that skates on the surface of possibilities. With a *deep* ecological approach, however, the university will come to understand itself anew. Its 'ethic of environmental activism' will be one of 'solidarity' with the elements of the natural world (Plumwood, 2002: 202) It would be a stance that neither pretends to a total unity between humanity and the constituents of Nature, *nor* to a fundamental difference with Nature, *nor* even simply 'a love of Nature' (Hung, 2008: 362), *nor* even a view of Nature 'standing outside oneself' (Bonnett, 2012: 299), but rather would take on a sense of being imbued with Nature and having a due concern for it. It would be oriented towards 'a political ecology of things' which recognizes the 'independence possessed by things' that possess their own 'vibrancy'. In this deep ecology, it is understood that 'human being and thinghood overlap' for 'we are also nonhuman', and that 'things, too, are vital players in the world' (Bennett, 2010: 3–4).

So energized, the ecological university takes on a deep 'environmental ethic', an ethic that seeps into the university's being (its 'ontology') as well as its ways of coming to know the world (its 'epistemologies') (Hourdequin, 2015: 178). However, this would be an ethic that draws the university beyond mere environmental 'restoration' (as Hourdequin puts it) to having a concern and to acting so to contribute to strengthening the natural world itself.

Conclusions

The university is implicated in no less than seven ecosystems – of knowledge, social institutions, persons, the economy, learning, culture and the natural environment – inchoate as they are. These ecosystems are 'space[s] of flows' (Castells, 1996: 376–428), being zones in which the university can engage with its world, which is nothing other than the whole Earth. Here lie social ecologies *and* personal ecologies. And they are global, national and local – 'glonacal' indeed (Marginson and Rhoades, 2002). This university understands that it is ineluctably held within all of the seven ecologies, and has its being within them and among them. The ecosphere – of the seven eco-zones – is not out there, but is deeply within the university.

Accordingly, the ecological university would attend to its interior ecological presences, engaging deliberately with the seven ecosystems. And each university will take on its own *ecological pattern*, always moving here and there; always restless, exploring possibilities as they may be discerned. Inner and outer coalesce: a conversation between a university and a professional body that accredits its engineering courses is at once a conversation within and without.

The general form of the ecological university, therefore, is of the following kind:

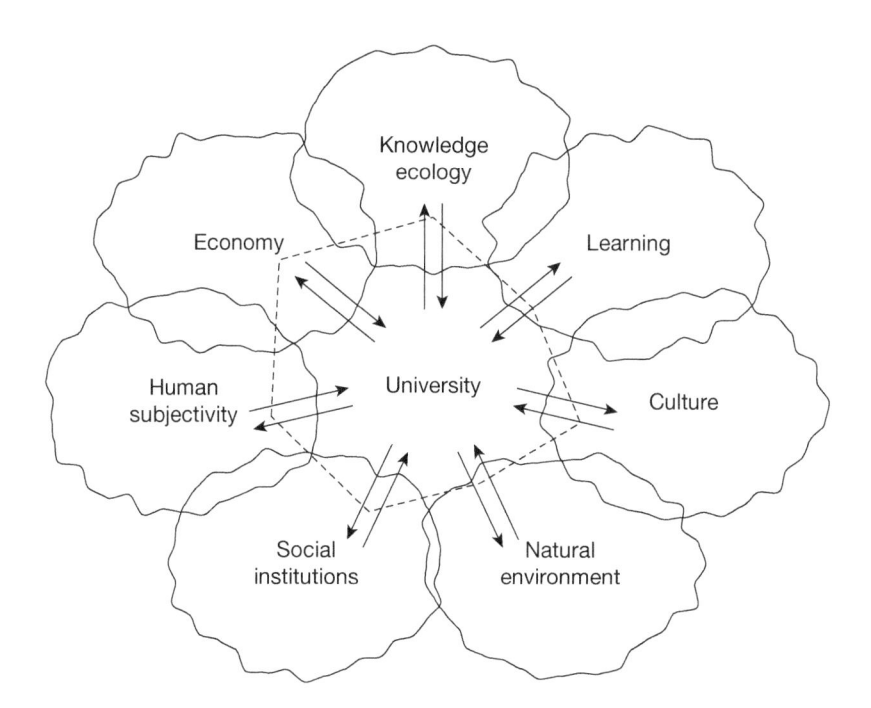

FIGURE 4.1 The ecological university

Note: The ecological university is heavily influenced by but intentionally acting on its seven ecological zones (with each university taking up its own ecological profile across the seven zones, a profile that changes over time as it imaginatively discerns new ecological opportunities for itself).

68 The idea of the ecological

This university is *ecologically* agentic, striving to fulfil its ecological possibilities in the world. It is a restless university, never content with its ecological reach. Nor is it allowed to rest, for its actions and the spaces it opens in turn conjure disputes and difficulties. There is no sure way forward for this university. But, being seized with a concern for its whole ecosphere, it maintains its energies and continues to search for new paths of becoming-ecological.

Notes

1 Just some of the more recent resources to begin such a task might include Bleiklie and Henkel (2005), Boutang (2011), Innerarity (2015), Irwin and Michael (2003), Kennedy (2015), Nowotny, Scott and Gibbons (2001), Peters (2013), Slaughter and Rhoades (2010) and Ward (2014).
2 Much attention is being given to the marginalization of the humanities, notoriously a threat (since rescinded) to withdraw funding for the humanities in Japan: www.japan times.co.jp/opinion/2015/08/23/commentary/japan-commentary/humanities-attack/
  The flight from the humanities is worldwide and is being seen in a disinclination among students to enrol on humanities programmes. See, for instance, a recent report from Canada (Chiosa, 2017).
  The theoretical and conceptual case for the humanities has been recently made severally (e.g., Cohen [2001] which contains Derrida's classic essay on 'the university without condition'; Nussbaum [2010]; and Small [2013]). Much less noted than the flight from the humanities are countervailing tendencies. For instance, Singapore has announced a substantial boost in support for the humanities and social science research: www.straits times.com/singapore/moe-to-put-in-350-million-for-social-sciences-and-humanities-research-over-next-five-years
  This warring between disciplines is far from new. More than 200 years ago, Kant (1992) drew attention to 'the conflict of the faculties' and the terminology of his analysis – in his speaking of the practical disciplines being guided by 'utility' while the more reflective disciplines were guided by 'truth' (pp. 45–47) – is not so far removed from today's epistemological situation.
3 Though see the works cited in note 1, of which here I would pick out Boutang (2011) and especially Peters (2013); and see also DeLanda (2015).
4 There is, therefore, a significant degree of 'indeterminacy' in the global age (Albrow, 1996: 123–128).
5 One database lists 26,368 universities: www.webometrics.info/en/node/54
6 The concept of 'machine' is central to Guattari's work in *Lines of Flight*, in which he distinguishes 'concrete' and 'abstract' machines. As I read Guattari, I would say that a university is both a concrete machine (with its physicality, instrumentality and financing) and an abstract machine (with its ideational and symbolic interweavings), and it is in this latter guise that the university is a '[machine] of pure potentiality' (Guattari, 2016: 121).
7 See, for instance, the report from the University of Manchester Post-Crash Economics Society (PCES) (2014); Yilmaz and Stockhammer (2015); Mitchell (2017).
8 Though see Fleming (2010), who argues that in order fully to assist the formation of a learning society (*à la* Habermas), the university has to become a mini learning society in itself.
9 That there are spaces available does not entail that wise action will be forthcoming. In the UK, government policies have led to a halving of part-time students, such students typically being also gainfully employed and/or otherwise contributing to the wider society. In theprocess, their learning is truncated and societal learning processes are harmed. See Hillman, 2015.
10 The idea of a common culture appeared in the report of a major national inquiry into higher education in the UK in the 1960s (the Robbins Report), 'the transmission of a common culture and common standards of citizenship' being one of four 'aims' to be served by higher education (Robbins, 1963: 7).

INTERLUDE

A social ecology of the university: Exposition, recapitulation and development

It may be helpful, at this stage in the present inquiry (between two parts of this book), to provide a very brief note by way of a stock-taking. In this note, therefore, I offer an exposition of the main argument, recapitulate some of its key planks and also inject a little development.

The ecological university has an ecological concern that goes well beyond the natural environment to embrace the world as such, including the social world, in all of its economic, epistemological, cultural, psychological and more strictly social aspects. It is the whole world, the Earth indeed, that comes into view within a fully ecological perspective. Second, the ecological university acknowledges that there are at stake legitimate human interests, although it does not especially privilege such interests. Third, it recognizes that human and particularly social responsibilities attach to matters that can be said to be ecological in character. To put this perspective briefly, all three concerns together denote a 'social ecology'.[1]

To draw on and develop the argument so far, components of such a social ecology perspective are:

- That there exist several largely discrete – if overlapping – ecosystems.
- Each ecosystem has a unity of its own to some extent, such that the elements have strong internal relationships. However, these relationships are not binding and elements or units within an ecosystem can be unplugged.
- There is a sense of actual or possible impairment. Any ecosystem can become corrupted or defiled in some way, such that it falls far short of its potential for assisting wellbeing in the world. (It may lose its diversity, its effectiveness in the world, its own flourishing or its spatial and nomadic qualities.)
- Each ecosystem has generative powers of its own so as to have continuity over time. It has self-reproducing and, more especially, self-organizing capacities.

- A recognition of a state of impairment imposes responsibilities, in the first place, to aim at a restoration of good order, but second, to go on working to advance the resources, energy and capacities of any ecosystem. (Self-reproduction and sustainability are not sufficient goals for an ecological perspective.)
- A social ecological perspective has three orientations, towards structures, agency *and* ideas. It acknowledges that structures are at work across the various ecosystems. It contains as an axiom a belief that humanity, in its various institutions (such as its universities), organizations and collectives, has (some) space for new paths of possibility and so possesses at least a limited degree of agency. And it grasps the point that new possibilities have to be not just discerned but imagined, and that humanity possesses the wherewithal to imagine new futures.
- An ecological approach considers that the elements which present themselves in the world do not necessarily constitute the totality of elements, whether impaired or not. Indeed, an ecological approach is predisposed to identifying absences in the world, elements that are not extant but which could plausibly be injected into the world.
- A social ecology necessarily involves ecological wisdom; that is, a stance that seeks transcendence from the world while remaining part *of* the world. This is a 'head in the clouds with feet on the ground' stance (Barnett, 2013: 134). It is a stance that seeks to be sensitive to the interrelatedness of elements in the world while remaining sensitive too to the individuation of the world (that each element in the world is unique).

   It is also a stance that is able to move purposefully forward amid competing value positions and readings of the world. It is a stance that exhibits collective judiciousness, sagacity and carefulness but which also exhibits resourcefulness and speculation.
- Especially for complex and open-ended institutions such as universities, ecosystems do not stand simply outside in the external world, but seep into institutions. Accordingly, an ecological orientation has to be inner-directed as well as outer-directed.

With these conceptual foundations establishing the ecological perspective in place, we can now turn, in Part II, to tackle in turn elements that contribute to the making of the ecological university; and we shall begin by setting out principles and maxims that might guide its formation.

Note

1 Among the first, if not the first, to use the term 'social ecology' was Murray Bookchin, whose approach – in its collectivism, democracy and broad conception of the potential relationship between humanity and Nature – resonates with the general argument here. So far as I can see, however, Bookchin had rather little to say about universities and higher education. See, for example, his (1980, 1996) books.

PART II
The ecological university

5

THE ECO-UNIVERSITY

Principles and maxims

Introduction

Part I of this book has attempted to uncover the potential of the theme of ecology and reveal something of the character of the ecological hinterland of the university. Against the background of those preliminary sorties, how might the university move forward, to begin to take on the mantle of the ecological university? How might the ecological university be recognized, if it was to be encountered? Which principles might be adopted by such a university? What orientations to *action* might it adopt? It is questions such as these that form the territory of this chapter.[1]

My strategy is as follows. First, I shall offer a framework – consisting of three axes – by which potential ideas of the ecological university could be placed and I shall nail my colours to an idea of the ecological university as being placed in a *certain* space within the conceptual terrain of those three axes. Second, principles – if they are to inject momentum to the ecological university – must be such as energize a university in challenging circumstances. To each principle identified here, I therefore attach a maxim, to provide a way of moving forward.

One principle proposed here is that of fearlessness, the suggested maxim of which is 'Hold fast to the university as a space of critical and open dialogue'. This is especially necessary in an age in which universities – for understandable reasons – are coming to censure themselves, and refrain from speaking out and even to limit their inner conversations. I, therefore, discuss institutional fearlessness and the ecological university as a thinking university. Thinking and fearlessness accompany each other in the ecological university.

A grid – and a cube

Two distinctions have been emerging. The first is that between sustainability and ecology. Both ideas are important, but – as we have seen (Chapter 3) – they are radically different, even if they overlap. Sustainability denotes a concern that the environment has been or may be weakened in some way, and is oriented towards restoring the environment. Ecology has no difficulty with these sentiments *per se*, but it is a richer concept. *First*, while it concedes that the environment may be deficient or impaired in some way, the ecological disposition would come into play *even if no significant impairment in the environment was apparent*. This disposition has a care towards the environment, irrespective of the actual state of affairs. *Second*, it is uninterested merely in restoring the environment to some pre-existing state of affairs (an impossibility in any event), but has a continuing interest in doing all in its powers to go on perpetually in helping to strengthen or improve the environment. It is always predisposed, therefore, to noticing and imagining ways in which the world is falling short of its potential and could, therefore, be taken forward, and its wellbeing advanced in some way.

The second distinction that has emerged from our reflections is that between the natural world and the whole Earth. To a large extent, both sets of movements that come under the banners of sustainability and ecology are concerned especially with the natural environment, whereas the idea of ecology being pressed here broadens to include non-natural systems, especially those of the human world. The dominant interest in the physical environment is understandable, against a background of its degradation. The ecosystems of the natural world have turned out to possess a precarious character and are in jeopardy, a degradation that has come about to a large extent due to actions of humanity.

The idea of ecology is sympathetic to these considerations but, as intimated, goes much further. It stretches the concept – somewhat metaphorically – to refer to collectivities present in the human world (of social institutions, knowledge, culture, persons and so forth). It sees those collectivities as interconnected and as having systematic characteristics, however loosely, so generating forms of social complexity. And it sees the ecosystems that it picks out as open systems, with strains of openness that provide spaces for human imagination.

Accordingly, the following grid – with its two axes – suggests itself:

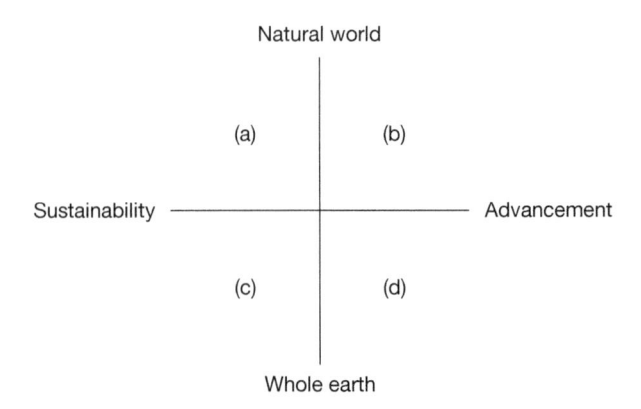

FIGURE 5.1 The ecological university: two axes

Much of the ecological movement has surely been located in the top left-hand quadrant (a) – of concerns about sustainability in the natural world. This way of thinking has been carried over into work on 'the sustainable university' and the 'eco-versity' – both in the literature and in actual developments[2] – which primarily have a dual focus: (i) the university's profile in relation to the natural environment; and (ii) wanting to see concerns with the natural environment finding their way into both the teaching and research functions of the university. Certainly, a large canvas opens for both teaching and research, as research endeavours and curricula and pedagogies are now reoriented in the direction of environmental issues across the whole planet. Large matters also arise over the turning of a university in those directions; and social-material perspectives are called up in aiding such a project (Hopkinson and James, 2013; Luna and Maxey, 2013).

The argument here, however, is located in the lower right-hand quadrant (d), in which the ecological university understands itself as moving across a set of ecosystems in the human and natural worlds, with an orientation *not* towards sustainability but to the strengthening of the (seven) major ecosystems in which the university is implicated. There is an institutional reflexivity here too: the ecological university *intentionally* works at its possibilities in advancing the wellbeing of the whole Earth.

There is, though, a third axis simmering under the surface of these considerations, namely an instrumental–transcendental axis. The clustering just observed, in which an interest in the natural world allies itself to concerns about its sustainability characteristically stretches towards an *instrumental* mode of being. In this orientation, the world is held to be separate from humanity and the dominant interest becomes that of determining actions, technologies and systems that might repair instances of environmental degradation. In contrast, the ecological approach being urged here is that of a depth ecology in which the world and humanity are understood not as separate but as bound up in each other. The energies contained within the complex and open systems of the world include humanity which, in turn, can infuse additional energies as it considers its trajectories. These can fairly be understood as a transcendental outlook: the ecological university has a transcendental spirit that energizes it in and towards the whole Earth, as it imaginatively attempts to discern its possibilities.[3]

There is, as befits an ecological perspective, a large space opening here, with three coordinates – sustainability/advancement; natural world/whole Earth; instrumentalism/transcendentalism. This space has something of the cube-like structure shown in Figure 5.2, with the ecological university *in situ* in the corner marked by 'advancement', 'whole Earth' and 'transcendentalism'.

Notwithstanding sightings of a grid and axes, this is an inchoate and fluid space, a cloud formation. The ecological university finds its ways uncertainly in this hazy space and with nothing that amounts to a compass to hand; there is no fixed point. At best, it only has its own ethos (a term now fallen into desuetude and much worth restoring) and principles to offer it some kind of guide.

76 The ecological university

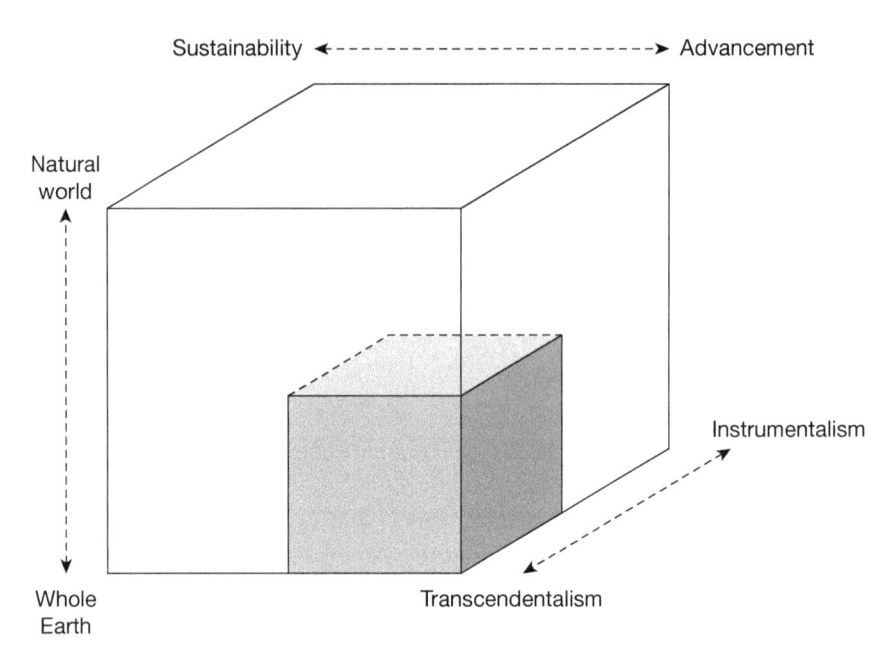

FIGURE 5.2 Three axes of the university and the position of the ecological university

Ethos

The ecological university is oriented towards the totality of the Earth's ecosystems, and especially the seven ecological zones picked out here. It understands itself as already implicated in those seven ecosystems. It moves in those ecosystems and has effects (an 'impact') on them. The ecological university deliberately and self-consciously has a care towards its movements across those ecosystems. It is concerned not only that it has influence in relation to those ecosystems, but seeks imaginatively to discern possibilities for aiding them. Such a university sets itself apart from those universities that pursue their self-interests, and/or that are concerned only with their position in the ecosystem of the economy, and/or move within excessively limited horizons.[4]

We may note that *the entrepreneurial university* is characteristically anthropocentric. It is self-absorbed. It frames its understandings of the world through its own interests and projects and hopes for itself. And it is a surprisingly parochial institution: it might position itself as global but, being concerned with its own positioning, its sense of its possibilities is unduly limited. The ecological university, in contrast, has no less than the whole Earth – social, natural, cultural, personal and so on – in its sights. More than that, it is an anthropocosmic institution (Mickey, 2016), displacing itself such that the interests of the whole Earth come to the fore as it shapes its endeavours, academic and non-academic.

The ecological university, accordingly, lives – has its being – for the 'Other' but, here, the 'Other' has to be understood in the broadest possible way. The ecological university asks itself (*in relation to the knowledge ecology*) how it can widen and nourish understandings of the world and bring them into more fruitful relationships with each other – for just as languages are dying off amid globalization, so too are knowledges gradually being extinguished (and not just the knowledges of the 'South' or of indigenous peoples but within the academy too, as the humanities and non-mathematical modes of understanding lose their legitimacy). The ecological university asks itself (*in relation to the learning ecology*) how it can help to advance learning through the lifespan, perhaps by enabling the wider community to have access to its resources; and also across the lifeworld, perhaps by encouraging its students to develop their 'lifewide' learning and even, if the students wish it, recognizing that extra-mural learning. The ecological university asks itself (*in relation to culture as an ecosystem*) how it might become a space for the intermingling of cultures and their contrasting symbol systems (not least by opening spaces for its own students from many backgrounds to engage more with each other or by developing curricula projects that encourage them to engage with a multicultural local community).

In understanding such a university, as intimated, we surely have to call up that long-unused term of ethos. As noted, 'ethos' has dropped out of the educational lexicon, including that of the academic community. It has too many resonances of tacitness, mutuality, tradition, understanding, interpretation and trust for an age now saturated with beliefs in explicitness, measurement, planning and goal-directedness. To put it formally, 'ethos' stands in a hermeneutic approach to life as compared with a technical–instrumental approach.

Perhaps the nearest modern equivalent to 'ethos' is that of Bourdieu's notion of 'habitus', originally deployed to refer to individuals' structured dispositions that 'construct [a] situation as a complex whole endowed with meaning' (Bourdieu, 2000: 138–139), and which has been extended to allow for the idea of an organizational habitus (Palardy, 2014). 'Habitus' is a powerful idea but it does not suffice for our purposes. The ecological university is not just situated by chance, as it were, in an ecological situation. Its ecological leanings are not principally structured from without. To the contrary, the ecological university is *intentionally* ecological from within itself. It reflects on itself, it builds its ecological leanings into its whole way of approaching and interacting with the world. Such leanings reflect and exhibit its values and deliberately expand its ecological reach.

This is no mere habitus, for the ecological university has an ecological *spirit*. It lives *from* the Earth and strives to do all it can for the whole Earth – especially through its implicatedness in those seven ecosystems. It seeks gaps and possibilities where its ecological credentials can be realized. Its collective value position is all the time stretching this way and that, as the ecological university spreads itself unevenly across its seven ecologies. There is no neat patterning here. But the ecological university is energized in an ecological direction.[5] And it is sensitive to the point that 'what really educates is the whole atmosphere of a . . . college [or university]' (Williams, 2003: 114). It possesses an ecological *ethos*.

Principles and maxims

It is apparent that the ecological university lives by certain principles; and principles that hold across all seven of its ecosystems, such as those of:

1. *Active concern*, the maxim of which is '*Strive to live out your concerns for the world*'. The ecological university has a concern for the whole Earth, and lives out this concern, with the difficulties that this concern will bring. It will bring, for example, not just strategic challenges – in just which of its ecosystems might a university place its major efforts? And in which ways? *But* it will also bring challenges, as values and interpretations collide in and across each of its ecosystems. Having a concern for persons may open a university to claims from its students not to be unsettled or discomfited, when controversial issues appear in a curriculum, but its concern for persons' learning ecologies fully to flourish orients a university towards deliberately placing students in a pedagogical environment that may be personally stretching and discomfiting.

2. *Exploration*, the maxim of which is '*Continue always to explore possibilities for realizing the potential of the university in the world*'. The ecological university is an exploring university. It is never content to reside within its own present boundaries – of knowledge, academic identity, understandings, position, relationships with the world or pedagogical relationships. It is always self-critical, exploring possibilities for itself in the world ('world' encompassing both its internal workings and its external relationships). It ventures forth, stretching into new spaces.

3. *Wellbeing*, the maxim of which is '*Aim continually to increase wellbeing in the world*'. The ecological university is guided most of all by a determination to increase wellbeing in the world, especially the wellbeing of each of the seven ecosystems in which it is especially implicated; but to say this is to open the university to profound difficulties. There will be disputes, both within the university itself and in the wider world, over both the meaning of wellbeing and its source and legitimation. That disputes of this kind erupt in a university is testimony to the vitality of a university.

    'Wellbeing' is open to multiple and conflicting interpretations – whether drawing inspiration from rules, religion, utilitarianism, a virtues sensibility or considerations of justice – but it is far from being an empty signifier. To the contrary, 'wellbeing' acts as an ideational umbrella, under which competing insights can coexist, even if uneasily. The ecological university not only strives to increase wellbeing in the world, but also does so by holding itself open to disputations about the very idea of wellbeing.[6]

4. *Epistemological openness*, the maxim of which is '*Go on opening yourself to new insights, new ways of conceiving the world and countervailing frameworks*'. All research units, academic departments and even whole universities take on a characteristic epistemological footprint. They become known for certain epistemic stances towards the world. The ecological university is reflexively conscious of this

limiting tendency and works to maintain and encourage epistemological openness.

An openness in its knowledge frameworks is essential if the university is to go on working against the horizon of its ecological potential, and across its ecosystems. Disciplines have self-enclosing tendencies – even if, in an internet age, their boundaries have become more porous. And, as implied, academic groupings acquire their own accoutrements, maintaining their own epistemological signatures, with their favoured theorists, frameworks and epistemic assumptions (over, for instance, knowledge as being contemplative or action-oriented). The ecological university, accordingly, will work towards opening its knowledge groupings to each other, in the hope that new epistemic trajectories will take off. This, of course, is far from easy.

5   *Engagement*, the maxim of which is '*Engage with all that or whom you encounter*'. The idea of engagement is elusive (Fransman, forthcoming) and has been taken up much of late to legitimate a limited instrumentalism, but also to encourage public-spirited stances among universities (notably in Watson et al., 2011). The concept of engagement can be stretched in this way quite easily, for not only does it possess belligerent connotations – where the enemies engage with each other – but it also harbours harmonious leanings, as when the lovers become engaged. Gears, too, may be engaged but rather with difficulty – or, with a little oil – more easily. The very idea of engagement, therefore, is another concept (relevant to our theme) that opens to multiple interpretations and so, in its laying the basis for a foundational principle and maxim, yet again, difficulties arise to which the ecological university has to be sensitive.

6   *Imagination*, the maxim of which is '*Develop and put to use your imaginative capacities, at all levels of the university*'. Across the world, universities have become bureaucracies with corporate tendencies. In both guises – as bureaucracies and as corporations – their imaginative powers shrink and such tendencies need vigorous counter-action if they are to be combatted. At its best, a university's corporate strategy is none other than a set of hopeful fictions (Barnett, 2011: 81), for it represents an imaginative discernment of the university's possibilities. A university's possibilities are not there, in the world, waiting to be read off. They are not even to be discovered, for the idea of discovery implies their existing presence.

A possibility, in this sense, has its feet on the ground; it has an ontological robustness. It is grounded in what it is that the real world affords. It is really possible. But it exudes, in the first place, from the imaginative mind, even if that be a university's collective mind. It is not already there. It emerges as an image of what might be; of what could be.

Nice questions immediately arise about the relationship of the imagination and the world, so far as a possibility for the university is concerned. To what extent might a possibility be revolutionary, carrying with it attempts to usher in a new world, if only for the university; if only for *this* university? To what extent might it be utopian, glimpsing a kind of university quite different from those present (perhaps formed around entirely democratic inner relationships or being really open in particular ways or only having an interest in serving society)?

The ecological university is a feasible utopia (Barnett, 2016), not yet present, but yet still conceivably real in the best of all possible worlds. Embryonic examples may be spotted across the world, perhaps idiosyncratic small-scale ventures, or perhaps even at departmental level in established universities, or even at the level of a university as an institution, as it seeks to establish new kinds of relationship with the wider society.

This is, accordingly, a practical imagination, with its eye on discerning and creating projects for and of the university that just might be realized and which would herald changes, however limited, not only in the university but in the world.

7 *Fearlessness*, the maxim of which is '*Hold fast to the university as a space of critical and open dialogue*'. The university cannot hope to be an ecological university unless it is fearless in protecting itself as a space of critical reasoning. Unfortunately, the university is censuring itself and its members. Closure is to be seen within the university and at deep levels. As MacIntyre has observed,

> The contemporary research university is . . . by and large a place in which certain questions go unasked or rather, if they are asked, it is only by individuals and in settings such that as few as possible hear them being asked.
>
> (MacIntyre, 2011: 174)

Academics as researchers shrink from taking on established paradigms of thought, for they have an eye to securing their next grant and they are hesitant both to disturb the present consensus among those who will be reviewing their research project proposals, and hesitant to run counter to any emerging assumptive world (Sabri, 2010) on the part of funding bodies and other powerful agents. Nor will academics want to run foul of the dominant institutional *Weltanschauung* adopted by its senior managers, on whom they are dependent for career advancement. And as teachers, it would be understandable if academics avoided the use of unsettling pedagogical approaches that might lead to reduced student satisfaction scores.

The fearlessness of the ecological university

That last principle and its associated maxim are especially complex and warrant further consideration. The ecological university is fearless on several levels. It is fearless as an institution: in seriously opening itself to and in encouraging debates, it will frequently run against the nervousness of interests in the wider world, which would rather see tight boundaries characterizing the ways in which the university disports itself in the world (whether explicitly voiced or subtly present from political, state, instrumental, religious or ethnic directions). It is fearless among participants in debate who will not shrink from running against the party line in their own disciplines or in ways of understanding controversial issues. And it is fearless both in the willingness of a university to allow criticisms of itself within itself and in the willingness of its members to exploit and even press at the boundaries of that discursive space.

Fearlessness is absolutely necessary for any serious understanding of the ecological university. Being ecological betokens neither a harmonious environment nor a comforting adornment. If the ecological university is to advance the wellbeing of its seven ecosystems, it will be obliged to confront established and powerful interests at play within those ecologies. That is evident. But more subtly, the university remains a key institution in society for the growth and circulation of ideas and offers a space in which ideas can be rigorously examined. Anything that threatens to draw in the boundaries of the university as a space of critical reasoning will put the ecological university in jeopardy. It has to be a space not so much of reason (Bakhurst, 2011) – since reason is more a characteristic of truth claims – but more a space of reason*ing*, understood as a quality of the university as a discursive space.

An immediate response may be 'of course', but it is not readily understood just how subtly these boundaries are sometimes being tightened. Quite unrecognized by itself, a course team might be energizing a course with a number of assumptions, not only epistemic or pedagogical assumptions but assumptions about the world. In the professional areas (which now often account for the majority of a university's programmes), a course may be sustained on the basis of assumptions about the institutions to which it is oriented, say, in law, medicine, accountancy, engineering, pharmacy, social work or education. The course team may hold a set of tacit assumptions and its course may come to have its own ideology.

The fearlessness of the ecological university, accordingly, calls for an inner culture of openness, such that a critical awareness and critical messages are encouraged. This fearlessness is not a matter of individual courage, but is a matter of an institutional stance and collective dispositions. Perhaps Jurgen Habermas (1989) came closest to intimating the essential conditions of such an institutional space of critical reason with his presupposed 'validity claims' of an ideal speech situation, in which participants are unconstrained but yet communicate within dialogical conditions of sincerity, appropriateness and truthfulness. It was, though, never entirely clear why just these conditions should be given special consideration for they should surely be supplemented by yet *other* conditions – say, of openness, courage (one may have all the space in the world but lack the courage to participate), respect for persons and listening capacities.

In the culture of modernity, fearlessness all too often implies a readiness to speak out, and to be declarative in promoting one's self. There are times when such a disposition is appropriate and even necessary. But a space of fearlessness and critical reason is far more than a space for participants to engage vocally and visibly – and even volubly – with each other. Ultimately, fearlessness implies a willingness to give way, to hear the Other, and to open oneself to fearless self-questioning and even self-doubt.

There is here a direct connection to the idea of the ecological university, for the ecological university is, *par excellence*, a university that is relational (cf. Rustin, 2013), connected to the total world, and understands itself in this way. To draw on Buber (2002/1947), 'the goal of [its] becoming is . . . the entry into a relation' (p. 58) and so it must be for its discursive situations. Buber talks of 'the Single One in responsibility' (pp. 81–83) and this relationship has to be characteristic of the ecological university, both at the institutional level and in all of its innermost parts. And, as Buber continues, given this being-responsible, one 'is bound to be opposed and if possible refuted once for all by that point of view' (p. 83). And, we may add, in being *seriously* responsible – for itself, for and towards the world in all its manifestations – the ecological university is itself 'bound to be opposed' and 'if possible refuted'.

There is a call here for the ecological university to exhibit a fearlessness in entering openly into the Other. It is a fearlessness born not only out of a wonder and awe and sheer surprise at what may be uncovered in the Other, but also, as intimated, a fearlessness that makes possible an inner openness to itself. The ecological university is able, therefore, fearlessly to turn critical reason onto itself.

The philosopher and theologian, Emmanuel Levinas, is helpful here. As he puts it, 'Being is exteriority' (Levinas, 2005/1969: 290). The ecological university knows this. It lives not in-itself and for-itself, but lives in and through its exteriorities, as well as its interiorities (and the Trojan horses that may sit *there*). But to do this, the ecological university has to be fearless, of inquiring into the Other and of wanting the wellbeing of the Other. It is not only that the Other will issue forth in strangeness – which it will – but that a genuine encounter with the Other calls for a willingness to leave oneself behind. The ecological university fearlessly yields to what it finds, what it creates and what it communicates. The ecological university is devoid of that preciousness that marks so many universities, intent on their 'branding' and projecting themselves as this or that.

A thinking university

The idea of a thinking university has become something of an oxymoron. Indeed, it is doubtful whether the university is clear as to what might count as thinking. Early in his (2004/1954) book, *What Is Called Thinking?*, Heidegger suggested that, 'In universities especially, the danger is still very great that we misunderstand what we hear of thinking' (p. 13). And his book, indeed, consists of a forensic inquiry precisely into what is called 'thinking'. Heidegger cautions us not to jump to a belief that we do think. 'Thought-provoking is that we are still not thinking' (p. 4).

The ecological university is and has to be a thinking university. But what is it to say this? Heidegger identifies several questions that arise from an interrogation of thinking:

1   What does the word 'thinking' signify?
2   What does the prevailing doctrine mean by thinking?

3   What is needed for us to accomplish thinking with essential rightness?
4   What is That which calls us into thinking?

(Heidegger, 2004/1954: 157)

Some brief answers might be essayed in response to these questions so far as the university is concerned. In *this* context, unfortunately, the word thinking (Q1) signifies very little, if anything. 'Thinking' as a concept is rarely given thought in the university. One would look for a very long time before seeing it in a university website. It is not a category to be seen in university mission statements or corresponding documents. The term 'critical thinking' is occasionally to be seen, but it is too rarely given thought; and in countries with heavily marketized higher education systems, even this phrase is increasingly less in evidence, in a relentless shift to a performative culture. Accordingly, the prevailing doctrine means little by thinking (Q2), for thinking rarely comes before it for scrutiny. This leaves us with (Q3) and (Q4), which we may take in reverse order.

That which calls the ecological university into thinking (Q4) is the identification of problems in the world (which include the university itself). Problems may be *theoretical*, concerned with frameworks for comprehending the world, or *ontological*, concerned with uncovering features of the world, or *practical*, concerned with effecting changes in the world, or *aesthetic*, concerned with creating new symbolic patternings in the world. Thinking is provoked by the discernment of problems that call for some kind of resolution. And not uncommonly, problem resolution may draw on admixtures of such kinds of thinking.

For the ecological university, too, thinking is provoked through its having a care for the world and for its ecosystems. Thinking is provoked especially when some shortfall or impairment of an ecosystem is discerned or when it is sensed that the world could be strengthened or taken forward in some way. Perhaps it is a matter of cities not working well or health systems being ineffective or of life chances unduly diminished within an education system or the university undermining itself through its diminution of cognitive freedoms. This thinking of the ecological university is a thinking-through, a thinking with a continual remainder, a thinking that is always *un*satisfied (cf. Adorno, 2014/1966: 5). It is resistant to seduction. It declines, for example, to be seduced by the idea of smart cities, a term that is bewitched by interests in efficiency, in data accumulation, by mathematical measurements, by surveillance and centralized decision-making. The ecological university, instead, would seek to identify deep and even hidden features of cities that deserve attention, such as massive inequalities, a poverty of experience of many, a segregation of communities and an impoverished aesthetic environment (cf. Wilson, 2016). The ecological university would look into dark spaces that lie hidden beneath prevailing ideologies (cf. Bengtsen and Barnett, 2016).

What, then, 'is needed for us to accomplish thinking with essential rightness?' (Q3). This is the key question here. For the ecological university, essential rightness of thinking is thinking that is disposed towards the wellbeing of the world, particularly through the seven ecosystems in which the university is especially implicated. Certainly, this cannot be an exclusive criterion. There are other forms of right thinking for and within the university. As intimated, rightness of thinking includes thinking that brings to the surface hidden ideologies, that exposes power structures, that widens frameworks of thought, that critiques thought, and that brings imagination to bear in creating new ideas. But the overriding principle here will remain that of a concern for the wellbeing of the world, all the while conscious that that very principle is open to rival interpretations.

Conclusions

The ecological university is a principled university. It not merely recognizes certain principles and axioms that are consonant with the idea of ecology but it lives out those principles and axioms. This is extremely difficult. There will be occasions when the principles clash. There will also be occasions when enacting its principles runs counter to the prevailing climate and the hegemonic powers of the state, of cross-national agencies, of corporations and so forth. In turn, academics and universities minded to take on the kind of ecological dispositions being contended for here are potentially vulnerable to the forces of suppression and may be subjected to incarceration or worse. There will be occasions when internal activities find themselves energized by rivalrous interests, as when an interest in criticality runs against an interest in wellbeing (witness the rivalries in student unions between those who would no platform speakers and those who would offer open platforms).

The seven principles and axioms proposed here are a series of *aides-mémoire*, reminding the would-be ecological university as to its responsibilities, and its way of being and perpetually becoming a university. This is no blue-print philosophy, pointing a certain way forward. The ecological university maintains its credentials uneasily.

It may be politic for the ecological university not to brandish its ecological stance too widely or too loudly abroad. It may be better served by keeping a low profile, while still sticking to its own mission. On occasions, the ecological university can sometimes be most effective by working under cover, surreptitiously outflanking the big battalions.[7] But this would be a temporary tactic, in a particularly constraining situation. For the most part, much more is to be gained by institutional openness on the part of the ecological university.

The ecological university is, perforce, a fearless university, and its fearlessness will have many facets. It not only presses forward, and engages with the world, but it also opens itself to scrutiny. It resists the dominant forces by working immanently, espying their self-contradictions and silent callings, and using their latent energies to deflect their trajectories, and veer in a new direction. It is, thereby, a thinking university in that it opens a space for thinking critically both about the world and about itself. The ecological university, therefore, orchestrates its capacities for self-reflection and self-scrutiny. After all, it can only live out a care for the world if it goes on extending itself as a thinking institution. The eco-university lives both in the (ontologically) real world and in the world of ideas.

Notes

1 Against the background of Chapter 2, another way of registering these opening questions is this: what 'new and different assemblages' might be created, so far as the university and its total environment are concerned? (cf. Hroch, 2016: 8).
2 In the UK, 'Ecoversity is the name given to Bradford [University's] strategic programme for sustainable development': www.lancaster.ac.uk/educational-research/research/our-research-and-its-impact/research-impact-stories/sustainability-initiatives-in-higher-education/
3 The concept of spirit is a most difficult concept, opening to numerous interpretations and perspectives, to *inter alia* a grand Hegelian sense of Spirit, as the steady march to the realization of universal reason; to an anthropologically and ecologically sensitive sense of spirit – and 'spirits' – as alluding to 'an enveloping and sensuous earth [as] the dwelling place of both the living and the dead' (Abram, 1996: 14); to a Christian sense of spirit as 'the embodiment of the divine' (Clayton, 2003: 211) or 'as living consciousness proceeding into the determinate otherness of the world' (Williams, 2007: 42); to a Bhaskarian Mark 1 as a dialectical process of negating absence (2008a); to a Bhaskarian Mark 2 as a transcendental movement towards a universal unity (Bhaskar, 2002a); and to an atheistic confrontation 'with the infinite, the eternal and the absolute' (Comte-Sponville, 2007: 136). I use it here to take on something of a more mundane character as a kind of organizational will realized as a vibrant and collective playing out of an institutional journey, and exhibited to a significant degree in the working lives and sheer being of its members. Schopenhauer, Heidegger, Habermas, and even Žižek, may all be additionally helpful in fleshing out an adequate concept of will along these lines, although I suspect that we are short of an account that satisfactorily meets the bill.
4 The concept of horizons has played a significant part in phenomenology and existentialism – including Husserl, Merleau-Ponty and Sartre. Perhaps its most significant treatment in recent work has been that of Gadamer (1985/1965: 269–273), but that account seems to me to be far too person-centred. We can speak sensibly of institutions – such as the university – having horizons *and* we can speak of structures impersonally imparting horizons (often unrecognized) to persons *and* to institutions.
5 See Fung (2017) for an excellent portrayal of a worked-through exemplar of an institutional project that goes quite some way in this direction. (My own Foreword [Barnett, 2017] attempts to identify some of its key ecological features.)
6 See the set of 'dialogues' on *Contingency, Hegemony and Universality* among Judith Butler, Ernesto Laclau and Slavoj Žižek (2000), in which the three authors seem united that universality is not marked by agreement but forms a space in which disagreement may be expressed. The concept of wellbeing can surely be said to constitute just such a universal.
7 Pertinent here is Gary Rolfe's plea (2013) for the university to arm itself with 'subversive' tactics.

6
ECOLOGICAL INQUIRY

Introduction

For the ecological university, it is the knowledge ecology that must have the largest claim on its attention – for the category of knowledge remains at the heart of the university, even if a little tarnished these days. However, the phrase 'knowledge ecology' now travels with much baggage and is no longer helpful, tending to fly in several directions at once. It is used to refer to the management of knowledge resources 'in ways that are more efficient, more fair, and responsive to human needs' (Knowledge Ecology International website) and so betrays an *overly* human-centred focus characteristic of the Anthropocene age – and against which the ecological spirit must contend. It embraces concerns about the ways in which intellectual property is controlled in the interests of large corporations. It is aligned with the concept of an 'innovation ecoystem' (Papaioannou, Wield and Chataway, 2009). It is used as a framing concept in discussions about 'ecological learning in social software environments' (Pata, 2009: 241). And it is deployed at both organizational and individual levels of action (such that some individual consultants even term themselves 'knowledge ecologist').

Some of these interpretations of 'knowledge ecology' embody a wish to improve matters and, to that extent, there is a link with the idea of ecology which I am pressing here. But even then, there are significant differences of meaning, the term 'knowledge ecology' being deployed both to refer to the development of knowledge systems and, much more directly, to improve the lot of humanity through a better circulation of knowledge. More particularly, in some of these understandings, the idea of knowledge ecology betrays an instrumental–technical systems approach that is in tension with the whole direction of travel here.

Strikingly, too, there has been little attempt to bring the concepts of university and knowledge ecology together. Where it has, the term 'knowledge ecology' has tended to take on a more descriptive sense. We are told, for instance, that 'German research universities still have a long way to go to adapt to the changing knowledge ecology' (Rhoten and Calhoun, 2011: 369). Here, the term is being used to refer to new patterns of knowledge production and research financing in advanced economies and regions.

Our challenge in this chapter is to branch out, and to develop a concept of knowledge ecology that at once does justice to the conception of ecology being advanced here, and to the university interweaving with the knowledge ecology. It will be a concept in which the university is intentionally striving to develop the knowledge ecology, sensitive to possible impairments that that ecosystem is facing. It will be disinterested, the university not working in the interests of any particular sector, but rather in the collective interests of the whole Earth. Given the inchoateness of the idea of 'knowledge ecology' on the one hand (and even the idea of 'knowledge'), and our concern with the university, we need a different term. I shall opt here instead, therefore, for 'ecological inquiry'. This fluid term will offer us options and be more fitting for the territory ahead.

First considerations

We require a conception of ecological inquiry that will help to reorient universities in the direction of the world. It would help to redirect universities away from a preoccupation with their own fortunes. But it would be more than this; it would involve a *turning* of universities' values. It would be an idea of knowledge inquiry such that universities (to borrow a much more general point of Guattari) 'don't profit anyone, but in the long term are the conduits of a processual enrichment for the whole of humanity' (Guattari, 2005/1989: 65). The very notion of profit, even if widely drawn, has to be ditched: not profit, which betokens a benefit to the self or corporations, but rather collective enrichment: this is a goal for the ecological university.

Guattari's next sentence is decisive, and central to the whole project of this book: 'It is the whole future of fundamental research and artistic production that is in question here' (2005/1989: 65). But notice how he runs together the ideas of 'fundamental research' and 'artistic production'. This is crucial for the ecological university: its inner notion of inquiry has to bring artistic creation and fundamental research together in the same epistemic space. For the ecological university, knowing efforts are understood also as imaginative efforts, indeed, in part, precisely as 'artistic production'. If such endeavours are to be turned out to the world, to enrich 'the whole of humanity', imagination has to be understood as an essential component.

In Chapter 4, I drew attention to the early work of Jurgen Habermas, in his discerning three interests that were at work in the formation of knowledge. Instrumental interests gave rise to technical knowledge; interests in human understanding gave rise to hermeneutic knowledge; and an interest in emancipation gave rise to critical forms of knowledge. Notably, Habermas did not allow – in this schema – room for an interest in knowledge 'for its own sake' or, as Newman (1976: 97,

103–104) put it, as its own end. For Habermas, there was always an end beyond (if, indeed, not behind) knowledge itself. Two questions arise, therefore. Does the idea of knowledge for its own sake make sense? And: might there be an interest – or end – *in addition to* the three that Habermas identified?

Two quite different answers suggest themselves in response to question one. A first answer is to glance it away. Yes, human beings can be inquisitive; they can simply delight in exploring their worlds and gaining richer, wider, understandings of it. Knowledge can be pursued 'for its own sake'. But this reflection can run on to a second answer. When it is sustained within a university system, with its complex institutional structure, the idea of 'knowledge for its own sake' becomes an ideology, explicable as the collective interests of an academic class granted considerable academic autonomy. The idea of knowledge for its own sake, in such a milieu, is an expression of the self-interests of the academic class. It becomes a 'dogma', a basic presupposition of the whole enterprise (Nisbet, 1970). It is liable, too, to generate a kind of 'scholasticism', shorn of concerns with the wider world (Bourdieu, 2000).

This reflection is not to undermine the idea. Ideologies, after all, have some reason on their side (Gouldner, 1976; Barnett, 2003). The idea of knowledge for its own sake has its own value, as the expression of a legitimate knowledge interest outside of power structures. The university purports to provide a space of argumentative reasoning independently of extra-mural forces, which would otherwise bend it to its purposes. And, indeed, the ecological university can and should embrace such an *epistemological stance*, nestling within its larger knowledge orientation towards the whole world. But this stance – of disinterested and argumentative reason – is merely a necessary and by no means sufficient condition of the ecological university.

The ecological university evinces a care towards knowledge, in all of its creative, humanitarian, professional, artistic, embodied and scientific forms. Knowledge, as a collective set of insights into the world that have gained some broad assent, is hard won. The knowledge of the poets, the philosophers, the scientists, the anthropologists and the theologians is won only with struggle. Knowledge, accordingly, has *truth-as-consensus* as one of its components; but so it also contains *truth-as-dispute* and *truth-as-struggle*.[1] No struggle and no dispute, then no truth!

'Post-truth', we should note, is a misleading term of art here. Rather, truth as 'truthfulness' is more helpful (Williams, 2002); truth can only be located, if at all, in an institutional space that prompts relatively disinterested, *conflictual* and never-finished inquiry, guided by truth as a value rather than as an end-point.

These considerations are important for the ecological university: its capacities to live adequately in and for the whole of humanity depend on its willingness to hold itself out as a space not merely of reason but of epistemic struggle, openness and forthrightness. For part of the context in which the ecological university has its being is that of epistemological contamination, in which massive ideological forces would bend the university to their own interests. Indeed, the ecological university acknowledges and works against the horizon of power structures.

These reflections point towards the second of our questions: might there be an interest *additional* to the three that Habermas felt he had identified? An answer has already been glimpsed. The ecological university is indeed energized by a further interest; namely, an interest in enriching the world, *tout court*. But then we face a conundrum. On the analysis so far, the epistemic orientation of the ecological university is both disinterested *and* interested. It is both fearless in its search for collective understanding and offers a *dis*interested space in which contending viewpoints can have their day, *and yet* it has an interest in enriching the whole world, and strives in that direction. Can this conundrum be resolved? Can the university be both disinterested *and* interested? Unless this conundrum can be resolved, the whole idea of the ecological university must falter.

Both disinterested and interested

A tempting ploy – in resolving this disinterested–interested conundrum – is to propose that Janus-faced, the ecological university looks in two directions at once. Or, to use another analogy, it hops – rather uncomfortably – from one foot to another.[2] But these are linguistic ploys that are inadequate to the problem. The problem is real. We are talking here of real stances on the part of the university: does it hold itself open disinterestedly, *qua* neutral umpire (Montefiore, 1975), allowing all rival views to the party, or does it seemingly foreclose on inquiries held in its name, and orient them 'ecologically'? Can a university both open its doors (metaphorically but also literally) and facilitate fearlessly the voicing of rival views – some of which may be seeking to impose or reflect dominant ideologies – and also maintain and pursue its ecological interests?

A preliminary answer has already been foreshadowed. The ecological university *needs* disinterested inquiry. Disinterested inquiry, born out of an open space for critical argument, is crucial for the ecological university to realize itself. The ecological university cannot speak truth to power unless its profferings have *epistemic legitimacy*. But then we run into what might be termed the Weber–Bourdieu debate.

In his classic essay, 'Science as a Vocation', Max Weber – one of the founders of sociology – boldly decreed that the integrity of the scholar lay in a purity that focused only on the facts of the matter, especially 'inconvenient facts' (Weber, 1991: 147), and so avoided any pronouncement that contained a value element. Science (that is, systematic knowledge) could only inform means to ends, and not the ends themselves. Weber accepted both that the individual academic 'will not succeed in eliminating his personal sympathies' (p. 146) and that 'no science is absolutely free from presuppositions' (p. 153), but science should not be asked to give an account of its own value-base. 'Science does not ask for the answers to such questions' (p. 144) and 'no science can prove its fundamental value' (p. 153). It is simply to be lived as a 'vocation'. This was an epistemology that, despite its leakiness, attempted to draw a tight set of boundaries around itself and its place and possibilities in the world.

Surely such epistemic self-enclosure was in Bourdieu's mind in his critique of 'scholastic reason'. He remarked that 'only the illusion of the omnipotence of thought could lead one to believe that the most radical doubt is capable of suspending the presuppositions' (Bourdieu, 2000: 9). Far from leaving its presuppositions undisturbed, Bourdieu suggests that 'the most effective reflection is the one that consists in objectifying the subject of objectification', by which he has in mind that form of reflection 'that dispossesses the knowing subject of the privilege it normally grants itself' (p. 10). And Bourdieu goes on to identify 'different orders' of such presuppositions and various aspects of academe's 'disposition to set up [a] distance from directly perceived reality' (p. 17). Bourdieu extends these thoughts in a separate essay. For him, the scholastic mind has its own 'logic of practice', which was 'separate from . . . practical experience'. It was, in short, nothing other than a 'scholastic ethnocentricism' that 'cancels out practical logic' (2000: pp. 50–51).

Values cannot be cancelled out, but they can at least be brought out into the world. Even though they cannot be raised from the dead, they can be raised from the silent, so to speak. Such self-scrutiny then becomes an additional means by which the university blocks undue contamination in its epistemic processes. The university allows and, indeed, encourages a more or less free generation of ideas and contestation between them, *and* permits a self-scrutiny of the underlying values and interests at play in those conversations. (That, in practice, each of these elements falters in the university and has been critiqued over the past century, can be put on one side, in the present *conceptual* task.) This step, then, provides us with much of what we need. The university becomes fully ecological to the extent that it permits – and even better encourages – critiques of its being ecological. An absolute condition of being the ecological university is precisely that it interrogates its own ecological leanings.[3]

Institutional self-scrutiny

Institutional self-scrutiny is triply desirable for the ecological university. *First*, self-scrutiny is desirable especially here because it would help to unite theory and practice. To borrow from Bourdieu (2000), such academic self-critique would help 'to rehabilitate practical reason and to subvert the social division between theory and practice in representations and in practices'. And he added that, 'This opposition, deeply rooted in the scholastic unconscious, dominates the whole of thought' (p. 80). Being ecological on the part of the university – with the scope proposed here – is in the first place a *practical* project. And it is a project of and partly born out of practical reason.

This is a project, too, of the widest scope. The ecological university lives from and for the whole Earth (and the 'whole Earth' includes the university itself). But if such nostrums are not to be empty, they need constant revisiting and reinterpretation, and at all levels, global, national and local. Each university has continually to be working out its ecological challenges and its ecological options

– again, across the broad swathe of ecosystems identified here. And such reflections are exercises in *collective* imagination, but also call for reason, at once empirical, logical and practical. Imagination, theory and practice all need to be united in this collective project of the university. That overused Marxist term 'praxis' has a fitting application here.

Second, institutional self-scrutiny on the part of the ecological university would open a space for a *continuing* working through what it means to be ecological. Which resources might be brought into play in filling out a university's understanding of the idea? Might they be drawn from the physical sciences, from systems theory, from philosophy (and there primarily from ethics, ontology or metaphysics), from social science or from theology (and possibly particular religious traditions) or even from economics? All of these frameworks offer resources that at least provide provocations and steers in an individual university charting its own ecological possibilities. Further, they conflict, or at least run into each other at awkward angles. Philosophy – in some of its forms – may speak an inner strategy of pure reason while religion may speak for a mode of being of active care for every element in the environment; systems theory may conjure a sense of open fields in movement and colliding with unpredictable results, while social science may prompt a concern with the Other and differential power structures.

In short, the ecological university has bewildering and conflicting options, both intellectual and practical. And the consequences of taking up any particular stance will be freighted with unforeseeable consequences. Continual vigilance and self-examination are necessary ingredients of being an ecological university but they cannot be sufficient. A certain amount of courage is necessary too.

Third, the ecological university will be interrogating its options at different levels. The ecological university understands that it is a 'glonacal' institution (Marginson and Rhoades, 2002), being at once global, national and local; and its ecological possibilities will need to be not just identified but also imagined, and turned into institutional strategies at each level. Doing so, it will be pulled in different directions. Can it both set up an international observatory on *global* poverty and a centre offering short courses largely to individuals in the *immediate* locality on personal wellbeing? Can its academics be both public intellectuals, putting their thoughts and ideas primarily into internet networks *and* be engaging with the political sphere, with the different communication registers that may be required? Can it position itself as playing its part as a critical and independent voice in the public sphere *and* be engaged as a participant in social reconstruction (say, in a developing country)? Can it spend time and resources in experimenting with different kinds of curricula and in opening quite new kinds of spaces to students, while its academics are encouraged to work at the global 'cutting edge' of research? In practice, in a large multi-faculty university, different units and departmental groups may be oriented in several such directions at once, *even if apparently counter-posed to each other*.[4]

In forming itself as an ecological university, each university will, therefore, move in different geographical spaces, with contrasting admixtures of ideas and practice. And it will call upon differing epistemological resources in doing so. But such spaces are more than geographical. For ultimately, they take on universal characteristics. In being ecological, the university places itself and sees itself against categories of openness, justice, freedom, equity, emancipation and so forth, categories that have a universal reach. This is not to say that such categories yield unifying or absolute principles, still less explicit guidance for action. To the contrary, universal categories open themselves to multiple, rival and proliferating interpretations. So, again, being an ecological university calls for powers of institutional self-criticality.

Ecological inquiry

In this chapter, we have largely been involved in skirmishes on the outer fringes of our topic, engaging with the matter of the institutional conditions under which a university might orient itself to ecological inquiry. But what should ecological inquiry look like? Certainly, it would exhibit 'forms of research, and engagement with knowledge that transcends current realities' (McArthur, 2014: 132). But more specific responses at different levels are warranted.

Empirical instances of ecological inquiry have already been intimated and can be readily extended. *Prima facie*, ecological inquiry is present when the university attends, either in its research or in its programmes of study, to matters of poverty or inequality or social justice and it is present when it seeks to *widen* what might count as knowledge – for example, by encouraging professionals to reflect on their 'embodied knowledge' (Loftus, 2015). It is present where 'participatory research' is conducted as an 'action strategy' sensitive to the community-based knowledges of indigenous cultures, and so tacitly widens the epistemologies of the West (Hall and Tandon, 2017). It is, self-evidently, present when it takes up issues concerning the apparent degradation of the natural environment, and it is present when it puts such material on its websites and so enables the wider public to advance its understanding of such (complex) issues. It is manifestly present when, as in South Africa and elsewhere, the university plays its part in using its epistemic resources (in law, in the technologies, in policy analysis) to aid projects of societal reconstruction (World of Learning, 2014). And it is present when it reflects on what it is to be an academic, and on the responsibilities that might attach thereto.

Such a list of examples could readily be extended but, even in this list, we can see ways in which the university can readily be active in each of its seven ecosystems; namely, the knowledge ecology itself, social institutions, persons, the economy, learning, culture and the natural environment. This reflection confirms our starting point in this chapter that in attending to the knowledge ecology – or, as I am preferring to call it, ecological inquiry – the university has a gateway towards playing its part in *all* of the other ecosystems in which it is implicated.

There is, however, an important codicil. The list was preceded by the qualification, *'prima facie'*. Examples of the kind just listed are *not* in themselves instances of the ecological university at work. They take on that status fully when they are backed by an *intention* to be ecological. This point returns us to Habermas (1978) and his conception of 'knowledge-constitutive interests'.

Each of the examples just listed *could* be pursued through energies fuelled variously by the three interests identified by Habermas: instrumental–technical, understanding –hermeneutic and emancipatory–critical. A university concert hall *could* be managed so as just to put on events that were likely to make a financial return and so generate resources for the university's mainstream academic activities. Reflections on knowledge and a university's epistemic footprint *could* be conducted with a view to identifying activities that were not much assisting the university's position in the worldwide rankings and comfortably could be pruned. Short courses *could* be mounted for professionals so as to enable them to work more efficiently or simply to master new techniques. And so on and so on. In all such cases, activities *could* be undertaken that were energized by instrumental and technical interests.

So the interest structure is crucial for the ecological university. It becomes fully ecological not just in taking on challenges and conducting activities that are overtly ecological, but in conjoining such activities with ecological intentions. Accordingly, we are entitled to add to Habermas' three interests that of an *ecological interest*. The ecological university is driven in part by just such an ecological interest. This would amount – to use Habermas' (1978) term – to an *additional* 'knowledge-constitutive interest'; and its general structure, in comparison with the three knowledges and their interests as identified by Habermas, is set out in Table 6.1 (overpage).

The ecological interest would be constitutive of the ecological university's knowledge activities – its ecological inquiry; but we can also add that this interest would, of course, be constitutive of the ecological university itself.

Sustaining such an ecological interest will be far from easy. Judgements will need to be made and they will characteristically be controversial. It might be held that there was value in maintaining a concert hall that brought peoples together to celebrate cultural efforts, perhaps representative of local traditions, even if it was something of a loss leader, whereas the university maintaining an expensive sports stadium would be just a little more difficult to justify under the sway of an ecological spirit.

Ecological inquiry and the public sphere

A knowledge ecosystem is irredeemably intertwined in the wider knowledge society. In such a society, knowledge and indeed inquiry are ubiquitous; they are not dependent on any particular institution – such as the university – for its epistemological resources. Consequently, questions arise immediately about the ways in which knowledge is produced across society and its circulation. To what extent do organizations, groups and individuals have access to the knowledge resources that they need? To what degree are their own efforts to produce and disseminate knowledge recognized and accorded due respect? The idea of 'cognitive capitalism' (Boutang, 2011) suggests that knowledge is often imbued not just with interests, but with the interests of the economically powerful and is unduly oriented towards instrumental ends.

TABLE 6.1 The interest structure of ecological inquiry, compared with the interest structure of other forms of inquiry

Form of understanding	Empirical–analytic sciences	Historical–hermeneutic studies (cultural 'sciences')	Critical studies	Ecological inquiry
Interest structure	instrumental – technique exploitability	practical interest (collective self-understanding)	emancipation	betterment of whole Earth
World orientation (ontology)	separation from nature	oriented to life-world (society as nature)	reflection on distorted consciousness	intermeshed with world
Epistemology	general laws	context-bound understanding	critique of ideology	relationality: listening to/attending to the character of each ecosystem
Presumed value structure	value free	belief in mutual understanding	human autonomy	intrinsic value in whole Earth
Legitimation	objectivist (illusion of pure theory)	understanding of collective meaning	intersubjective agreement	removal of absences plus imaginative discernment of possibilities
Efficacy	separation of understanding from cultivation of persons	bound up with self-reflection & self-cultivation	shedding of illusions	advancement of ecosystems
Fundamental stance	control	empathy	critique	active concern

Source: This table re-constructs and extends Habermas' typification of 'knowledge-constitutive interests' (1978: 301–317).

The university is implicated here: to what extent, for example, can it outflank the knowledge interests of the state and large knowledge-based corporations? Can it enlist the wider society in its own epistemological efforts? How far does it put the fruits of its own inquiries into the public realm and so become a 'university without walls' (Finnegan, 2005)? Do research groups reach out to the wider public, not just to share their ideas and results, but to engage dialogically with members of the public?

In front of us here is precisely an ecosystem, in the senses being advanced here. Knowledge inquiry has systematic features, it has elements that are more or less contiguous (even if they pull against each other), it is of considerable value to the world, and it has degrees of wellbeing in itself. It may be impaired (it may be narrowing, or non-reflexive, or unduly reflecting the interests of the academic tribe), and so matters arise as to how the knowledge ecology can be strengthened.

The ecological university is assuredly implicated here, for such a university will want to identify and realize ways in which it can play its part, say, in helping the growth of public understanding. Scientists in the Victorian age did just this (Gordon and White, 1979), without any qualms, speaking to public audiences and seeing it as their responsibility to do so. As the academic class became more powerful and less reliant on public esteem and largesse, that public orientation faded. Recently, there have been signs of a return in that direction, with academics (across disciplines) taking advantage of the communicative possibilities represented by social and mass media.

Some of the vocabulary for writing up the contemporary story here has been intimated through the work of Jurgen Habermas. Here is the prospect of a 'transformation of the public sphere' (Habermas, 2005/1962) in which the university acts so as to advance societal 'learning processes' (1987) and so, in turn, help to form 'the rational society' (1972), not least in widening society's symbolic resources (2001), while perhaps maintaining 'the reasonable attitude of keeping one's distance from religion without closing off . . . the perspective it offers' (2003: 113). At issue is not only the circulation of knowledge resources, but their form. Can the university communicate with the wider society such that there is genuine communication, involving a reciprocity between citizens and the university? Can the university engage with the public sphere in an internet age, in which there has come to be much reliance on social media for 'news' and information? Can such forms of interaction between the university and the wider society obey something akin to Habermas' ideal speech situation, such that there is upheld an equality of respect between the participants?

We need, however, to press on beyond Habermas' insights. For, in contemporary society, there is not just one 'public sphere', but several public spheres, each with its own register and favoured mode of communication (Barnett, 2015). This simple point outstrips the contemporary debate about university engagement with society, and it at once presents the university with a challenge that it must find difficulty in meeting. Just how, if at all, is the university to reach out to multiple publics, in different socio-economic classes and different kinds of organization (from local small-scale to mega multinational enterprises), and favouring multiple knowledge 'modes'?

The questions answer themselves in this way. There are bound to be limits to the extent to which the ecological university can reach out to multiple publics. In turn, the extent to which the university can aid the development of society's learning processes is always going to be limited. It seems that, while the ecological university may harbour the hope of advancing the wider knowledge ecology, its efforts are bound to be inadequate when measured against the theoretical possibilities.

At this point, a pessimistic and self-limiting countenance can all too easily befall the university. A hope-less pessimism often characterizes much contemporary critical commentary on higher education. Pessimism has good grounds on its side (Dienstag, 2006); but undue pessimism is to be avoided (Tallis, 1999). After all, when placed against the totality of its place in the world, an infinity of options opens. Totality and infinity are conjoined, as Levinas made plain; but they differ. 'The idea of totality and the idea of infinity differ precisely in that the first is purely theoretical, while the second is moral' (Levinas, 2005/1969: 83). The totality of the world stands before us; it is a pure idea. Infinity, however, invites a response, perhaps withdrawal, perhaps a living-with, perhaps a will-to-change; and so it is for the ecological university.

The ecological university engages – not instrumentally but empathically – with the Other, with the totality of the world. It does not shrink from this infinity that such a stance opens. It can never do justice to the potential that stands before it – to aid the world, culture, persons, institutions and so on. But it marshals its energies relentlessly in that endeavour. This 'awakening comes from the Other' (Levinas, 2005/1969: 86) and brings a sense of the university's 'own imperfection' (p. 84). This awareness of the Other calls the ecological university forward.

What does this mean here, in relation to the knowledge ecology? The knowledge ecology actually comprises several sub-ecologies, with their own publics – or potential publics. This is a totality with an infinity of challenges and spaces that stand before the ecological university. With what spirit might it respond? With timidity, having but a limited view of its resources and possibilities? Or with fortitude, striving imaginatively and energetically to orchestrate its resources to advance understanding across its knowledge ecosystems?

Practical matters impinge here. In the UK (in 2016), universities were understandably concerned that the outcome of a nation-wide referendum would have deleterious effects not only on their relationship with continental Europe (the 'EU'), but also even on their standing in the world. A matter not raised by universities is whether they might have played a larger part – over the past half-century – in helping to advance public understanding about the EU and so raise the general level of public understanding of a complex matter. Universities – as ecological universities – have capacities to advance the knowledge ecology more than they commonly recognize.

Conclusions: epistemological abundance, profit and surplus

Knowledge swims in the world. Certainly, it flows in *competing* pools, and claimants continually come forth, asking for the title of knowledge – and well beyond the academy. Lyotard got it awry: what we have been witnessing of late is not a dissolution of the category of knowledge but the burgeoning of a surfeit of knowledges (not least in the wake of the digital revolution with both its screen-based form of cognition and private and public communication companies marshalling transactions). Complementary medicine, embodied knowledge, professional knowledge, corporate knowledge, problem-based knowledge *in situ* (so-called Mode 2 knowledge [Gibbons et al., 1994]), the knowledge of think tanks and management consultants, political 'research' and the networks of conversations in social media all claim the status of knowledge. Issues arise about 'the legitimation of knowledge' (Gellner, 1974). What, in a society that is dependent on knowledge, is to count *as* knowledge? Just how, in a technological age, might the epistemological status of the humanities be construed? Once, the academy could have been at least posited as the arbiter of knowledge, but now such pretensions are passé, in a world in which knowledge is produced widely across society.

This is a complex knowledge ecology, which is fragmented across knowledge producers and its recipients, among whom awkward patterns may be seen. Knowledge producers work in different registers, with different criteria as to what is to count as knowledge. Knowledge recipients have greater or lesser access to the various pools of knowledge *and* greater or lesser understanding and powers of discrimination in relation to the testimonies that come their way. Accompanying these inchoate movements are hierarchies of knowledge, with counter-intuitive fault-lines. The young may know more than their elders, the individual hacker can disrupt the knowledge systems of great corporations, and the lone amateur can still make discoveries that add to the sum of knowledge. Only awkward phrases, such as 'ethno-epistemic assemblages' (Irwin and Michael, 2003) are available, it seems, in attempting to do justice to this haphazard milieu.

The ecological university is implicated in this epistemological abundance.[5] To what degree does it make its own knowledge wares open to the wider world? In what ways does it widen public understanding of complex matters? Does it speak in ways that are as comprehensible as they might be to the widest sets of publics? More broadly, is it deliberately aiding the circuits of understanding – even within itself – and so addressing their impairments, both manifest and latent? Is it helping the growth of world understanding, both in volume and in diversity?

What is in question here is nothing other than the *epistemological interest* of the university. Is the university simply taking it upon itself to put its knowledge resources to work in ways it defines for and by itself, and so secure its own *epistemological profit*, ***or*** is it making its knowledge resources available to the world for different constituencies to use ('appropriate') in ways defined by those wider constituencies? New technologies are opening opportunities – but still barely understood – for the university to develop just such an epistemological stance. Some speak of the coming of 'socialist knowledge' (Peters, Gietzen and Ondercin, 2012) but, paradoxically, that is suggestive of a certain kind of governance and control. Perhaps a happier phrase is precisely that of *democratic knowledge* (cf. Innerarity, 2015). 'Demos', after all, has connotations of commonality, of sharing, and of what is common across a people.

The ecological university has a *democratic* interest in promoting understanding across peoples and so playing its part in helping the peoples of the world to live together. It looks out into the world and works with the understandings of the world, so as to develop those understandings. It has about it an epistemological *otherness*. It operates with a new sense of profit, that of a democratic *epistemological surplus*, in which public understandings multiply and take on energies of their own but are always able to draw on the knowledge resources of the academic world. The promotion of this epistemological surplus would constitute an *ecological knowledge policy* for universities in the twenty-first century.

Notes

1 Habermas rather overlooked at least the last of these three, if not also the second, and perhaps too easily linked an absence of power with the formation of a consensus. By the way, in a 'post-truth' era, we seemed to have moved towards a conception of *truth-as-assertion*.
2 'The university will have to go on two feet, left and right, each foot having to support the other as it rises with each step' (Derrida, 1992: 31).
3 Derrida (2001) famously posed the idea of the university 'without condition', a somewhat absurd notion. There are always conditions of the university, both conceptual and empirical.
4 This internal differentiation reflects the 'loosely coupled' character of large research universities (Clark, 1983: 70).
5 There are significant links here to Feyerabend's philosophy (2001, but also 1975) of epistemological 'abundance'.

7
BEYOND LIQUID LEARNING TO THE ECOLOGICAL LEARNER

Introduction

Students increasingly live in multiple spaces, many of which call at least for informal learning on the student's part. Not infrequently, students work in employment while they are studying, they take gap years out before, during or after obtaining their degrees, they are involved in voluntary work (perhaps overseas), they may try their hand at small entrepreneurial activities, and they take advantage of leisure opportunities (perhaps even playing in university sports teams of some kind). So-called mature students often continue with work and have responsibilities both at home and in their wider professional life. Students, therefore, are portfolio learners, in which each one's learning is a *singular* composite of learning and developmental experiences. And these life*wide* learning experiences abut onto multiple ecosystems in the economy, students' own lives as persons, society, culture and so on. Students are liquid learners, moving across different learning spaces, each with her and his individual journey.

Students, in short, are becoming ecological learners and on two levels. On the one hand, students become involved in and concerned with the *sustainability* of their *individual* wellbeing. That wellbeing is increasingly interconnected with networks and learning spaces. So there is an ecology of students' personal learning. Students become managers of their own learning ecologies. On the other hand, students are global learners and even global citizens and agitators, traversing the world physically and virtually. Just as students are on their way to adding to the world's knowledge capital, so they are in a position to add to its global wellbeing. Students, and graduates, have the potential to enhance the world's capacity to ameliorate if not improve its condition.

Teasing out the related ideas of the student as liquid learner and as ecological learner is, therefore, the task of this chapter. My thesis is that students are inevitably liquid learners and have openings to become *ecological* learners, but that is by no means an assured further step.

Liquid learning, liquid learners

Part of the context here is that of massive and fundamental forms of change in the world – in the nature of work, but in most if not all other spheres of life – and the implications for learning that derive from such a context. Work is increasingly *similar* to other spheres of life in certain respects that are pivotal here. To put it in Habermasian terms, the lifeworld and the technical–instrumental worlds are no longer tightly differentiated.

The relevant features of the world are well enough known, and they include rapid change as such (so that skills once acquired may – relatively quickly – become obsolete), an increasing presence of activities that are heavily dependent on research-based knowledges, an interconnectedness of and porosity across activities, a social 'disembeddedness' (Giddens, 1995) such that individuals are being asked to take on multiple identities, and a proliferation of discourses and representations of the world that are often in tension, if not actually incompatible, with each other. Some of these changes amount to systems complexity that could, in principle, be resolved (given enough time, effort, thought, resources and goodwill), but others point to complexity in narratives of the world that are incapable of *any* resolution. This latter phenomenon we may term *super*complexity (Barnett, 2000).

These features have produced a liquid world and a liquid life, a world of dissolving boundaries, uncertain and competing currents, and turbulence (Bauman, 2000). Such a liquid world calls for liquid learning and, therefore, for *liquid learners*. We might be drawn here to metaphors of Deleuze and Guattari and instead speak of 'smooth' learning, a learning that has 'nomadic' qualities, as learners roam freely across learning zones. But a smooth journeying implies a security of surfaces, whereas all surfaces are in motion. The metaphor of liquid learning is more apt, therefore, for in liquid learning, *both* the voyaging and the medium are on the move. There are no secure surfaces, and no stable location or narrative on which the learner can rely.

Liquid learning calls for certain kinds of *disposition* so as to sustain oneself in an uncertain world, and six especially stand out. They are those of (i) a will to *learn*; (ii) a preparedness to encounter the unexpected and to *explore*, even though one doesn't know what might be round the next corner; (iii) a preparedness to *listen* to the world, acutely to hear its messages; (iv) a desire to go on journeying and to *engage* with the world; (v) a determination to *frame* possibilities for oneself; and (vi) an orientation to *appraise* the world and to form critical judgements on one's experiences (cf. Barnett, 2007). Liquid learning *also* calls for certain kinds of *qualities*; namely, those of steadfastness in the face of turbulence, a care for standards, self-monitoring (self-critical) capacities (partly so as to yield and even transform the very standards in question), courage, humility, empathy and humour (in its old-fashioned sense of being of good humour, so as to make the best of all situations).

Such dispositions and qualities crucially differ. *Dispositions*, as identified here, have a *universality* to them. The six picked out are features of being that the world, in all its complexity *and* supercomplexity, calls forth *tout court*. Qualities, on the other hand, are much more personal and so have a degree of *optionality* about them.

They denote an individual person's particular unfolding and developing character in relation to the world in all its vicissitudes.

Whereas it makes sense to expect that the six dispositions, so identified, should be enhanced across higher education, across *all* disciplines, institutions and nation states, qualities in contrast are ways in which individuals can come to acquire their own selves and develop their uniqueness. Such qualities will legitimately *differ* across disciplines and programmes in higher education and they will also vary across individual students, *even within the same cohort* on a single programme of study. This schema of dispositions and qualities offers properties both of *universality* (in the six dispositions) and of *singularization* (in the extendable and variable qualities).[1] In this way, students may come to inhabit *both* a universal space *and* their own unique individual spaces.

Much is required, therefore, of liquid learners in this depiction – and separation – of dispositions and qualities. Two features stand out. The first feature is double-barrelled, both negative and positive. The more *negative observation* is that, in those lists of dispositions and qualities, neither the term 'knowledge' nor the term skills appears. This is not happenstance. In a liquid world, knowledge and skills are still required but they recede in significance. They remain necessary but by no means sufficient conditions of what it is to be an ecological learner.

The *positive observation* is that the liquid world calls for certain kinds of human being, able to assimilate to and to accommodate new worlds. To put it formally, in an age of supercomplexity, learning becomes more an ontological matter than an epistemological matter or even a practical matter: it is more that learners be certain kinds of person – that they take on certain kinds of *being* in the world (as framed by the six dispositions) – than that they know certain things and are able to perform certain tasks in the world. After all, both their knowledge and their capacities to perform (their 'skills') will be sorely tested: their knowledges will become redundant, or inappropriate or recognized as faulty in some way; and their skills will be felt to be passé or not wanted on board or gauche or bad form or even, in a globalized world, outré in another culture. What *is* required for sure, though, is that individuals possess the six kinds of dispositions *and* have developed their own panoply of qualities that are going to energize them as their own persons and take them through an ever-present turbulence.

There is a second feature of liquid learning. The kinds of dispositions and qualities required to enable learners to thrive amid changing and contested interpretations of the world – dispositions of a will to go on, to encounter the unexpected, and a will to listen to the world; and qualities of carefulness, integrity, steadfastness and courage – are ethical in their nature. They are 'epistemic virtues' (cf. Brady and Pritchard, 2003), virtues that derive from a serious effort to understand the world and to offer interpretations of the world amid change and contestation.

The arrival of the lifewide learner

As observed, the liquid learner lives simultaneously in multiple learning spaces. This is so for younger students and so-called 'mature students' alike. Learning spaces are of infinite variety, both virtual and physical. The United States has long had a tradition of service learning, in which students are encouraged to be extra-murally active, beyond the physical walls of the university. Elsewhere, extra-mural learning is often more informal. Voluntary work, perhaps in the developing world, working in a school, working with autistic children, educational courses (learning a language either on or off campus), being involved in sports, learning a musical instrument, teaming up with other students to produce musical compositions, engaging in small-scale entrepreneurial activities, taking a first-aid course, and running a student choir are only examples (Barnett, 2010). Students now roam the world, if only via the internet: social networking is accompanied by more cognitive networking.

Such lifewide activities are not lightly to be dismissed for they may generate severe experiential challenges. Students may be undertaking an additional course or training programme in their own time; they may have embarked on their own personal development (perhaps as performing musicians); they may be training for an arduous sports or other endeavour; or, being economically active, they may have some position of responsibility in the world of work.

Issues arise as to the character and even the health of a student's total learning ecology. Do the various learning experiences contest against and even undermine each other? Does the individual have a set of fragmented learning experiences or do they aid each other? Do the disparate learning experiences contribute to the individual's wellbeing or do they confound it? Does the student have the glimmerings of a coherent learning ecology as she/he moves through the world? (cf. Jackson, 2016)

The writings of Paul Virilio are testimony to the intersection – in the contemporary world – of information, technology, time, space and understanding (cf. Virilio, 2005/1984; 2008/1995). In their pedagogical functioning, universities have barely begun to intuit these cultural and epistemic transformations; admittedly for good reason in a way, in that these transformations are barely understood. If liquid learning takes place simultaneously in multiple learning spaces, those learning spaces have different characteristic rhythms (cf. Lefebvre, 2004/1992); and those rhythms overlay each other, with learners developing their temporal preferences. It is hardly surprising that students in the lecture theatre seek the more immediate and even instantaneous responses that the latest technology in the palm of their hands has to offer, even or especially during the lecture.

Such students are life*wide* learners (Skolverket, 2000). Simultaneously, their learning ranges across multiple spaces of their lives. This is learning amid a changing life, but it is also a learning that is prompting a changing life. This is a lifeworld that is never still and it is a lifeworld that, for all its collective nature, is partly of the student's making. In this liquid learning, personal and social learning often intermingle, in both time and space. Being a student is now less a designation of a place (of learning) and more a matter of juggling multiple learning spaces (Savin-Baden, 2008) and of trying, however vainly, to discriminate between those learning experiences.

Authentic horizons

A helpful concept here is that of horizons. The concept was pursued in phenomenology and existentialism – by Merleau-Ponty, the early Sartre and Heidegger, but especially by Gadamer (1985/1965). But in all those treatments, it was surely given a somewhat romanticized view of the individual forming agentically his or her own horizons. We need to embrace a sense both of horizons being formed independently of persons, through large societal structures and ideologies, and of horizons being messily negotiated between persons and structures. Horizons are not only in the mind but are also present in the world – as ideologies, they have a robustness – and often impose themselves on persons and social groups. Learning horizons should be understood, therefore, as both individual and collective, and as being always-in-formation, negotiated and struggled over.

Horizons are always on the move, characteristically widening but sometimes – although rarely admitted – drawing in. New learning ventures are typically espied and tackled; but sometimes shunned and even withdrawn against one's will (by an employer, a parent, a university, a state). An individual's learning biography betokens multiple learning horizons, ever enlarging and shrinking (Barnett and Guzmán-Valenzuela, 2016).

We noted that universities have barely begun to respond to this learning situation in which their students are placed and in which they have placed themselves. Universities still deceive themselves that they are entirely responsible for thestudents' learning. Two influences are at work here. *On the one hand*, debate about students being prepared for the transformations that they are about to face – in the world of work and through life – is framed as a pedagogical responsibility of universities: universities are asked to modify the educational experiences that they offer students so as to facilitate students' transitions and develop their 'graduate attributes'.

On the other hand, it quite suits universities to be put on the spot in this way for this pedagogical demand confirms them in their belief that the nature of students' learning may be construed as a matter of the relationship between universities and their students. It is as if students' learning was hermetically sealed within the university. Insofar as it is acknowledged that students might have learning biographies outside the university, such learning is often repudiated as having nil learning value. It is what happens in the academy that counts. There lie real standards of right knowing and of deep understanding, or so it is felt.

In a sense, universities can be forgiven for turning a blind eye to their students' extra-mural learning, for universities are repositories not so much of knowledge or even learning but of *standards*. However, this ostrich-like stance towards the students as multiple learners lets the universities off the hook. Universities excuse themselves from asking awkward questions such as, 'How does the students' extra-mural learning relate to their learning inside the academy?'; 'Could it just be that some of that extra-mural learning is educationally worthwhile?'; 'Might it even be that some of that extra-mural learning is *more* pedagogically worthwhile than the learning being encouraged in the university?'[2]

In asking such questions, there are two dimensions at work, those of education and of psychology. *Educationally*, it just might turn out that the student's extramural life is *more* worthwhile than her learning experiences afforded by the academy. Some of her experiences in her wider life might offer her greater autonomy, responsibility, accountability, interpersonal demand and cognitive variation than those in her university life; or (say, in working with autistic children or teaching children in a developing country) may call for considerable emotional investment on the part of the student. Nowadays, the 'university of life' may just be living up to its billing even while the student is a student.

Psychologically, her wider learning spaces may generate several significant changes. Those learning experiences may bring 'disjunctures' (Jarvis, 1992, 2010; Bagnall, 2016) that prompt worthwhile learning. Due to the features just noticed – their cognitive complexity, the level of responsibility they offer or the personal investment they call for – those wider learning experiences may generate a high level of attachment on the part of the student. Students may come to feel that it is in those learning spaces, which are more under their control and in which they are investing themselves, that they can be more fully themselves. Those wider learning spaces become spaces of authentic learning (Kreber, 2013); and, therefore, the source of *authentic horizons*.

The coming of the self-sustaining learner

Higher education is marked by a level of autonomy it affords its students. This autonomy varies across disciplines and national pedagogic cultures but there is an inherent openness in both curricula and pedagogies. Curricula are rarely determined by state authorities or by third parties but are usually designed in the student's immediate locale.[3] Disciplines vary in the extent to which the student's time is formally structured (with science courses requiring a high number of 'class contact' hours per week), but students characteristically have many unstructured hours to determine their own study patterns. Digital learning, too, brings more autonomy as the formerly tight teacher–student relationship is dissolved. It is intuited, too, that the development of self-critical dispositions heralded by higher education requires a degree of student autonomy and self-reliance. In higher education, then, the pedagogical frame possesses a high degree of openness and the crafting of the learner's *learning biography* in large part becomes his or her own.

This relatively high level of autonomy afforded by higher education is coupled with an increasingly variegated learning experience. Within the student's programme of studies, attempts are made to encourage a wider set of skills, both within existing programmes and as part of multidisciplinary new programmes (for example, music design technology). Work-based learning, community service, research-based learning, modules in partner institutions, problem-based learning, an organized use of social media, and virtual learning (with a growing use of 'second life' across disciplines) are just some of the experiences being opened to students.

In addition, as noted, students have access to an ever-wider range of learning and developmental opportunities outside their programmes of studies, both on campus (through the students' union, private companies serving the university and via the university itself) and off campus (both private and public sector and freelance activities, where students are engaging in activities by themselves).

This is here an extraordinary but largely unremarked phenomenon. Students are now *self-sustaining learners* in that they are having to sustain themselves as learners. Students live amid multiple learning spaces, on their programme of studies, on campus, in the wider university and beyond the university, perhaps in other countries. To recall Castells' (1996: 376–428) imagery, the student has her or his pedagogical being within a 'space of flows'. This presents practical problems of time management, but the feature of significance here is the student as a manager of his or her own learning spaces.

A problem that such learners have is that of forging and sustaining the self as a person. Can the learner cope with all of these learning spaces and learning challenges? Which has priority? And why? What decision-making processes come into play in handling these multiple learning spaces? They overlap each other; they may even be in tension. There is a precariousness here, as the learning self strives for personal coherence but stands perpetually on the edge of incoherence. Over time, priorities may change as value preferences change or the profit and loss calculations change. Sustaining these learning options is a matter of self-management; it is the self that has to be managed.

These demands of managing a learning self may become overwhelming. Much as the student may try, it may prove impossible to bring all of her/his learning experiences into a single narrative. In this disjointedness, one or more learning tasks may have to be abandoned. Or the student will adopt a stance of bad faith: the work in the supermarket may be almost disowned as 'simply necessary' even as it is continued. Or he or she opts entirely for the world of work.

In construing the student as a manager of his or her lifewide learning spaces, in the continuing construction of his or her lifeworld, the category of student changes. It becomes an option to be picked up or put down. The learning spaces that are associated with a student's formal programme of studies are only part – and not necessarily the major part – of the individual's learning tasks and accomplishments. So the very depiction of an individual as 'a student' becomes problematic.

Nomadic learners

Learners are embedded in the world and their being and becoming in the world have a fragility. Sometimes their learning will take the form of realizing that a certain kind of learning space (in working, say, for an electronics company or in an accountancy office) is not one in which they wish to continue and they may instead decide to become a primary school teacher. Sometimes, their values may be put to the test. Faced with criticism from an employer or from a customer, their sense of their self may be impaired. A liquid world of learning is likely to bring fragility. Something that Badiou says is relevant here:

> All multiple presentation is exposed to the danger of the void: the void is its being. . . . the void . . . cannot . . . be presented as fixed. What Heidegger names the care of being . . . could also be termed the situational anxiety of the void, or the necessity of warding off the void. The apparent solidity of the world of presentation is merely a result of the action of structure . . . It is necessary to prohibit that catastrophe of presentation which would be its encounter with its own void . . .
>
> (Badiou, 2007/1988: 93)

The learner, accordingly, is faced with the task of warding off the void that is the result of exposure to multiple representations (which is precisely the condition of being a learner in the modern world). The learner has to cope with a continuing and radical fragility.

This learner fragility has three aspects: a fragility of *learning* itself, in a realization that no secure epistemic position is ever available; a fragility of the *self*, in a realization that no stable place is within reach; and a *worldly* fragility, in a realization that the learner's interconnections with the world are liable always to be unsettled. These considerations usher in a sense of the learner as ecological, but multiply so, moving reflectively but uncertainly across a complex and personal *learning ecology*. World, self and learning intermingle and interconnect with the several other ecosystems in which the university is implicated (knowledge, the economy, culture, social institutions and so on).

One dimension of this fragility is the world's interconnectedness. We know the linguistic signs of this interconnectedness and its fragilities: 'globalization'; 'the network society'; the 'virtual society'; 'chaos theory'; the 'global knowledge economy'; 'cognitive capitalism'; 'post capitalism'; 'assemblage'; the 'dissolution of the self'; and even 'post-humanism'. Opposed readings are possible here. On the one hand, John Donne's suggestion that 'no man is an island' is implicit in all of these concepts, appealing as they do to forms of collectivities.[4] In contrast, cultural theory suggests stories of separateness, of many cultures finding it difficult if not impossible to engage with each other and even of individualization and identity politics.[5] This is an explosive admixture, where peoples are required to intermesh, but lack the resources for mutual comprehension.

Perhaps this extraordinary juxtaposition – of simultaneous interconnectedness and separation – has not yet been sufficiently explored.[6] It just may be that there is here the potential for a spiralling of mutual incomprehension, in which the growing interconnectedness of peoples *heightens* the incomprehension and mistrust. Be that as it may, there lie here in this interconnected world challenges for learning: what is to be learnt? Is it facts of the matter? Is it skills to get by? Or/and is it dispositions for cooperative living? Can one *learn* how to live with strangers and to accommodate the 'Other', even as a form of 'conditioned hospitality'? (Derrida, 2006: 99; cf. Ignatieff, 1984; Eagleton, 2009).

This wider landscape of learning is crucial here. For students are not just *embedded learners*, embedded in their immediate learning spaces on and off campus, but they are implicated in this wider global world of learning. They are implicated directly, with many students engaging in a large range of learning milieux that bring them into contact with differing social classes, status groups, age groups and ethnic groups, and people in contrasting situations of dependency and powerfulness. The sheer range of learning encounters involved – quite apart from the absolute numbers of people – is almost bewildering.

Precisely because students are in a relatively unstructured and fluid part of their lives, they are in a phase of absolute fluid learning – and *un*learning. That is to say, turmoil is a fundament of their learning, as they move across learning spaces and often with little pattern. Across national borders, private and public sectors, and self-directed or other-directed, and engaged on individual or group ventures and projects, and whether for social, sporting, leisure, cultural or economic purposes: within the compass of a very few years, students encounter and live – if only fleetingly – in multiple worlds of learning.

Students do not just prepare for transitions; they are perpetually learning amid multiple processes of transition. They have become *learning nomads*; and they are *becoming-learners*, to draw on and to adapt two constructions from Deleuze and Guattari (2007/1980). They are always going on learning, being challenged unintentionally and intentionally, putting themselves into new situations (culturally, socially, economically). Their learning is never quiescent.

Inevitably, students are global learner-travellers. They are perpetually coming into contact with groups and classes and networks that are in turn linked to the wider world. And this contact is both physical and virtual. Physical travel, across the world, expands. Universities build in travel abroad as part of programmes of study, they make available modules or years out in other 'partner' institutions in other countries, and they work with student unions (if only because of insurance requirements and the mitigation of risk) in facilitating voluntary and charity work overseas; and students themselves venture forth, individually or in groups, to experience travel to and across other countries (for leisure or for sporting purposes). Parents are reminded that they have an emerging function as quasi-travel agents in assisting such cross-national travel among their (adult) offspring, even to the extent of acting as host to some of it.

The coming of the ecological learner

The idea of the ecological learner works at two levels: within the individual *and* between the learner and his/her wider environment. *Within the individual*, the ideas of lifewide learning and the learner as inhabiting and moving across multiple learning spaces – as noted – bring in the idea of the self-sustaining learner. A dual task incumbent on the lifewide learner is that of maintaining the learning *in* those various learning sites and of sustaining a more or less coherent self *across* those learning sites. Is the student all at once able to learn practical skills, acquire capacities for solving immediate problems, reflect in an abstract way, engage with the public realm in a spirit of philanthropy, earn money, live in spaces of pure freedom and be judged and judge others? Here, the learner is a learning ecology in her/himself, a set of learning ventures that are in relationships – harmonious or discordant – with each other (cf. Jackson, 2016).

But the learner is also a learning ecology at a further level; namely, that of the interlocking of her/his own learning ventures with the learning processes of the wider world (cf. Habermas, 1987). As remarked, the learner is often directly interconnected with those wider learning systems of civil society, in its cultural, economic and social domains; and nationally and internationally (graphically so, where student radical movements involve public demonstrations explicitly aimed at combatting state policy). The fragility and increasing openness of those national and global learning systems have an impact on the learner's own systems.[7] Indeed, given their increasing openness, the looser term 'network' could be more apposite.[8] Being a learner is to be implicated in the openness of those wider networks.[9]

There are, therefore, interconnected layers of learning systems, wellbeing and sustainability, at the individual, student–student, and societal and global levels.[10] In a sense, the lifewide learner cannot help but become an ecological learner. At least, much prompting in that direction is present. The lifewide learner has the conjoint task of sustaining her own learning systems and her *learning wellbeing*; and also of interconnecting with wider societal and global learning endeavours.

This project of becoming an ecological learner can self-evidently occur at both tacit and more self-reflexive levels. The learner can simply struggle to keep going all her many sites of learning in all their complexity, on both their personal and much wider societal (and even global) levels; or the learner can become conscious and deliberate about the many learning challenges with which she is faced. Being a geology student, how might the student comport herself on an overseas field trip, being based in an indigenous community with its non-routinized and ethically demanding challenges? In prioritizing her course options, should she seek to maximize her income potential, even at the price of her own authenticity? Should she captain the University's sports team, even though a major match is due to take place on the very afternoon that she is also being invited to participate in a local charity event? Should she take up the opportunity to take a year's placement on her course, given that to do so will deny her the chance of spending time with a parent who is suffering from a life-threatening disease? Should she become an employee (even if only on a temporary and part-time basis), if she does not agree with a company's investment policies? The self-sustaining lifewide learner becomes fully an ecological learner insofar as these reflexive processes, and the ethical choices that they betoken, become conscious and become part of the individual's learning biography.

Being an ecological learner

'Being', as Heidegger pointed out, is always 'being-possible' (Heidegger, 1998/1962: 185). Where there is being, there are always possibilities before being. Being, therefore, is always in the process of becoming. Being is always becoming-being; struggling to be and to become. Opening here, therefore, is much more than an 'ecology of pedagogical knowledge' (Thompson, 2015). Rather, coming into view is also an ecology of *pedagogical being*.

We see all of this in the ecological learner, not least as he or she struggles to bring new learning pursuits and experiences into a coherent self-narrative. The idea of the ecological learner works and has its possibilities in several domains. *First*, the idea of the ecological goes well beyond a concern with the natural environment. The ecological learner is implicated in her own learning ecology, in social ecologies, in ecologies of knowledge and of media. In short, the ecological learner has a concern for all of her environments, plural, and has possibilities for future growth in all of those environments. *Second*, that wider environment is layered. At its centre lies the learner herself. Progressively, it extends outwards to include layers of interpersonal relationships, work, culture, the material world, the global world and the natural world. The idea of students as global citizens, as becoming global citizens, has its full meaning only in terms of such a layered and expanding sense of the student's responsibilities and possibilities. The general form of this ever-widening sense of the ecological learner and its relationship with the student as a global citizen is shown in Figure 7.1:

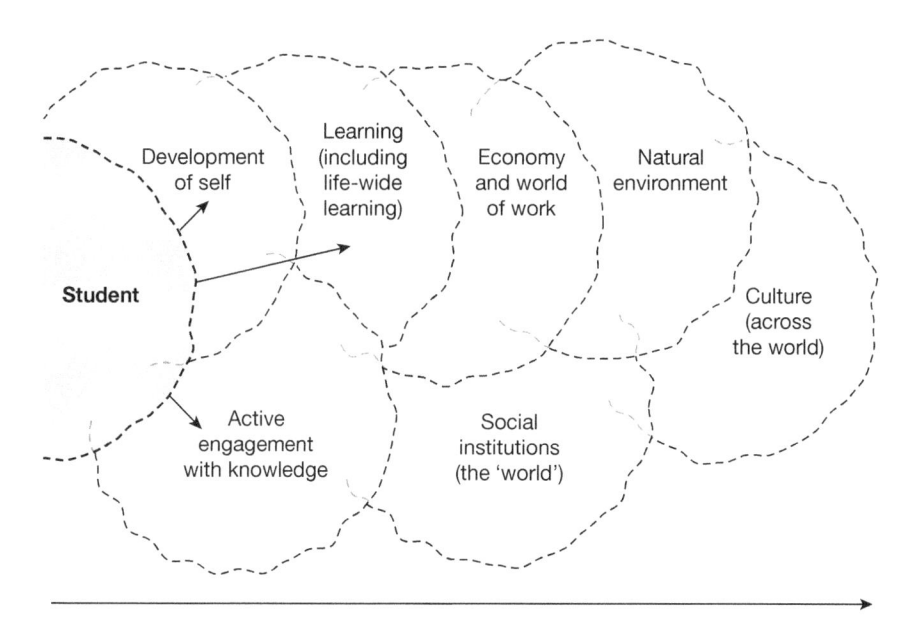

FIGURE 7.1 Development of student as a global citizen (going well beyond the world of work and entrepreneurialism)

Third, the student as an ecological learner has her being in time. (Heidegger insisted that being is always in time and has its possibilities across time.) We cannot understand the student as an ecological learner outside the handling and, indeed, the juggling of different and even competing timeframes of learning extending over time. *Fourth*, this unfolding of the student's being in time is Othered. The ecological student is not merely networked, but comes to have an abiding care or concern towards those networks, human, material and physical, both actual and potential. (Again, care, understood as concern, was another key category of Heidegger.)

In such a depiction of the student as an ecological learner, we see unending possibilities for the student's becoming; for the unfolding of the student's 'ecological self' (Bragg, 1996). All her learning is part of her emerging and continuing construction of her lifeworld. All of that learning has the potential for being integrated in her life's narrative; or, at least, to be objects for critical self-scrutiny.

We may note, *en passant*, that, some years after graduation, a student can often reflect back on her formal programme of study at university and extract meaning from it that is quite different from that which it held at the time *for that same student*. The reflective learner has the challenge of trying to make mutual sense of her various learning endeavours, scattered across manifold learning spaces. It may not be fully possible. The student may be living amid or may have lived through utterly conflicting learning challenges, with such competing values that they never could be brought into an integrated relationship with each other. But the ecological learner tries valiantly to see how far such integration is possible. And against the new horizons that an elapse of time offers, the graduate may see her student learning in changed ways. New patterns, new trajectories and new possibilities may emerge.

Here lies an endeavour not just towards self-sustainability but towards self-*re*organization (to pick up and to develop a distinction from Chapter 3). Inevitably, as new situations are encountered, so the self-reflective juxtaposing of the individual's learning experiences undergoes continual reconfiguration. It is hardly surprising if the surface meanings of the student's higher education – its formal structure, its assessment requirements and its employability outcomes – give way to deeper insights into the dispositions and qualities that it helped to nurture. And, in turn, resources flow through which the ecological learner can embark on a lifelong process of self-reorganization.

Conclusion: the university and the ecological learner

In this liquid age, individuals are called upon to be learners, as they move from one experience to another. They become liquid learners and are always in transition. Transitory learning is simply the state that characterizes human being in a liquid age.

Consequently, students – as a particular group of learners in society – are always in transition. There is hardly any feature of their situation, as learners, that marks either their entry into or their exit from higher education as being particularly special transitions, other than the status and symbolism that attach to being a student in or a graduate from higher education. Human beings in a liquid age are faced with transitions all the time.

What is special about a student's transitions in learning is the juxtaposition of a heightened complexity of learning spaces that the student inhabits, coupled with the particular formative period of life in which these learning spaces are experienced. (While this point has particular force for students as they move through, say, the decade from 17 to 27, it holds also for students of *all* ages.) Students are but lifewide learners, engaged in learning across multiple learning sites and seeking to make a continuing and integrated life-story out of those manifold experiences. *Qua* students, too, they are characteristically in a pedagogical environment that prompts reflection on their individual experiences.

Here opens the prospect of the ecological learner, at once bound up in the many networks that the spaces of lifewide learning affords, engaged on his or her own self-sustainability, and coming to have a care both towards herself and her own learning ecology. Here, too, we may glimpse the possibility of the learner as a global citizen, becoming reflective about the dimensions of the world that are opening to her through her multiple learning experiences. The learner's own self-sustaining efforts – or even self-reorganizing efforts – become interlinked with the world's self-sustaining efforts.

The ecological university can assist the formation of just such an ecological learner. Spaces are opening for the curriculum to be broadened in ways that would bring on just such a learner, both directly and in recognizing the student's wider learning across manifold ecosystems; and in which links are made to the student's lifewide learning. At least for the moment, the ecological learner is in sight, albeit on the far horizon.

Notes

1 'Singularization' is a dominant concept in Guattari's (2005/1989) *The Three Ecologies* – and its deployment there is directly applicable to the present argument; e.g., 'It is in [the] multiplication of antagonisms and processes of singularization that the new ecological problematics suddenly appear' (p. 33).
2 In the UK, some scores of universities have established schemes to recognize and give credit for their students' informal learning achieved alongside a student's programme of study. A particular development here is that of the 'digital badging' of such achievements (Law, P and Law, A, 2014).
3 Certainly, especially among the private sector of universities and among those that make particular use of digital learning, courses may be designed by third parties, commissioned by a university or even imposed by a parent company; but the generalization here about local autonomy still holds water, I believe.
4 Cf. 'No human group . . . can organise itself . . . independently of a series of types of "collective equipment"' (Guattari, 2016: 11).
5 Robert Putnam's (2001) book, *Bowling Alone*, remains a powerful and poignant argument.
6 Among pertinent texts here are those by Lipovetsky (2005) and Stiegler (2014).
7 Aided by an internet age, there are both dynamism and creativity at the societal–individual level, such that some speak of a 'country's creative learning ecosystem' (Crosling, Nair and Vaithilingam, 2015).

8 In a very helpful synoptic paper, and drawing especially on the work of Gregory Bateson, Peters and Araya (2009) draw threads between the ideas of ecology, learning (and so 'learning ecologies'), networks and culture, and see, in 'peer-to-peer' networking, opportunities for 'flat' learning exchanges that can be and are already being taken up in higher education.
9 Opening here is an 'eco-psychology', an interplay between an individual's psychology, cosmology and ecology, all of which is brilliantly explored at some length by Roszak (2001/1996).
10 For a vigorous argument spelling out such a multi-dimensional context, with its themes of care, citizenship and an 'ecologically viable Earth' (and which connects with much of the present argument), see Wals's (2016) account of 'learning for socio-ecological sustainability'. As implied here in Chapter 3, however, there must be a concern that the emphasis there on 'sustainability' either unduly limits horizons or underplays the radical nature of the envisaged action, since the situation calls for continuous repair, improvement and strengthening of learning ecosystems; and, indeed, Wals's account tacitly contains such radical components.

8
SIGHTINGS OF AN ECOLOGICAL CURRICULUM

Introduction

As with all higher education curricula in the twenty-first century, the ecological curriculum is an assemblage, a loosely fitting collection of elements. However, to count as an ecological curriculum, it has to have certain kinds of elements. But which elements? By which kinds of criteria might the ecological curriculum try to abide? And towards which kinds of values might it be oriented?

A complex assemblage

My suggestion has been that the university is implicated especially in seven ecosystems, those of knowledge, social institutions, persons, economy, learning, culture and the natural environment. 'Implication' takes two directions. Being caught in these ecosystems, the university is influenced by them, whether it realizes it or not. But then, especially if it has a care for the world, the university is impelled to turn towards these ecosystems and bend its resources in assisting their advancement. Just such is the ecological university.

This thesis holds, *pari passu*, for the curriculum. Currents swirl in and around the curriculum, not least from the energies exerted by the seven ecosystems. The university has been sensitive especially to the claims of the economy and has shaped its curricula accordingly. But, in unduly paying heed to such claims, the university has succumbed to the blandishments of economic reason. The mantra of 'knowledge, knowledge, knowledge' has been replaced by 'skills, skills, skills' (and perhaps even that latter mantra is now being replaced by cries of 'employability, employability, employability'). In universities around the world, curricula have been increasingly constructed to yield economic value. This is but a form of instrumental reason. There *is* a rationality here, but it is a limited form of reason.[1]

A task, therefore, for the ecological curriculum is that of reflecting *ecological reason*. This curriculum would be shaped to connect with its ecosphere. These ecological leanings and possibilities will vary from course to course, from university to university and from nation to nation. In every case, considerations can enter as to how a curriculum might engage with the wider society, and not just with the natural environment, but with knowledge, with learning and so forth. Different paths may open and deliberateness is called for; imagination indeed. In turn, the curriculum becomes an educational space for stretching the student into unfamiliar and even unsettling spaces. *The ecological curriculum entices the student into venturing across the ecosphere of the university.*

And so the forging of a curriculum becomes the assembly of an assemblage. Just which elements might come into view? And with what pattern or, at least, with which organizing principles might they be put together? An infinite array of options opens but yet there are boundary markers. The ecological curriculum, after all, is shaped so as to lead the student on into new and wide spaces across the regions of the various ecosystems, such that the student is brought to a realization of her/his possibilities in the world.[2] These possibilities are not only instrumental, but also provide the student with cognitive, practical, experiential and ethical resources.

The chemistry student might be encouraged to explore – with some study in the field – the place of the chemical industry and its effects on the total human and natural environment (cf. Gomes Zuin and Lopes de Almeida Pacca, 2012). The geology student might be required to engage with peoples in a traditional culture in settings for field trips. The philosophy student might be led to consider the place of philosophy in the evolution of society and its ideological tendencies, and critically to examine the character of reason in the contemporary world. The student in nursing studies or medicine could be invited to reflect upon and give a systematic account of his/her felt experiences of clinical exposure to hospital settings.

Such paths as these are not to be understood as 'lines of flight',[3] for 'flight' is characteristically either an escape from the field or a route to a journey's end, and a line is far too linear! Either of these metaphors – line or flight – is illicit here. The kinds of avenue being suggested neither lead the student from an undesired place nor towards a definite end-point.

Each ecological venture can characteristically be a voyage across *two or more* ecosystems. The geology student on a field trip in a distant land is at once venturing across multiple ecosystems of knowledge (crossing disciplinary boundaries), of society, of culture, of her/his own person and own learning ecology. This is a curriculum of discovery, with no end-point, but only a continuing opening out across ecosystems. This is a curriculum characterized by *paths of possibility*, but of the kind within a maze.

There is ecological fluidity here. The ecosystems themselves flow into and across each other, and the ecological curriculum becomes a set of spaces (plural) in which the student moves, doubtless often with some hesitancy and even trepidation. It follows that such an ecological curriculum cannot be tightly specified. Talk of 'learning outcomes' are otiose in this situation. Indeed, that phrase is redolent of precisely the kind of deterministic and instrumental thinking that the ecological curriculum seeks to combat. The ecological curriculum is literally a stretching curriculum in that it stretches the student into strange, demanding and open settings. It opens to *a pedagogy of strangeness* (Barnett, 2007: 76).

This curriculum opens, too, spaces for the student's own responses. It affords the student an arena to discover and to develop her own voice, with all the vulnerability thereto (Batchelor, 2006). And just as there may be two sopranos (as in Delibes' 'Flower Duet' in *Lakmé*) or two tenors (as in Bizet's *The Pearl Fishers* duet) on the opera stage, still they both hold their own lines and project their distinctive voices developed over the course of time.

The ecological curriculum, therefore, is a complex assemblage. It is composed of heterogeneous elements, bringing different ecosystems – of learning, of society, of personhood and so forth – into mutual contact and playing on their interconnectedness. In turn, this juxtaposition of elements creates pedagogical uncertainty. It cannot be foretold precisely what the student might stumble upon, cognitively, experientially, socially or subjectively. To attempt to predict the journey that the student might take and the sights that he or she might see would prejudice the *raison d'être* of this curriculum. And so the ecological curriculum is complex pedagogically, for it presumes an openness in the pedagogical relationship as the dynamic between student and tutor unfurls, taking on different colours and intensity, with the student's foragings and the curricula spaces jostling with each other. *Any* curriculum has to be realized in action (Barnett and Coate, 2005), and take on a vibrancy of its own, but this is especially so for the ecological curriculum. After all, this is a curriculum that is doubly emergent, allowing for openness and creativity, both within the curriculum and in the pedagogical relationship.

The encouraging of nomadism

In their extraordinary book, *A Thousand Plateaus*, Deleuze and Guattari (2007/1980) make much play with the contrast between 'smooth' and 'striated' spaces. Smooth spaces are associated with nomadism; striated spaces are associated with a sedentary disposition. There are, of course, intermediate situations: some occupations – they mention smiths (p. 456) – are itinerant; always on the move but going intentionally from place to place.

The ecological curriculum is all and none of these. As described, in the ecological curriculum, the student is challenged to venture across borders. They may be disciplinary borders, they may be borders in the student's mind or they may be pedagogical boundaries (where the tutor might give way to the student as she or he brings forward a new encounter in their learning experience). There are striations here, therefore, real boundaries and borders that are independent of the pedagogical setting – they are not just in the mind – but the student is encouraged to take courage and stride, or at least sashay, across them. But there are also smooth areas, where the student finds herself on home ground, and feels that she knows the rules and methods of self-propulsion. The ecological curriculum is both striated and smooth.

In the ecological curriculum, therefore, the student must be both nomadic and sedentary. But the metaphors don't work entirely comfortably. Missing is a sense, not of direction or movement, but of challenge; of the student being enticed into a strange place, even despite his or her will, and being encouraged to confront awkward experiences. The ecological curriculum puts to the student disconcerting challenges, as he or she is enjoined to attend to cognitive, experiential, cultural or environmental discomforts and offer an authentic response.

A happier set of metaphors might be that of explorer and discovery, with a topography of thickets across the borders. Once the student has left familiar ground, the landscape will appear to be dense and heavy going. It is not just that challenging 'threshold concepts' are bound to be encountered (Meyer and Land, 2005); rather, it is a matter of a whole unfamiliar perspective and sets of sensations crowding into the student. Seeing the world through the lens of another discipline, or being confronted with value issues not normally on the agenda, or being displaced into concerns for the world and for persons (when one would rather focus elsewhere), or being asked to imagine and to act out a chemical reaction, or being put into challenging practical situations (whether on campus or in the clinical situation or on a field trip) or being invited to reflect on one's experience in a self-study may be discomfiting. It is a *troubling mode of being* that confronts the student.

Heidegger talked (2004: 15) of the educational requirement towards the students to 'let learn'. But it is not a presupposition of the ecological curriculum towards its students that they be let learn. And not even, say, to let be. Certainly not. There is a responsibility upon the educator (the tutor, the course team, the teaching group, the university as such) purposively to bring the student out of him/herself, and into strange lands. A higher education requires that. It cannot be an education that leaves the student in the same place – it cannot be a letting learn in *that* sense. It is a curriculum to 'let explore' or even 'dare to explore'.

It may be thought that such reflections might, at best, have application in relation to students whose main studies lie in the social sciences or the humanities. In the physical sciences, however, surely such considerations have little purchase for, there, the cognitive structures are so tight that the idea of explorations by the student in multiple ecological spaces cannot get going. There are also pertinent matters of risk (both to buildings and to persons). This defence in favour of retaining tight boundaries must be scotched. Science and mathematics (and technologies) open naturally to the university's ecosystems, to explorations of culture, knowledge, society, learning, the natural environment and so forth. But we cannot speak of a genuine higher education unless the learning achievements are the student's own, willed, interpreted and owned by the student to some degree.

In turn, the student becomes something of an explorer, with the 'scariness' that will follow:

(beginning the student journey) is [an entry into] a scary, exciting and fascinating world . . . We need . . . self-belief to survive and prosper . . . I remember thinking . . . this is amazing, exciting, exhilarating and downright terrifying . . . Working with a complex world is . . . about . . . not giving up when you feel overwhelmed . . .

What's fascinating about [my tutor's] courses is the amount of panic, you know, that surrounds the essays and I felt it personally . . . It was a very, very scary thing to do because . . . there were no right answers.

(taken from interviews between two students and the author, held at two quite different universities)

There is nomadism here, but not without its own boundaries. The learning experiences and the spaces of this curriculum have to be not just held together, but swirl in and across each other. There will be connecting threads, at times gossamer-thin, and almost invisible, but still there. Serendipity *and* discipline are conjoint markers of this assemblage. It is a kind of confined nomadism, tempered by connections across the curriculum. For instance, the concept of perception could be explored through the lenses, the practical situations and the *emotional* experiences opened by many disciplines (across the hard sciences, social sciences and humanities), but then those insights and experiences can be co-mingled, in all their 'disparateness' (Žižek, 2016).[4] There are possibilities for coherence and integration here, however loose the components. An ecological curriculum, in exhibiting its diversity, will call – in short – for the student to be able to handle disparateness, unresolvable clashes of perspectives, concepts and evidence, and emotional unsettling.

This is a curriculum that calls for courage from both teacher and taught. The nomadic tendencies of the ecological curriculum put the teacher on his or her mettle. In the first place, the student is accorded space to challenge the tutor. A fundamental axiom of the idea of the university expounded by the English academic and literary critic, F R Leavis, was that ideas should be put before the student in a spirit of 'this is so, isn't it?' (Leavis, 1969: 6).[5] The student was thereby challenged to make his or her own assessments of the situation. That is all well and good. But in the ecological curriculum, the student is permitted to put the same question back to the tutor! The tutor has to be open to examining his or her presuppositions and to being a learner. Both the student and the tutor become continually open to challenge, therefore. It is a curriculum that produces a *pedagogy of mutual risk*.

In the second place, the student is permitted here to venture off down an unpromising path (to make his or her own mistakes). Courage is called for – from the tutor *and* from the student – as the student threatens to veer off well-followed paths. Will the student get lost, if she/he goes off piste? Will the learning be coherent? Will the student find her or his way back? Will the student be able to make sense of her/his resulting set of inchoate experiences? Is this an *unsustainable* set of encounters?

These elements of openness, challenge, freedom, boundary-breaking and journeying are abiding elements of the ecological curriculum. This is a curriculum not just sensitive to the ecosystems attendant on the university but also one that becomes an ecology *in itself*.

Commenting on the board game Go, Deleuze and Guattari observe that

> it is a question of arraying oneself in an open space, of holding space, of maintaining the possibility of springing up at any point: the movement is not from one point to another, but becomes perpetual, without aim or destination, without departure or arrival.
>
> (Deleuze and Guattari, 2007/1980: 389)

Compared to the regulated, highly rule-bound, 'striated' space of chess, Go – we are told – offers a 'smooth' space. This is the character of the ecological curriculum, at once a heady space, characterized by diversity, and open to daring sorties; but not without its own tacit rules of engagement.

Academic freedom: being compelled to be free

Let us situate these ideas in the context of themes in relation to the university curriculum, both old and new; and we may start with that rather tired expression of 'academic freedom'. (What, after all, might that mean in an internet age?)

It was an axiom of the Germanic idea of the university that both the professor and the student should enjoy academic freedom. The professor should be able to teach as he or she wished – *Lehrfreiheit*; and the student should have a freedom to learn – *Lernfreiheit*. There were always question-begging aspects to that dual conception: either the freedom to teach had implications for the boundaries and character of the student's learning, in which case, the student's freedom to learn was necessarily constrained; *or* the student really did have complete freedom to learn as he or she wished, in which case the professor's teaching was independent of the student's learning, a rather thin idea of teaching. The idea of the student's learning freedom, then, warrants some consideration.

The ecological curriculum affords the student a right, a freedom and an inducement to roam. The ecological curriculum is a set of spaces, open in the views they afford and in their pathways. It is a mansion with many rooms, presenting varied vistas to students, as it opens onto the various ecosystems. In her tasks, her reading, her activities within and beyond the university, in field trips, in cross-disciplinary sorties, in placements and in intercultural experiences, the student ventures into the university's ecosystems. This is a curriculum with no definite territory. It is de-territorialized. And 'the process of deterritorialization constitutes and extends the territory itself' (Deleuze and Guattari, 2007/1980: 411). Such a de-territorialization will produce a limited and measured *destabilization* within the student, as she/he is displaced.

To build on a concept identified especially with Basil Bernstein, the higher education curriculum undergoes not just one or two 'recontextualisations' (1996), but several, as it plays between discipline(s), profession(s), external audit regimes, internal management systems, and academics *and* the seven ecosystems. Perhaps a better term would be 'iterations' or 'negotiations' as the student zig-zags across her manifold experiences.

However, the academic freedoms associated with the ecological curriculum are not forms of freedom *carte blanche*. Boundary conditions attach. There are two kinds of boundaries, one concerning the ground to be covered and its justification (the curriculum) and the other concerning the manner of that venture (the pedagogy). It is important that academic freedom cannot – within an ecological curriculum – denote a freedom to construct a curriculum without certain considerations coming into view. Every curriculum is guided by considerations – values – of one kind or another. Significantly, however, the ecological university is explicit about those that guide it, especially its concern for the whole world. Choices over the curriculum cannot be value-free.[6]

Neither can it be a curriculum chosen entirely by the student and nor is it a lone voyage – it is not a form of independent study. As it has been remarked, 'Self-will, self-motivation or auto-didacticism is counter-productive because the fullness of truth can never reside in an individual' (Robinson, 2004: 92). An ecological curriculum is guided by a care towards relationality, a relationality that extends beyond students being obliged to take account of each other. In the ecological curriculum, a student comes to sense a connectedness to all things and to acquire an interest in such interconnectedness. Doubtless, the student will have her or his main studies, a focus of interest. But, in an ecological curriculum, the student will be led to glimpse connections between her disciplinary or professional field and at least some of the ecosystems that circulate in it, and acquire an interest in those interconnections.

Within these boundaries flow an infinite set of curricula and learning possibilities, and it is essential that students be granted significant pools of freedom to make their own explorations. Much of the curricula temper of the present age runs against such a proposal. Learning outcomes, audits, markets, busy-ness on the part of academics, a separation of university research and teaching functions, a management need to maintain and even improve retention rates, an eye to the student's future employability and a desire to receive trigger warnings of challenging experiences: all conspire to produce a safe and a narrow curriculum. In this milieu, students may have to be compelled to be free (Macfarlane, 2017), to form curricula choices of their own and to come to their own understandings. But so, too, do those who teach in higher education have to loosen – and be allowed to loosen – their own tight hold on the curricula and pedagogical reins.

A new general education

'[G]eneral education represents a minimal construction of a curriculum that seeks to direct students to the knowledge the educated men and women should have as they embark on their adult lives' (Schudson, 2011: 28). Perhaps it was Robert Hutchins who, as a young President of the University of Chicago in the 1930s, was the first educationalist to espouse this cause. Amid a major and fast-growing city, with its very many cultures, it was not surprising that Hutchins saw virtues in a common curriculum built upon the great books (Hutchins, 1936). It offered a kind of common culture (to steal a phrase from the UK's Robbins Report of 1963), and so provided many with cultural capital that was otherwise denied them. But that 'great books' gambit – Allan Bloom (1987) is a more recent and notorious exponent – opened itself to the charge that the chosen texts constituted a question-begging canon of a cultured elite. Why those texts? For many, such a general education seemed to be a form of entrapment.

Since then, efforts to derive a general education from within the higher education curriculum have taken several turns – and in both developed and newly emerging nations. Modular degrees, contextual studies, a breadth requirement such that a student should study a discipline quite different from her chosen subject, multidisciplinary programmes and so-called liberal arts for scientists have all been on offer. Strikingly, all of these options have sought to confront an epistemological narrowness, since university curricula have been commonly constructed on the basis of a single discipline and its immediate cognate fields.

More recently, a different approach has been voiced, variously termed 'transferable skills', 'graduate attributes' or 'general capabilities'. This is a radical shift towards a performative approach to curriculum construction, concerned not that students should have insight into multiple fields of knowledge, still less understanding, but that they should be able to *act* appropriately. It is a shift from knowing to performing in the world. Such a shift, too, marks a movement from modernity to postmodernity, a state of affairs acutely observed in Lyotard's (1984) analysis of 'the condition of knowledge': the test of the student's understanding has become not 'what does he know?', but rather 'what use is it?' (p. 51).

This latter development in the story of general education should be understood for what it is. If Hutchins' (and Bloom's) great books option could be criticized on the grounds of its tendentiousness – who was to decide what was to count as the great books? Only those who were supremely cultured, of course – the contemporary transferable skills option tacitly holds to *an automaton view of human being*. The same few skills – for example, communication skills – will hold across all domains, all settings, all fields, all situations, accompanied by a silence over understanding. It is a context-free account of human being. Far from being a general education that might open the student to multiple experiences, the idea of transferable skills bequeaths a universality of response to the world. Here, the infinity of nuance, of the subtleties of culture, of social situations, are airbrushed away. Particularities of experience are slid over. Despite its rhetoric – of an education for the complexity of the world – this is an impoverished approach to curricula that ultimately spells over-simplicity, imposition and even domination.

The ecological curriculum offers a general education of an entirely different order. It is a curriculum that, whatever the student's main focus, opens the student to a sense of the infinite interconnectedness of her studies to many ecosystems, of society, of knowledge, of the economy and so on. In fact, the term 'general' does not do justice to this curriculum. The ecosystems are infinite spaces and so the student's potential experiences are infinite in their variety. It is a curriculum that might link a class, say, in civil engineering to a corresponding class in another country and so jointly explore what it is to be a civil engineer in different societies and cultures (Pillay and Lavern, 2016). It is a curriculum that might invite students to act out their empathic imaginings of the entities that they are studying, be they wars or molecules (cf. Monk et al., 2011). It is a curriculum which explores contested value issues that their field prompts. It is a curriculum that delves into the connections between a field of study and the economy, and examines the ideological threads that are assuredly present.

Such a curriculum is ecological in three senses: it encourages a wide learning repertoire in the student, calling for imaginative, emotional, bodily and cognitive responses, connections between them then being brought forward. It encourages an embeddedness in the wider world, to place, to Nature, to other peoples. And it encourages a connectedness to other students. This would be a curriculum marked by an imaginative and active social ecology (Wright, 2010; Judson, 2010). In this heterogeneous assemblage, the student's main field of interest is held steady as the body of the student's experiences. But it goes on to exhibit diversity. In turn, its arms are stretched across the ecosystems, in all manner of ways.

Deleuze and Guattari observed that the 'arborescent' metaphor of tree trunk and branches is far too structured to account for the world; it is a 'sad metaphor' (2007/1980: 18). But their own suggestion, of a rhizome, is itself far too limited, even with its labyrinthine lack of structure and sprawling tendencies; even though 'any point . . . can be connected to anything other' (p. 7). Much more apt are metaphors that reflect continual and *rapid* movement without limit, in time and in space. (Students are already moving in these ways, not least via social media platforms.) The ecological curriculum invites the student to be on the move, always in search of a home that is rarely to be found (*and never with any permanence*). If the metaphor of rhizome is inadequate – in space and time – can a more suitable metaphor be found? Is the image (suggested in Chapter 1 in relation to the university) of the curriculum as a *squid* too threatening, too suggestive of darkness and envelopment?[7] At least, it conveys a sense of a shell (the main field or discipline) and potentially fast and far-reaching movements in several directions, into small crevices and within a fluid medium; and then the capacity of the body to move in a definite direction (as the student finds him/herself in a new place).

So the ecological curriculum helps the student to realize that her studies are but an opening to the infinite, and to the connectedness of all things. This is no general education, ordinarily conceived, for 'general' has connotations of vagueness, superficiality and non-specificity. In *this* curriculum, the student is opened to encounters with specific matters across the many ecosystems. Particular knowledges, institutions, feelings, communities, settings and timeframes come into view. In the process, the student is – to draw on a phrase of John Henry Newman from the

1850s – brought into 'a philosophical habit of mind' (1976: 57), but in a way that Newman could not have conceived. It is a curriculum that promotes a broad, generous and interconnected mode of being and understanding within an inchoate and fluid situation. It would be a general education for the twenty-first century.

Global or universal?

As the twenty-first century unfolds, much is being made of the idea of the student as a global citizen. It seems to be an idea whose time has come. In an age of mobility (the graduate could work anywhere in the world), a shrinking world (with its compression of time and space), and interculturality, the idea of the student as a global citizen has much appeal. However, the idea has come under attack. It is observed that the idea is taking off in higher education systems that are particularly marketized. What is on offer, so the claim goes, is an idea of a global *economic* citizen, a student who can confidently make his or her way as an economic entrepreneur wherever in the world he or she might be (cf. M A Peters, 2018). The implicit image is that of the free-wheeling individual, acting as a strategic operator, being globally successful in the business sphere. This economic critique wins its case rather easily partly because cases for the student-as-global-citizen that offer any substance are thin on the ground.[8] Perhaps the idea of the ecological university offers a way forward.

The curriculum of the ecological university draws the student into the world. It does so not so much by displacing the student physically into the world but by bringing the world *to* the student. The student's world enlarges, even as she retains something of her home; and, in turn, her home enlarges. She comes to see herself in a wider 'cognitive perspective' (R S Peters, 1966) that helps to impart an ontological enlargement of the student as a person.

Some universities – especially the larger research-led universities – are intent on *all* their students gaining some kind of international experience, such that, whether as a formal part of the curriculum or in their wider voluntary activities, their students would actually visit other countries, and preferably distant lands, speaking their hosts' own languages at that. This is to be applauded, but geographical travel is not necessary for the student to become a 'global citizen'. Bertrand Russell (1967: 93) spoke implicitly of himself as a 'citizen of the universe'; Hamlet observed that he could be 'bounded in a nutshell and count himself king of infinite space'; Kant rarely ventured beyond Königsberg;[9] and significant works have been written from behind the bars and walls of prisons (one thinks of Bonhoeffer and of Gramsci). What is in question here is not external place but interior *space*.

Much is being made of the potential of modern technology, with both its interactivity and its open source materials. This set of claims believes that 'an avalanche is coming' (Barber, Donnelly and Rizvi, 2013), which turns on an image of free-floating individuals in a learning market-place. Much less is made of the educational potential of such new technologies to help to realize the student-as-a-global citizen.[10] Now, the world – the galleries and museums, other cultures, other societies, cross-national data, and the offerings of global scholars and researchers – can come into the classroom and into the mind and being of the student. Student classes can be in touch with each other across the world. A worldly consciousness can naturally form. The world can come to be felt as a small place.

The idea of the global citizen implies a concern with and sense of responsibility towards the world. It betokens a kind of hermeneutic consciousness, a felt regard for the world, and a willingness in principle to form a close understanding of its manifold parts. The ecological university helps to realize this hope. Its curricula open imaginative global spaces to its students and oblige them to venture into those spaces (Fanghanel and Cousin, 2012). Accordingly, it is concerned if its international students are keeping to their own national groups and will seek to draw project teams from across a university's cultural groupings.

In its interpretation of the student-as-a-global-citizen, therefore, the ecological university offers its own way through the age-old universality/particularistic problem. Its curricula would open windows that invite the student to go on expeditions across the ecosystems. The student is extended cognitively, socially, empathically, culturally. She comes to see her own studies from the outside, so to speak. In the process, she develops her own qualities and makes her own responses to all that she encounters. And, at moments, she may experience an unalloyed personal disclosure when, in the words of the theologian, Ian Ramsey (1957: 23), situations 'come alive' and 'the penny drops'. She comes to be her own person. We see this transformation not infrequently in higher education, and it may happen suddenly. (And it is her *individual* qualities that her professors try to recall when they are approached for a job reference months or years after the student's graduation.)

But this open-ended voyaging brings to the student a tacit sense of inhabiting a shared world; a shared Earth indeed. As well as particularity – the student as her own person – there is universality here too.

It follows that whereas 'global' speaks of this physical planet, and its total geography in its cognitive, social, economic and cultural spaces, 'universal' points to different and even metaphysical considerations. As noted (Chapter 7), I suggested that there are six and only six dispositions that are foundational in becoming a student: a will to learn; a preparedness to encounter the unexpected and explore; a preparedness to listen; a will to engage; a willingness to hold oneself open to experiences and to frame possibilities for oneself; an orientation to appraise the world and to form critical judgements on one's experiences. These dispositions are irreducible to each other and are necessary conditions of a proper higher education. Here, we can add that, in acquiring these six dispositions, the student will become open to the world and will, thereby, enter a universal space potentially shared by all. Whatever her individual *qualities* (of criticality, courage, creativity, carefulness, resourcefulness – or whatever), these six *dispositions* are universal properties of going on in the world. So the ecological curriculum offers particularism and universality, both spaces for students' individual becoming *and* an entry into a universal mode of being.

But more deeply, the ecological curriculum is itself a universal space. Indeed, the theme of the ecological invokes the universe, with nothing standing outside it. To experience higher education at its fullest is to enter a state of being in which one understands that one is in the whole universe, and is connected to it, and comes to have a concern for it. One enters into a tacit and quiet state of awe towards the universe, but yet is given resources to keep going.

We see just this in that assertion of Bertrand Russell (recalled a moment ago) that he was a citizen of the universe. He understood that he was in the universe and that the universe had claims upon him but yet, spectacularly, he kept pressing on (despite being imprisoned by the British state on more than one occasion and experiences of near-bankruptcy, not to mention being overtaken philosophically by the 'genius' – as he put it (Russell, 1968: 99) – that was Ludwig Wittgenstein). Russell was not paralysed into inaction. So the curriculum of the ecological university is an educational space that opens to a universal, all-encompassing, space. It is, *ipso facto*, a space that one shares with others, and so there is a universality of (human) being that is intimately associated with the ecological university.

Conclusion – the encouragement of ecological being

The curriculum of the ecological university is open to the world and offers openness to the student. The student may be understandably daunted by such openness, for it impinges on the student's very being. *This* openness – *the openness of the ecological university* – seeps into the student's hold on the world. It is a principled openness that invites nomadic wanderings on the part of the student, but also encourages a concern for the world.

There are, therefore, profound differences between digital reason (or, as DeLanda [2015] tellingly calls it, 'synthetic reason') and ecological reason. Paradoxically, digital openness *can* offer avenues, and ways of proceeding, to that more deep-seated openness that the ecological curriculum offers. In his or her coming to inhabit ecological reason, the student heightens his or her awareness of the whole world. This is not a vague generalized awareness, but has its own structurings, as the student's mind is opened into the seven ecosystems, each with its own entities and issues. The ecological curriculum does no less than promote a concern with the whole world, the Earth indeed. Or, in other words, it seeks to bring on, in each student, an 'ecological intelligence' (Stratford, 2015), an intelligence marked not only with a concern for the planet and biosphere, but with a concern for the whole of life in all of its manifestations.

Not uncommonly, we see just this. We see students acquiring a concern not even just with their own society but indeed the whole world, energized by concerns with social justice, freedom and democracy; a concern expressed by students even at risk to themselves in the face of state oppression. The ecological curriculum is not far off. It can already be sighted, and in various guises.

Notes

1 Disentangling and critiquing – and discerning relationships between – different forms of reason was central to the Frankfurt School of Critical Theory. See, for instance, Horkheimer's (2004) *Eclipse of Reason* and Habermas' (1978) *Knowledge and Human Interests*. In the latter, see especially the brief section on 'Reason and Interest: Retrospect on Kant and Fichte', in which Habermas weaves between reflections on reason, knowledge, theory, practice, (his idea of) knowledge-constitutive interests, self-reflection and emancipation. An implication of Habermas' analysis has to be that instrumental reason is but one of several (at least three) forms of rationality.
2 It follows that I am in sympathy with suggestions that higher education should become more environmental in the sense of encouraging a sense of the 'otherness of nature' (Grun, 2005), but – as I hope is clear in the argument of this book – I see the educational environment as going far wider than the natural environment.
3 'Lines of flight' is a phrase to be found in the philosophy of Deleuze and Guattari (Deleuze and Guattari, 2007/1980; Guattari, 2016) and has been much taken up in philosophy and philosophy of education. As I try to explain, the metaphorical content seems to me to have some major limitations, much as the overall argument here draws on their works.
4 According to Žižek:

> At its most radical, disparity does not refer just to the gap between parts or spheres of reality, it has to be brought to . . . include the disparity of a thing with regard to itself. . . . A is not just not-B, it is also and primarily not fully A, and B emerges to fill in this gap.
>
> (Žižek, 2016: 21)

Perhaps 'the ecological university' can help to fill in the gap between the pretensions of the university and its actual character. The ecological university would probe the gap between actual and possible perceptions, not least in a 'post-truth' world.
5 See Steven Cranfield (2016), *The Creative University*, for a brilliant account of F R Leavis's thought in relation to the university.
6 On values in higher education, see the collections of: Astley et al. (2004), perhaps especially the opening essay by Ian Markham (pp. 3–14); Robinson and Katulushi (2005); and Heap (2017). Each of these volumes implicitly offers guidance as to curriculum markers, such as world community, citizenship, the common good, virtues and values. More important still is the language that characterizes each of those volumes.
7 In contradistinction to the (Deleuze/Guattari) metaphor of a rhizome, I first mooted this idea of the university as a squid in *Being a University* (Barnett, 2011). However, I see I am now joined – in a way – by Žižek: 'What seems to offer itself is . . . "rhizome" . . . However, . . . I am tempted to propose . . . the . . . disturbingly disgusting image of Kraken, a gigantic squid' (2016: 2). My squid, in contrast, has benign possibilities.
8 The essays by Annette and McLaughlin (2005) and Parameswaran (2011) are exceptions to this general observation.
9 That Kant *never* left Königsberg is described as a myth: www.kant-online.ru/en/?p=265
10 For a rare educationally oriented account of the possibilities of learning in the digital age, see Maggi Savin-Baden's (2015) beautifully written book.

9
TOWARDS AN ECOLOGICAL PROFESSIONALISM

Introduction

Professional life may be considered to be an ecosystem, in possessing a loose assemblage of elements, of systems and ethics. Material and expressive elements are here in plenty, and, as with ecosystems generally, so too diversity, self-sustaining capacities and impairments are all in evidence. It can fairly claim our attention in this total inquiry on two quite separate grounds. First, much of university education is a preparation for professional life; and, second, the staff of universities may be understood to be professionals. Here, I shall focus on the first of these considerations, the larger of the two, the matter of professional life in general and what it means to educate *for* professional life.

At the heart of this chapter is the question: what is it to be *an ecological professional*? On that basis – and only on that basis – we can turn our attention to the further matter: what is it to educate for ecological professionalism? In this investigation, I shall also tease out a number of related concepts – such as the 'being' of the professional (as in 'professional being'), 'liquid professionalism', the 'networked professional', 'registers' of professionalism, professional 'responsibility', professional 'authenticity' and professional 'sustainability'. This chapter is, therefore, an essay in the philosophy both of professionalism and of professional education.

The professional in space and time

The modern professional has her being in multiple spaces *and* multiple timeframes, and these spaces and timeframes interconnect. Professional being looks forwards and backwards, as well as to the demands of the moment. It looks outwards to external spaces and inwards to interior spaces. Part of today's professionalism lies in the handling of the juxtaposition of the interior and the exterior callings.

The spaces themselves characteristically have their own rhythms and pacings, and these can collide. We see this in the competing timeframes within the doctor–patient relationship. On the one hand, the doctor works within timeframes set by the local and national performance indicators and the resourcing envelope of the doctor's practice. On the other hand, the patient has a different timeframe, drawn from his or her personal needs and even anxieties. These timeframes collide, their being reflective of differing clinical spaces; on the one hand, a space of professional care and understanding (and even empathy) in which the patient is especially located; and, on the other hand, the bureaucratic–technical space in which the clinical practice is placed.

But the doctor is also placed in *widening* time–space complexes. She may be a member of international medical communities of practice, or of local and more informal networks of this kind; she will be subject to local and national and even international norms of medical practice; she will be receiving several journals, each with its own rhythm of publication, reporting on studies perhaps taking several years of research; and she will be bombarded daily with data and news and information (on new drugs, new routines, and new clinical practices and audit procedures). Here and now, distant and in the past and into the future; overlapping and colliding: the modern professional somehow manages these time–space complexes and her place amid them.

When, therefore, it is said that the modern professional is challenged in managing her time, that phrasing stands duty for complexes of time–space *being*. What is it to live amid multiple spaces, each with its mix of discourses, voices, ideologies and understandings? What is it to live in the future – the 'extended present' (Nowotny, 1996: 103) – as well as the actual present? What is it to live amid multiple timeframes, at once short and fast, and long and slow, the pressing moment and the distant future (as long-term projects are contemplated)?

This professional identity is an assemblage, a loose mixture of different elements. Perhaps a bureaucratic identity (a number on a professional register or a nodal point in resource management); a clinical identity; a quasi-pedagogical identity (for much professionalism lies in helping others to advance their understandings of the world); and distributed both horizontally, perhaps across other countries, and temporally.

There is no hiding place in this welter of identities: the modern professional is on show, her actions transparent to the wider world and subject to account from diverse directions and manifold stakeholders. Increasingly, corporate and bureaucratic 'analytics' effect their intrusive surveillance. The modern professional's identity is less under her control and more subject to the perceptions of others and the various resource, accountability and communicative structures in which she has her professional being.

While straddling these time–space complexes, the modern professional endeavours to construct her own subjectivity. How does she see the world? Is there available to her a stable horizon of values? Or, rather, does she inhabit several ethical territories simultaneously, to which she is subject, and with little overlap and possibly much tension between them? Is it possible for the modern professional to have a personal and unitary hold on the world? Does the idea of *authentic professionalism* make sense anymore?

Surely, these challenges to modern professionalism are only going to increase. The modern professional lives amid a set of infinities of expanding accountability demands, resource challenges, global horizons of standards and developing techniques, shifting knowledges, and changing client relationships. And each profession will take on its own fluctuating patterning in all of this. No wonder that professionals take early retirement or, worse, commit suicide.[1] In this openness and contestability, the modern professional moves uncertainly and even hesitantly. Any overt confidence can only be a pretence of security, for the reflexive professional knows that she skates on thin ice. Her only hope is to keep moving so as to stay ahead of the cracking ice behind her.

The networking professional

Willy-nilly, the modern professional is a *networked professional*. The idea of 'network' here, though, takes on complexity. Three distinctions should be observed. First, network here is both *verb* and *noun*. The professional 'networks' (verb): she engages with groups and communities, with a spread of interests. But she also is herself a node amid networks (noun) (cf. Castells, 1996: 470). The modern professional, indeed, may be construed as just that: a meeting point of a number of networks, which vary across professions. At the conjunction of a particular set of communities, agencies and groups, each with its own force and influence, sits a particular professional. This *structural* conception of professional life, as a set of interlocking networks, has a certain poignancy, for the idea of professional contains precisely the idea of allegiance to wider constituencies. The individual acquires a professional self only insofar as she interconnects with and acknowledges responsibilities to wider communities. There can be no *alone-professional*, no Robinson Crusoe professional.

A second distinction is that between *agent* and *subject*. As an agent, the professional works at extending her networks. The doctor may reach out to certain pharmaceutical companies, to other professionals in certain specialities (perhaps even across the world), to particular kinds of client in extending the client base and to other groups (in the political and bureaucratic domains) which might help in developing the practice's infrastructure. In all of this, the professional is intentionally networking: she networks *strategically*. The practice's website will be continually updated, in projecting certain kinds of image and resonance so as to reflect the networks that are deliberately being fostered. But this *agentic* networking also is liable to bring on the professional as a subject, for she will be drawn into reflecting on her career motives and plans. Both through her strategic networking and through the perceptions she senses of herself from around the world, she becomes more networked in her conscious being; in how she construes herself. (Certainly, in this 'reflexivity', she may conclude that the global professional game is not worth the candle and opt for a better life–work balance.)

The third distinction is that of *systems* and *discourses*; a kind of hard–soft distinction. On the one hand, the professional has her professional being among *systems* of client interaction, resource provision, disciplinary knowledge, bureaucratic accountability mechanisms and physical infrastructures. But, on the other hand, the professional moves within softer networks, of discourses, conversations and ethical horizons. These *discursive networks* are networks of ideas, concepts and beliefs. 'Soft', of course, is a relative term, for discourses always have aspects of power and exert their own constraints on professional thinking and behaviour.

These two features – systems and discourses – overlap but they are discrete and even contending. The professional, in the single clinical encounter, interacts with the client or patient as a centre of reflective consciousness (a human being to whom care is extended), but in the same moment, conducts that encounter against the background of an ever-constraining resource envelope. The patient is perceived both as a human being *and* as a consumer of expensive resources (not least the time of the professional herself): the ten-minute limit serves as an unspoken horizon to the consultation and quickens the latter's tempo. These days, both doctor and patient may feel an inner clock ticking even during the consultation. But this is to imply that the clinical encounter is conducted within intermingling – and competing – swirls of ideas and considerations.

A matrix of networks could be plotted here, its two axes being those of soft–hard networks and intended–unintended networks. But any such grid-oriented temptation should be resisted: even if its vertical and horizontal lines were to take a dotted form to reflect their porosity, still the grid would suggest a too definite sense of orderly structure. Even a more sophisticated spider diagram, showing differential engagement in multiple directions, would be inadequate. Rather, this *liquid professionalism*, as we may term it, is characterized precisely by multiple fluid currents, both intermingling and colliding.

Five ecological registers

The concept of ecology is helpful here. We may recall that it refers to facts about the world – notably its interconnectedness, its internal interdependencies, its diversity (or lack thereof) and humanity's part in sustaining (or injuring) those interdependencies – and to ethical dimensions, notably a sense that humanity has a responsibility in sustaining the ecological systems in which it finds itself. There is here an idea of stewardship, that humanity has been bequeathed powers and resources that may help to sustain the ecosystems of the world and so has a duty to do just that, over generations ahead. The idea of deep ecology goes even further, reminding humanity that the world is not out there, even as an object to be saved from extinction by humanity's efforts, but is of inherent value and that humanity is deeply implicated in its ecosystems.

We see all of this in professional life and professionalism, specifically in certain *registers*:

1 *The ecology of the professional self*: can there be a unity to the professional self or is it necessarily fragmented? To what degree and in what ways are its components held together or kept apart? Is there a sufficient diversity across the members of a profession or do they exhibit a homogeneity with moribund tendencies?
2 *The ecology of the client relationship*: what are the bonds of the relationship? To what extent might concepts such as duty, allegiance, trust and care have a bearing on contemporary professionalism?
3 *The knowledge ecology of professionalism*: which forms of knowledge come into view in the framing of professionalism? Does the term 'knowledge' even bear weight here, or should we not at least speak of contrasting knowledges? What is *their* ecology? Are some knowledges dominant with some even being suppressed (those of care and empathy, perhaps)? Are practical knowledges supplanting more discursive knowledges? Are yet others struggling to be born?
4 *The ecology of the professional environment*: what are the interconnections between the professional, the client and the wider physical, technological and societal environment? How might those interconnections be understood or even 'modelled'? Are mathematical models helpful or misleading?

Each of these four registers has already been implied in this chapter, but there is a fifth register within this ecological horizon, namely:

5 *The discursive ecology of professionalism*: what are the possible registers of ideas and concepts in conceptualizing contemporary professionalism? And from which disciplines might they be drawn: from management and organizational studies, ethics, economics, philosophy or even theology or anthropology? And what might be their connections and tensions?

The essence of the idea of the ecological lies in its dual features of interconnectedness *and* an ethical horizon. It is fact and value intertwined. The ecological professional has a sense of the *ecological registers* within which she has her professional being and their interconnectedness *and* has an orientation of care towards those registers. Those registers – of persons, systems, structures, knowledges and so on – do not present as discrete spaces but, to the contrary, are acutely felt as indivisible: in a single day, she juggles a wide array of professional challenges and responsibilities *and* possibilities that she sees for herself. Indeed, a single encounter between a professional and client opens an *infinite* array of possible lines of consideration.

In turn, the *ethical dimension* of what it is to be a professional presses itself. The professional is reflective about her professional self and its integrity across its registers; about the changing structure of her client relationships; about the developing knowledge structures within which her professional practices are situated; about the wider environment surrounding her professionalism; and about the ideas and concepts that contour the ideational territory of that professionalism. However, she goes beyond merely being aware of those registers and does what she can to sustain and even promote the integrity and wellbeing of those registers. This *professional sustainability* is turned both within and outwards to the wider world. The ecological professional does not just have an (inner) care for her own professionalism, but works out that professionalism in the five (exterior) registers of her professional life. She is her own severest critic as she works on her own continuing self-stabilization.

This is truly an ecological calling. Professionalism imbues an allegiance to the exterior; the exterior (clients, knowledges, practices) are not outside the professional's professionalism but are a part of it. The exterior in all its manifestations is not so much pressing on the professional but is held within her. It is a set of callings, inwardly felt. There is here a *soul of professionalism* (Freidson, 2001: 220–222), at once energizing the professional to hear and to respond to callings. The ecological professional has a care (Heidegger, 1998/1962: 225–273) towards the five ecological registers of her professional being and is moved to work towards their development.

An ecological responsibility

In the context of professional life, then, the idea of the ecological becomes a complex of ideas. It works in five registers, it connotes levels of professional being, it allows for varying forms of intensity and engagement, it has potential scope and it invites multiple perspectives; and these aspects – *registers*, *levels*, *intensity*, *scope* and *perspectives* – interrelate in inchoate ways; and so it takes something of the shape shown in Figure 9.1. It is hardly surprising, therefore, if – against this set of considerations – it is difficult to give a full or even an adequate account of professionalism in the present age.

Over decades, Charles Taylor (1969, 1991, 1992, 2007), has written on several of these themes, on ethics, authenticity and nature as a 'source of the self' and on yet other pertinent matters, including that of imaginaries of, and a value background to, social and community life.[2] Bringing just some of those strands together, we can – surely still in keeping with Taylor's thinking – suggest the idea of an *ecological authenticity* as providing a background ethical horizon to professional life.

The idea of an ecological professionalism presses this line of thought further, for the ecological professional is minded to try to improve the wellbeing of her environment, in all its networked complexity. But can the idea of improvement be conceptualized?

Here, the concept of responsibility regains an entrance; and it may be distinguished from authenticity. Authenticity is a matter of being true to oneself, an idea that may be further understood in two ways (cf. Cooper, 2002). One may be true to oneself through being unencumbered by unduly constraining forces and situations: here, one has the freedom to become oneself as one really wants and even needs to be. Alternatively, one may be true to oneself through venturing forward fearlessly, relying only on oneself and one's own resources and capacities. This is a more Nietzschean conception of authenticity, of striking out boldly no matter what the circumstances. On either conception, authenticity is that state of affairs

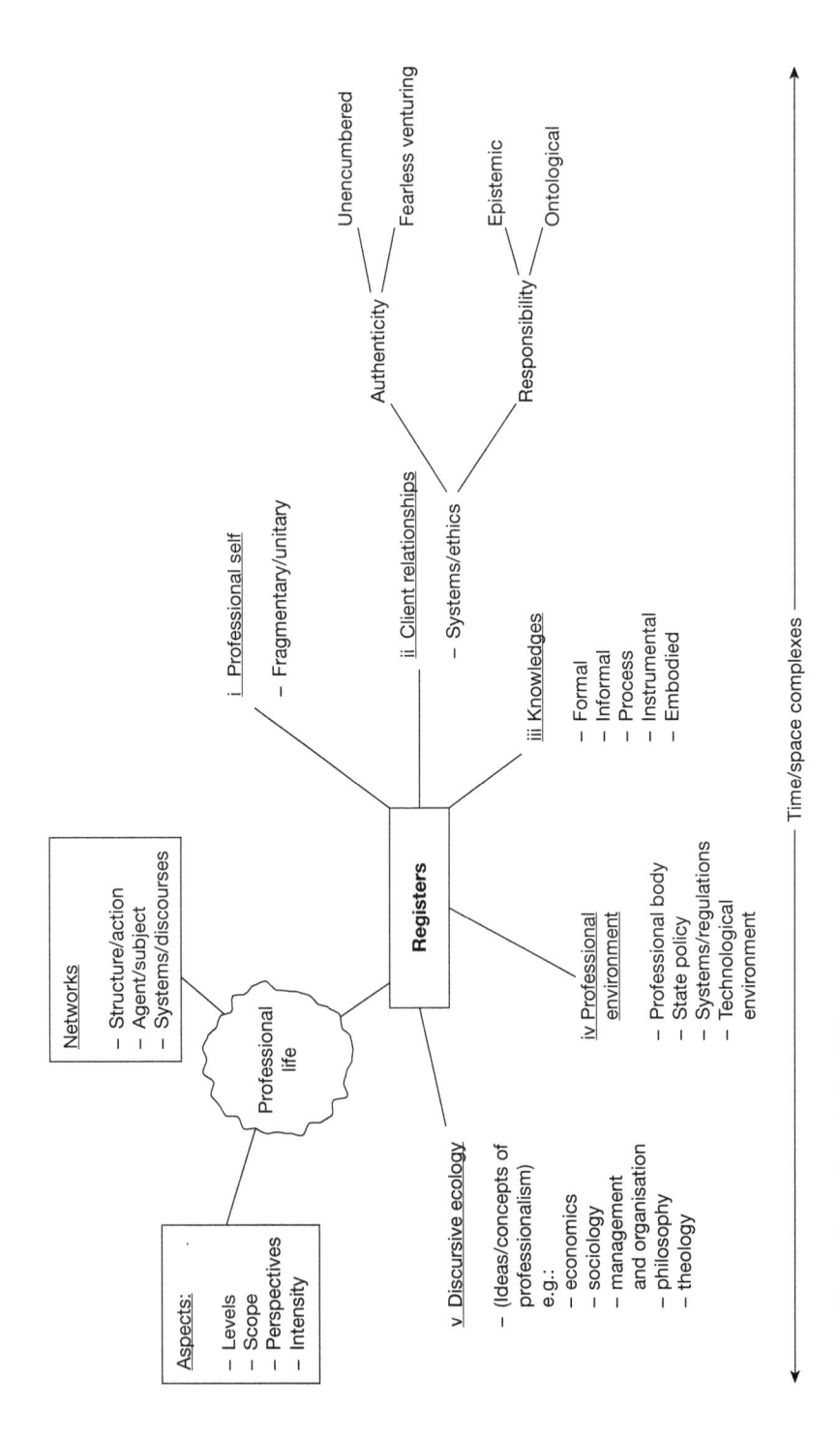

FIGURE 9.1 The ecology of professional life

in which one heeds one's own inner callings. Authenticity is crucial here, for in being fully professional, the professional has to be herself to a significant extent. Her acts and choices have to be hers. Such authenticity brings its own benefits. It has room and time for a mutual smile and flashes of humour, for authenticity opens spaces freed from the press of inner and outer forces. Both client and professional are put, and put themselves, at their ease.

Pit, then, responsibility alongside authenticity. If authenticity is a matter of heeding one's inner callings, responsibility heralds a regard for the exterior world; and almost a disregard for self. Responsibility calls precisely for *responsive*ness to the claims of the world. Again, in parallel with authenticity, two versions of responsibility may be distinguished. On the one hand, to each profession there attach certain kinds of responsibility towards the relevant field(s) of knowledge, in going on advancing her own and others' understandings therein. This is an *epistemic responsibility*.

On the other hand, there is the situation in which a professional does not just acknowledge responsibilities (and even act on them), but feels them as part of her own professional identity. They constitute her professional being. This is a form of *ontological responsibility*. It is the form of responsibility that comes to constitute what Heidegger called 'care' or 'concern', or what used also to be termed 'vocation', that state of self-*less* being in which individuals are called out to and yield to an inner calling. Such a calling has been especially associated with the so-called caring professions, in nursing, social work, the church or in teaching.

Both forms of responsibility are important *and* they are interrelated. Ontological responsibility – the felt responsibility – has to be anchored in a professional's epistemic responsibility, otherwise it is empty. Equally, her epistemic responsibility is sheer intellectualism unless it is given substance in the professional's own interior being. Her responsibilities impart a spirit that impels her forward into the professional fray. For this, there has to be an ontological responsibility at work; her professional being has to be layered with not just a *sense* of responsibility, but with responsibility itself. Her professional identity is structured in part by her exterior callings; her duty.

The ecological professional, accordingly, is always forging her own professionalism. She is conscious of the (five) registers of her professional being, which she is always exploring, and to each one she has, as indicated, an abiding care or concern. After all, 'Dasein's Being reveals itself as *care*' (Heidegger, 1998/1962: 227). More, since the domains of her professionalism are interrelated in ever-changing forms, her responsibilities as an ecological professional are always shifting, like patterns in the sand. This professional is something of a nomad, carrying her home into different places and spaces.

A professional ecosophy

In sketching his idea of the ecological environment in which humanity is embedded, Guattari spoke of 'a new ecosophy, at once applied and theoretical, ethico-political and aesthetic' (2005/1989: 67). Surely, we have seen such a 'new ecosophy' in this ecological professionalism. The idea of professionalism underwent a revolution – actually, it was an inversion – amid the arrival of the so-called new public management; from an autonomous professionalism founded on a command of a knowledge field interpreted in the interests of a client, to an accountable professionalism bounded by technical constraints and performance indicators, in the interests of systems and bureaucracies. In that imposition of professional technicization and bureaucratization, responsibility itself shifted from an immediate concern with profession and client *to* a responsiveness to external stakeholders and management systems.

However, within ecological professionalism, the professional has a horizon of a *worldly* responsibility towards the ecological registers of her professional being. We see this in the name of an international charity: 'Médecins *sans Frontières*' (emphasis added). This is a charity that recognizes no geographical borders. We see it too in graphic form when professionals of many kinds respond immediately to world crises – tsunamis, earthquakes, famines, floods – or to chronic world problems (such as physical malformations or diseases) and travel to distant lands to deploy their professional skills and care in alleviating suffering and pain. We see it too on the battlefield when doctors and others treat the injured of opposing armed forces, so exhibiting a universality in their professionalism. These professionals identify – *qua* professionals – with peoples across the world. Perhaps this stance was always there to some extent, but now – with modern communications and transport systems – this universality is doubly heightened, both in the professional's awareness and in the possibilities for her responses to the world.[3]

This worldly professionalism has yet other properties. Returning to Guattari, the earlier quotation is instructive. An ecological professionalism is itself 'at once applied and theoretical, ethico-political and aesthetic' (2005/1989: 67). The ecological professional, we may say, is a practising epistemologist *and* a practising ontologist: she believes that there is a world around her and it has definite forms and structures, even if their character is far from clear. She seeks to go on widening her understandings of the world, voyaging across different knowledges. *And* she acts in and on the world, and struggles to go on learning about the world in which she has her professional being.

But she has a care for, a concern for, the world: her professionalism has that '*ethico*-political' character of which Guattari spoke. She has a concern for all of the networks that mark out her professional life and the ecosystems in which she finds herself. She is mindful of her being within each of them, and tries in the first place to ensure that nothing she does or says brings harm to any of them.

Her actions and thoughts have too an aesthetic character. It is not too fanciful to say that the ecological professional is a professional poet – of a kind. For she imagines a world of beauty into being, as far as she can. In having a concern for the multiple environments within which she has her professional being, she makes her interventions with care, and with refinement, so as to advance the registers within which she works. Her concern has a natural aesthetic quality, which expresses itself in the micro aspects of her engagements with her world. It would be a near-contradiction to say that the ecological professional had a concern for the world, but yet was clumsy, inept, coarse or otherwise insensitive to the aesthetic character of her interactions with it.

This ecological professional has both dispositions *and* qualities; and these should be distinguished. In order to *be* an ecological professional, certain *dispositions* are called for. These include a will continuously to learn, a will to discern the world in all its complexity (its five registers), a will to engage, a will to be receptive to the world, a disposition of criticality (so as to evaluate and form judgements of her world) and a will to be creative. These dispositions propel a professional into the world, and with some care towards it.

To such universal dispositions (required of every ecological professional) are brought to bear numerous *qualities*; and here ecological professionals will vary as they interpret their callings as ecological professionals. Such qualities may include courage, resilience, energy, creativity, aesthetic sensitivity, imagination, humour and modesty.

These dispositions and qualities are embodied in the professional's being (cf. Loftus, 2015); but they crucially differ. To repeat, the enumerated dispositions are *necessary* and *universal* ingredients of an ecological professional, though they are not sufficient. Qualities, in contrast, are much more extendable and subject to individual take-up. The enumerated qualities are simply *examples* of qualities exhibited by ecological professionals, and ecological professionals will vary in their exemplification of such qualities. It is in their holding onto the necessary *dispositions* that individuals become ecological professionals *per se*; it is in their exhibiting certain kinds of *qualities* that such individuals form their own unique character as an ecological professional.

The ecological professional, therefore (and to pick up and extend Guattari's term) is a *professional ecosophist*. It may be that she would not easily be able to articulate her challenges and her aspirations as an ecological professional (although she may come close to doing so), but her professional being is held reflexively in this multi-dimensionality, in its playing out of the individual's dispositions *and* qualities in the regions of the ecological registers with their multiple timeframes and spaces.

No wonder that contemporary professional life is demanding. The ecological professional feels the call of the registers of her life, and responds, drawing on all her resources (cognitive, experiential, emotional, financial, empathic, and – yes – her time-management skills as she moves across multiple timeframes). Choices have to be made and ethical judgements reached and actions taken, as she extends herself across her ecological registers. This professional life is inexorable in the burdens it loads onto the individual. Not least, the life–work balance becomes ever more a fading prospect. Care exerts its ontological toll, as the emotional and existential demands *necessarily* outstrip the resources of the professional.

Supercomplexity

'Supercomplexity' is a shorthand for a particular set of challenges facing the ecological professional. Whereas complexity connotes the character and interwovenness of the manifold *systems* in which professional life is embedded, supercomplexity refers to the open-endedness of the *conceptual or narrative* challenges facing the professional as she works through and at her practices.

To some extent, what is at issue here is the hard–soft distinction that we encountered earlier; the hardness of systems as against the fuzziness of concepts and ideas through which the professional gains some kind of self-understanding and self-interpretation. On the one hand, systems are relatively tractable: they can be subjected to analysis and prediction and control. Their interwovenness in professional life produces situations of *real* complexity that often exert stress as professionals face an overload of tasks with inadequate resources. On the other hand, ideas, concepts and frameworks are relatively *in*tractable, yielding only dispute and never-ending interpretation (Barnett, 2000).

The question: 'To what systems of evaluation and accountability is the professional subject?' yields a confined set of responses such that there *could* be a consensus: the professional can comprehend the systems in which she is placed even if she does not support them. On the other hand, the question: 'What is to count as professionalism?' not only evinces a lack of consensus, but downright conflict. Here, the professional can justifiably suffer even some angst, as different interpretations of her professionalism conflict with each other. Questions as to (complex) systems *could*, in principle, yield agreement; questions as to concepts, ideas and frameworks could *never* yield agreement.

It is in relation to such utter open-endedness that the idea of 'supercomplexity' gains its purchase. But the idea takes on even more force in the context of the ecological professional. For, as we have seen, the ecological professional has her being among complexes of registers, of time and space, *and* of different ethical horizons. Her professional being moves on various planes – the local and the global, the performative and the therapeutic, the personal and the impersonal – and she is minded, willed even, to play her part in promoting wellbeing in the domains of her professionalism.

It is evident that the professional is all the time challenged not just to make decisions over systems and system-located actions, but also to make discursive, conceptual and ethical *choices*. Judgements just have to be made against a moving horizon of *competing* priorities and considerations. Just what might be meant by 'wellbeing' or 'effectiveness'? To what extent might a busy doctor concern herself with the home circumstances of each patient or the health needs of people in developing countries? To what extent might a doctor lobby for a change in health policy? Just how should the clinical relationship be construed (in a global and a digitized age, in which patients have recourse to all manner of resources and advice)? The ecological professional hears different ideas expressed in different languages – of virtues, performance indicators, rights, needs, resources – and responds to these voices through her own inner conversations (Archer, 2003). Living in a supercomplex world, the ecological professional is necessarily multi-lingual, but still has to *choose* her words and her acts.

Educating the ecological professional

Educating the ecological professional will involve stretching the student into the many zones of professional experience – human, social, epistemological, institutional, cultural, economic, environmental and her own learning too; in short, into and across the seven ecosystems. Judgements will need to be made by educators about the relative weightings to be accorded to each zone of experience. But, as we have seen, ecological professionalism amounts to more than a smooth gliding through fluid media; it is more than a transgressivity of nomadic wanderings. Rather, an ecological professionalism calls for an interconnectedness of the three moments of action, understanding and sheer being. In turn, the ecological professional exhibits agency and deliberateness, has capacities for critical and indeed wise judgement, and possesses a strong ethical orientation. And she does this all within an environment at once complex *and* supercomplex, and amid insecurity and uncertainty.

But even to say all this is not to exhaust the demands that professional education has a right to make upon students. For, as it will be recalled, the ecological professional not merely has an interest in the ecosystems of the world, but has a care towards those major ecosystems and is willed to play her part – however modest – in strengthening them. This ecological professional is concerned about the fate of the world and cannot just pass by, as it were. All her daily encounters and envisioned possibilities are set against this set of ecological horizons. Her relationships with her clients, her strivings towards her profession, her engagements with audit procedures and her interactions with private and public sectors are all played out with her ecological concerns. Understanding, wellbeing, probity, care and sheer professionalism are just some of her watchwords.

Accordingly, in this kind of professional education so conceived, both the curriculum and the pedagogical relationship set vital challenges. Only the broadest possible considerations can be suggested here, for they will need – in keeping with the wider thesis of this book – to be interpreted in local circumstances and persistently revisited amid changing exigencies. Still, certain practical principles suggest themselves.

A *curriculum* for ecological professionalism would be one that:

- takes the student into the zones of experience, cognitive challenge, and action;
- opens voyages to the student in time and place, across timeframes and across cultures;
- requires the student as a would-be professional to make judgements in circumstances of limited understanding and multiple interpretations of any such judgements;
- calls upon the student to accept increasing levels of responsibility for her/his words and acts;
- confronts the student with pertinent matters in each of the ecosystems – of knowledge, social institutions, persons, the economy, her own learning,

culture and the natural environment – and the intractable issues that arise from their co-mingling (in particular professional situations, what regard should be paid to human, operational, economic and cognitive dimensions, as they pull against each other?).

And such a curriculum would also be accompanied by *pedagogical relationships* that:

- accord both cognitive and experiential space to students, even in an education oriented towards those professions patently concerned to make judgements in which life itself is at risk;
- allow matters to be worked through collaboratively so that the university might become a space for 'encounter[s] for deliberative communication' (Englund, 2008). Such a pedagogical setting would approach an 'ideal speech situation' in which what counts is 'the force of the better argument' (Habermas, 1984: 25);[4]
- propel a student not only to reflect on and clarify her value stance, but to attend to it, to consider its presence within her professional actions and dispositions;
- advance accordingly her professional authenticity across both time and space.

This set of considerations puts any programme of professional education on its mettle. Any such programme would always be subject to being revisited, and to new possibilities being imagined for it, and for its balances to be reweighed. There would always be more that might be achieved and there would always justifiably be *less* that might be put the student's way (for considerations of the kind just enumerated would always act as a temptation to overload the curriculum). Less is more, even given the challenges identified here. Space is needed for the necessary good humour that will mark the pedagogical relationship of this ecological professionalism.

This set of principles may seem unduly ambitious, but the educator has a gambit up her sleeve. If a single encounter – say, in the clinical situation – can harbour infinite etceteras between and beyond the professional and the client, then it follows that a single student experience can open to multiple possibilities of insights and paths of human and professional development. The law student's encounter in a *pro bono* setting, helping to give advice to people in an impoverished inner-city setting, provides the basis for numerous considerations in several of the professional ecosystems.

Conclusions

An ecological professionalism is within reach, and it is already apparent in some professionals' lives. Some, if not many, are already living out its callings. They sense themselves as embedded in multiple timeframes and spaces, the local and the global, the short-term and the longer-term. And while they are bound to live amid performative discourses – of efficiency and cost-effectiveness and performance goals and indicators – they seek also to place those discourses against ethical horizons. This is an ecological professionalism that calls the professional self-reflexively to make choices continually, choices that bring instrumental strategies and actions to self-summoned ethical tribunals. In all this, the professional considers and acts so as to assist the wellbeing of the manifold registers that structure her professionalism.

This professionalism threatens to overwhelm individuals who heed its callings. All the time, this ecological professional senses a gap, even a gulf, between her perceived possibilities of a better world and the limitations of her actions. Such limitations are both practical and ethical. The ecological professional is aware always of other possibilities for her actions and utterances; she is acutely aware that she could have spoken and acted otherwise, and that her time and resources could have been deployed to further other registers (the interests of the client, collective practices among the profession, her own professional learning, the wider society and even the wider world). She is aware, too, of the power that lies behind the regulatory systems within which she works. This is a heavy load to bear; even an intolerable one.

But, as with the bringing off of a memorable performance of a musical concert, an ecological professionalism – for all its fragility – is possible. Like the musical performance, too, it also needs continual reflection, practice, effort, energy, creativity, imagination, authenticity, renewed performance and even, at times, political nous. Educating for this ecological professionalism is within reach. Much can already be glimpsed in the best of professional education in our universities. But, as always, there is much more to be done.

Notes

1. Over the past half-century or more, many studies have been conducted – separately in the United States, continental Europe and the UK – on suicide rates among doctors. While it turns out that there are significant variations across specialities, both men and women doctors generally show more elevated levels of suicide than the general population, with women doctors apparently showing a definite pattern in this way.
2. For a full examination of Charles Taylor's contributions to ecological debates, see Glen Lehman's recent (2015) book. While it associates Taylor's idea of ecology with the natural environment (in contradistinction to the fuller concept of ecology here), it is replete with insights directly pertinent to the argument here, not least the connections made between humanity and the wider environment. For instance, as observed, '[from Taylors' work], the key issue involves the development of deliberative structures throughout society to critically analyse, inform and nurture the significant values that shape our being-in-the-world' (p. 85). The present argument can be read as a plea for a conception and a reordering of the university precisely along these lines.
3. Pertinent here is the book by Bendik-Keymer (2006). It wears its heart on its sleeve but it brings together many issues directly relevant here, not least those of humanity, the Earth, citizenship, time, meaning and reason and ecology itself. Nor does it win its points with undue ease. For instance, 'finding moral reasons to respect life has been one of the difficult and contested areas of environmental ethics' (p. 100).

4 Certainly, this notion of Habermas – 'the force of the better argument' – has been critiqued; for example, the implication that such force can be generated in the absence of rhetoric (Ferry, 2012). Part of the difficulty, it seems to me, is that Habermas construed the validity conditions of the ideal speech situation – as a space for generating good arguments – rather narrowly.

10
ENGAGING THE WORLD

Introduction

The idea of universities engaging with the world has been taken up quite a bit in the recent higher education literature (Fransman, forthcoming), and I want to do so here too. I wish, however, to do so by pursuing two aims, to explore the very idea of engagement *and* to press those reflections into the service of our present topic. I shall try to show that the idea of engagement is especially helpful in fleshing out the idea of the ecological university, but that differences between distinctive *metaphors of engagement* need to be observed.

The very idea of engagement

When taken up in an academic text, the term 'engagement' is metaphorical. This gives it strengths and weaknesses. Its weaknesses are that it is non-specific, and so its intended meaning is unclear. Its strengths are that its very openness offers a space for the imagination to fill in meanings that might do justice to particular contexts. Just what might it mean, for instance, to speak of the university as engaging with the world or as having an orientation towards civic engagement? That the meanings of such expressions are not immediately transparent and, still less, secure universal understandings, invites exploration not just of meanings, but also of possible ways in which, say, a *particular* university might engage with the wider society. Institutional leaders and academics have an open canvas on which to exercise their imaginations, both over meanings and over actual courses of action that a university might pursue.

There is, too, a further advantage that accompanies such openness. As with many large terms, 'engagement' is open not just to different interpretations, but also to counter-views. Such differences would rarely be brought into the open because groups and individuals and even whole institutions can simply sign up to the idea of engagement without realizing that their sense of engagement might be radically different from another view. 'Engagement', in short, turns out to be a nice example of a contested concept (Gallie, 1956).

Let us briefly explore the idea of engagement itself. The term could carry with it a sense of gears engaging or meshing. With a bit of oil, they may work together with very little friction or, if ill-fitting in some way, they might screech and even judder to an awkward halt. Or the term 'engagement' could be harbouring a sense of a social relationship of engagement as a prelude to marriage; a getting-to-know-you-better period, which might be broken off, but which might lead to a long partnership and even happiness ever after. Or the term could be deployed so as to convey a sense of being totally immersed, as in being engaged on a task or in an issue. Here, one is emotionally engaged, energized and committed, and is developing one's identity as such. Or, last and perhaps unwittingly, military metaphors might be close at hand, as in armies engaging with each other. In fencing, too, during an encounter between two fencers, 'engagement' is 'the point at which the fencers are close enough to join blades, or to make an effective attack. Blade contact is also referred to as an engagement' (Wikipedia: 'Outline of fencing').

Three aspects stand out from these cursory reflections. *First*, a matter of *power*: on whose terms is the engagement being conducted? Is one party much more powerful than the other or is there a mutuality of resources and interests? This is an important matter for universities. Sometimes – as when a pharmacy or biochemical department enters into a relationship with (engages with) a global pharmaceutical company – the university may be the more junior, or weaker, partner. At other times, power can be present within the academic world itself – as when a top-ranking university forms a connection with a university in a developing country. Such inequality of academic power can harbour 'cognitive (in)justice' (de Sousa Santos, 2016) with effects on the minutiae of academic interactions, even expressed in forms of deference in interpersonal communication, both in 'private' emails and in more open academic events.

A key issue is this: how is the agenda of any such engagement being formed? Is it largely on the basis of the interests of only one of the parties? And so may arise egregious forms of *asymmetrical engagement*, where the parties are ill-balanced as they engage with each other, whether within the academic context or between a university and the wider world.

Second, there is a matter of *value commitment*. How whole-hearted are the parties to the engagement? In the academic world, the practice has grown of universities signing memoranda of understanding (MOUs) especially where two universities in different countries pledge to work together. All too often, these MOUs simply gather dust in a registrar's filing cabinet. They are symbolic texts and come to amount to very little, rarely being put into any kind of practice. Engagement seemed assured at the moment of the handshakes and photographs, but it turns out to be (literally) only paper-thin; a phantom engagement.

Issues arise here, therefore, of institutional identity and agency. To what extent might a university be committed to any process of engagement? What resources does it put to the task? And, much more profoundly, might a university's own identity be modified somewhat as a result of any engagement? Does it contemplate a change in itself? Is a particular engagement initiative seen (and even desired) only within the top brass of a university, while being neglected or even undermined by the academic staff?

Third, there is a matter of the *value structure* at work. Crudely, the notion of engagement harbours two contrasting value structures, associated with power. One is that of party x imposing its will in the engagement. It is that of a university, say, that seeks to widen its power and influence and, often too, its income streams. It is evident where a university puts itself at the centre of its own activities. It is a self-centred construction of a university's relationship with the world. Its corporate strategy is largely a list of targets as to how it will 'engage' so as to advance itself – its powers in the world, its world rankings, its number of students, its income base.

The other form of engagement is one in which party y does not merely take account of the world, but also listens to the world and tries to understand the world, and then tries to find ways of acting and interacting that do justice to what is heard. There is reciprocity here. This form of engagement is evident, for example, when, say, a team from a university's department of education goes into a developing country and spends time there – at all levels, from the Ministry of Education to local schools – gaining understanding, and working with schools, perhaps to try out some new educational ideas that are appropriate to the setting, and then, in action research, to evaluate them collaboratively with local people. To put it formally, there is a difference between an *instrumental* way of engaging with the world and a *hermeneutic* way of engaging with the world; of imposition and of understanding.

The first form of engagement is conducted in a way not exactly immune to the party being engaged, but that understanding extends only so far as is necessary in order to secure goals already identified. Such a university will engage with a local authority in the location and development of a new campus only so far as is necessary to secure its development. A more hermeneutic form of engagement would lead that university rather to work with the local authority and the local community, not just to avoid difficulties – for example, in disrupting the local housing market – but imaginatively to find ways of harmonizing the initiative with developments, say, in social housing locally.

It is that latter form of engagement – the hermeneutic engagement – that we may ascribe to the ecological university. The ecological university, after all, does not merely have a concern for the ecosystems in which it is implicated, but concretely works to understand and then to advance and even improve them.

Entanglement – and impact

There is a link here, to the concept of entanglement, that we may steal – and transpose – from quantum physics. In entanglement, the state of an entity cannot be stated independently of the entities that form a system as a whole. 'In entanglement, one constituent cannot be fully described without considering the other(s)' (Wikipedia: 'Quantum entanglement'). A measurement of one entity in such a system also constitutes a measure of another entity. One entity knows another entity without communication between them.

This is precisely the state of the ecological university. It cannot be described independently of its entanglements and, as implied, they exhibit different patterns. A true and full entanglement is evident when the state of play is such that we cannot speak of x university without also pointing to certain of its interconnections. Perhaps we could not properly understand a university without bringing into view its active networking with a local community; or its reaching out to the wider citizenry and helping to form it more into an informed public; or in its offering scholarships to prospective students from poor backgrounds; or its partnerships with certain corporations in the private sector. There is an *institutional semantics* opening here, in which the university *qua* institution takes on meaning and an identity that can be filled out only with reference to its hinterland.

It is important to understand the radical nature of these points. For the term 'entanglement' implies that we cannot understand that local community or that wider citizenry or those poorer settings or those corporations *unless* we bring a particular university into view. 'Entanglement' cuts both ways.

Moreover, a full entanglement is present when a university is actively working to deepen its entanglements by seeking to hear the voices of those with whom it is engaging. But this is not to say that in such an entanglement, a university subjugates its own voice. As in a duet in the opera house, each party retains its own voice, but the composition is not understandable without embracing each and all of the voices. Learning to hold one's voice-line, while listening to and engaging with the voices around one, is far from easy.

At this juncture, it may be helpful to compare on the one hand, the ideas of engagement, entanglement and, indeed, the ecological university with, on the other hand, the idea of impact. The idea of impact has recently come into the discourse of UK higher education in playing a part in the national research evaluation exercise (known at the time of writing as the Research Excellence Framework – or REF). The national funding council (the Higher Education Funding Council for England – or HEFCE) defines 'impact' as 'an effect on, change or benefit to the economy, society, culture, public policy or services, health, the environment or quality of life, beyond academia' (HEFCE website: 'REF impact'). Against the background of our analysis, a number of observations might be made.

'Impact' is a crude term in this context. It speaks of a mechanical collision, as when the proverbial billiard ball hits another, and has an impact on it. It is a revealing metaphor. It suggests an unyielding, a direct assault, a brutal collision, with considerable energy. It conjures an *instrumental* form of engagement and much less that hermeneutic form of engagement, in which a university listens carefully and sympathetically to the voices of those with whom it would interact, even, to some extent, *yielding* to the sources of those voices. There is no sense, as with the ecological university, of having a deep concern for the ecosystems with which it is implicated, and sets of relationships unfolding carefully over time. And so there is no sense of entanglement, of two entities being to some degree entwined with each other, even if somewhat apart. Quite the reverse: this is a connectivity that is devoid of a relationship. It is a sharp impact, at a moment in time. The flourishing and the taking forward of a mutual engagement are not on the cards here. Impact has no time for reciprocity. It is evident that the language of impact has to be not merely abandoned, but sharply repudiated, so far as the ecological university is concerned.

This is a real and pressing matter for those universities that are concerned to contribute to the wider society, not least against a background in which global rankings and a discourse of 'world-class' universities have taken a strong hold. Many such universities – especially in Asia, South America and Africa – are faced with dilemmas. Characteristically, they are caught in a fork, enjoined by their host state to take action designed to improve their standing in the rankings, but yet wishing to become much more engaged with the wider society in ways that will have no 'impact' on those standings. In a survey of higher education in Asia, the judgement is that, in such an 'ecology of higher education . . . [t]here are no easy "solutions" to the contradictions' that face such universities (Hawkins, 2016: 133).

Civic engagement – and the public sphere

There is much use these days of the term civic engagement. It is suggested that universities should take seriously their social responsibilities and should be involved (engaged indeed) in programmes of civic engagement. For example, the Talloires Declaration – of a freely joined group of universities from across the world – as the first in a list of 11 bullet points, states that the signatory universities agree to 'Expand civic engagement and social responsibility programs . . .' (Talloires Network website). Interestingly, that bullet point runs on 'in an ethical manner, through teaching, research and public service', as if it might be imagined that civic engagement and social responsibility might be conducted in a non-ethical way; but let that pass. The question before us is simple: just what might be meant by 'civic engagement'? Notably, it is rarely, if ever in such statements, spelt out.

In a way, it is understandable that the notion of civic engagement is left open. After all, it has had 2,000 years of history since the Greeks, with Aristotle developing a politics that was 'commensurate with the Greek city state characterized by a shared set of norms and ethos in which free citizens on an equal footing lived under the rule of law' (Wikipedia: 'Civil society: etymology'). But how might such ideas fare in the twenty-first century in the context of multicultural and diverse nation states and global movements and interchanges? This dimension is significant since all universities, even the most specialized, have become global institutions, inserted as they are into global discourses and circulations of knowledge and of worldly cognitive capital.

Let us be honest. In the context of universities, the phrase 'civic engagement' cannot be pinned down; but it should not abandoned. It is a suitably provocative term, provoking significant questions. The phrase seems to imply the presence of a civil society (with which the university might engage). But then, in an age of mass media and social media, where and in what form might we espy civil society, if at all? Can it, indeed, be seen or envisaged at a global level? Can it even be seen at a national level, modern society being so complex, with different social classes, nationalities and cultures intermingling? These questions are significant here, for just what might it mean for a university now to engage with civil society?

The matter becomes doubly more complicated. First, there have developed over time various ideas of civil society. A crucial point of difference lies in the market economy: some see it as potentially lying within, while others would place it outside civil society (cf. Calhoun, 2011). Second, the respective boundaries of civil society and the public sphere are unclear. For our purposes, I shall associate civil society with forms of organization and groupings that lie outside the state, being agnostic for the moment on the matter of the market. I shall associate the public sphere, on the other hand, with discursive exchanges in the non-state arena especially about society itself; for instance, its politics, its economy, the relationships between the state and individuals and so forth. Such a sense of the public sphere comes close to that of Jurgen Habermas, for whom the public sphere is much less a space – as we might say of civil society – and much more a process, a happening, a situation (McAfee, 2009). However, Habermas – whose book on *The Structural Transformation of the Public Sphere* (2005/1962) was first published in the 1960s – rather underplays the fact that, characteristically, modern society has recently come to exhibit all manner of public spheres (Barnett, 2015), which spill over each other in crazy ways but also contend against each other.

Yet further matters arise, in ferreting out what it might mean for the university to pursue a project of civic engagement. As implied, there is an issue as to whether civic engagement might be construed to include the market economy (or perhaps certain aspects of it). Notably, the Talloires Declaration does include mention of 'economic opportunity', but markets as such do not appear in it. It appears that the Talloires Network of universities understands civic engagement to lie in other spaces. The Network is intent precisely on encouraging the development of universities' civic engagement in 'contribut[ing] positively to local, social and global communities'. And there, too, we see that it does take seriously the idea of a global community, which presumably it sees itself as helping to form. Further, the Network wants to 'develop' communities and even more radically to 'transform' them. Precisely what such community transformation is supposed to look like, we are not told.[1]

These reflections point to an interplay across, but also distinctions between, the university being involved in civic engagement on the one hand and in advancing the public sphere on the other hand. To press the point, it is evident that the Talloires Network Declaration focuses its attention on universities' *civic* engagement. It is not just that the phrase 'public sphere' is not used, but rather that the very idea of universities helping to advance the public sphere is not seriously in evidence. The university as acting as a space for public debate, as extending public understanding of complex and controversial public issues, as advancing public reasoning by putting its research and scholarship into the public domain and by its academics playing their parts as public intellectuals or contributing to the advancement of evidence-based public policy: none of these is intimated in the Declaration. I am sure that such a programme of contributing to and of strengthening the public sphere would not be repudiated by the Talloires Network – but it is important that such a programme be explicitly acknowledged and grasped. For each university will have its own possibilities in relation to the public sphere and these possibilities have not merely to be identified, but imagined.

There is a final point. Such projects of civic engagement and of the development of the public sphere have ultimately to be realized in the real world. Given the distinctions just made between civic engagement and the development of the public sphere, it is characteristically much more common for interest to be registered in universities' possibilities for civic engagement. The contribution that universities might make to the public sphere, in contrast, has received surprisingly little attention.[2]

Engaging the world

Earlier, I proposed a hermeneutic approach in understanding what it might be for the ecological university to engage with its environment. But it is also apparent that engagement calls for much more than listening to, comprehending and taking the part of the other. Going back to our opening remarks about the metaphors of engagement, harmonious engagement calls not for yielding to the other or even inserting oneself – in a way – into the other. Rather, for a proper engagement, the parties need to engage *with each other*.[3] There is a danger that an entirely proper recoil against instrumental forms of engagement can lead to an over-determination to be sensitive to the other, and so unwittingly relinquish the university's full resources to help to strengthen the other.

We have glimpsed how the university might engage both socially and publicly (and the two were distinguished). The contemporary university has undreamt resources and new spaces are opening to it. It can help to advance the social realm, not least by extending life chances to students from poorer socio-economic backgrounds. It can actively work with local and regional communities and even communities in far-flung places. It can offer a space of reason in which a multitude of groups can come together to articulate the plight of indigenous peoples in the midst of globalization (cf. Pleyers, 2010). By putting its research findings and its scholarship into the public domain, it can help to widen public understanding of complex matters (should energy policy include the building of nuclear power stations? Should bioengineering extend to the fabrication of artificial rhino horns so as to destroy that market which is devastating the rhino population?). It can adopt a policy such that every open seminar and lecture is placed in the public domain on a social media platform, adding to the thousands of videos already available in which world experts can be seen and their ideas, perspectives and insights accessed.

But it can go further. It can engage with local and national broadcasting companies and host public debates on controversial issues. This is not the peer-to-peer situation that some advocates of open access call for (Peters, Gietzen and Ondercin, 2012); and nor is it a form of socialist knowledge, if by that is meant that all participants are on a communicative level, *à la* Habermas. To the contrary, it is the university bringing its expertise to bear and so enabling society to become more rational, enabling well-attuned debate among a more informed citizenry. Of course, there are difficulties in such a programme.[4] In putting themselves into the public domain, academics 'will be misquoted; they will not be able to explain important nuances; they will be attacked by aggressive phone-callers or internet posters [but even so] little steps may contribute to a public sense that, yes, the university does matter' (Bird, 2011: 70).

It follows that the university has a responsibility to consider ways in which it can engage with the world proactively; and the ecological university is a university that does precisely this. Each and every university has considerable resources available to it for engaging with the world, and those resources and possibilities will differ, from university to university. It is not enough, therefore, for universities simply to espouse, on their websites, a commitment to contribute to the world or even to engage with it. The hard work has to be put in, to identify the particular spaces in which it is well-placed to engage, and the resources that it has at its disposal so to engage. This is not a hidden plea simply for management to become ecological (in the sense adopted here). Rather, this ecological thinking has to run right through a university at all levels and in all of its activities.

Interventions

Part of the argument of this book is that, in the twenty-first century, willy-nilly, the university is implicated in a number of ecosystems. Seven have been identified, those of knowledge, social institutions, persons, the economy, learning, culture and the natural environment. A strategy of engagement, therefore, if pursued seriously and with vigour, would spread out to some extent across these ecosystems. A university could attempt to work up some kind of inventory of its resources and possibilities in relation to each of these ecosystems. And this would have to be a whole-university project, with all involved. Resources, of course, are not merely technical, but are much more to do with the epistemological imprint of a university in its centres and departments, and to do with the energies, commitments and academic subjectivities of its members. To what extent do they identify with possible wider callings and possibilities of the university and feel any obligations to reach out to the world?

This would be very much a university *in*-the-world, *from*-the-world and *for*-the-world. Some, seized of such a conception of the university, might wish to see the university placing itself under the banner of service as an additional function alongside teaching and research (Bourner, 2008); but this ploy, while common in the United States, is inadequate. Indeed, the ecological university would shun the term 'service'. For 'service' implies a relationship in which B gives to A that which

A desires or finds congenial. The situation is defined by A. It is not just a subservient relationship, but is unduly constrained by A's perceptions.

This is the situation in relation to the matter of student satisfaction, in which the pedagogical situation is framed increasingly by students' desires. The ecological university cannot be interested in limiting its pedagogical responsibility to that of satisfying students. In practice, universities tend to opt for a pedagogy that satisfices; that is to say, one which offers an optimum strategy given both an interpretation of students' satisfactions and the other pressing demands of time, audit, professional accreditation, research and income generation. The ecological university, in contrast, will have regard for the student's total wellbeing, over her or his entire lifespan. (As this is written in 2016, some students will be entering higher education who will be alive in the twenty-second century.) Far from satisfying students, the ecological university will seek to draw students into a pedagogy of strangeness or of risk, for it is such pedagogies that are likely to extend students so that they may be able to meet the challenges – at once, conceptual, ethical and technological – that the twenty-first century will assuredly face them with.

Take another example, that of culture considered as an ecosystem. Some universities are developing their physical estates as spaces of public art, perhaps displaying avant-garde works and art forms. Such a university is not 'serving' society but is widening the symbolic understandings circulating in society, and is at once challenging contemporary understandings and advancing the ecology of culture. More epistemologically, departments of anthropology, art, cultural studies, languages and history – perhaps in conjunction with regional museums and galleries – are all involved in exploring distant lands, cultures and languages. In so doing, they are not just, say, assisting re-evaluations of indigenous peoples or neglected artefacts, but are, at the same time, tacitly involved in widening – and so adding to the diversity of – society's symbol systems.

Neither serving society nor satisfying students, then, will be nostrums or gambits for the ecological university. Instead, it will carefully marshal its efforts actively to advance the wellbeing of each of the ecosystems in which it moves. A happier term might be that of 'interventions': the ecological university will purposefully intervene in its ecosystems, working to benefit, to enhance their inner diversity and to strengthen them.

A single set of acts may well aid more than one ecosystem. *As persons*, students can be extended by being encouraged to be active in the community, whether or not course credit is available for such efforts. In the process, the ecosystems of students as persons, social institutions, learning and even the economy can all be aided. As persons, too, students will be pulled out of themselves into a wider space and will acquire personal resources with which to dwell on and engage in life, not just with a wider 'cognitive perspective' (Peters, 1966), but with a wider emotional repertoire and capacities for being in the world. The ecosystem of *social institutions* will be aided as student projects both immediately and indirectly help local communities. Some projects may even help to revitalize neighbourhoods or provide direct support to groups in developing countries.

Learning ecosystems will be strengthened at different levels. Students' own learning ecologies will be strengthened, with their strands multiplying and interweaving – with no neat patterns – and the learning ecologies of the wider community reinforced as individuals and groups come to understand themselves through a wider array of information and concepts; for instance, as where students work with people in the community in the field of oral history. And *the ecosystem of the economy* may itself be strengthened as forms of exchange having a public and non-market character are deepened, perhaps through an engagement with non-governmental organizations and charities.

These can only be indicative examples. The hard work has to be put in at all levels of a university to identify its resources and possibilities in strengthening the ecosystems in which it is implicated. And these *paths of possibility* will vary not just between universities, but across departments within a university. As it works across its ecosystems, and across its departments, the ecological university is *ecologically differentiated*. And, since every university is, in several ways, a global institution, this differentiation splays outwards across its ecosystems, and institutionally inwards across its departments; and spreads out locally, nationally and across the world.

Worldly being

In this idea of a differentiated university, venturing out in varied patterns across its ecosystems and across its departments, there is an affinity with Bhaskar's (2002a: 150, also 50, 100) 'four-planar' depiction of social being *and* his seven levels of increasing non-duality, agency, awakening and transformation (Hartwig, 2010: viii). Bhaskar's notion of four-planar social being depicts *being* both as social and as moving on the four planes of 'material transactions with nature', 'social interactions between humans', 'social structure proper', and the 'embodied personality'. It is surely evident that the ecological university moves on all of these planes as it engages with, intervenes in and seeks to advance its ecosystems. Parallel to Bhaskar's notion of 'social being', we might then speak of the university's *institutional* being. As an institution, it moves on each of these four planes and the ecological university does so knowingly.

Bhaskar sees humanity as nested within a stratified universe, from the micro or personal level, through the meso or institutional level, the macro or societal level, the mega level of whole civilizations (including, presumably, features such as globalization), to the cosmological level.[5] An extraordinary feature of universities is that they simultaneously have their own agency at all of these levels. An eyebrow may be raised at that last level, the cosmological level. In what way is the university 'cosmological'? It may be recalled that in our unravelling of the very idea of ecology, we observed the significance of the concept of the Earth. The Earth has a double and interlocking meaning here, both that of a particular planet in a particular solar system in the universe and that of an interconnected set of ecosystems, including but going beyond those of the natural world. The university is implicated in this Earth, in both senses, and the ecological university strives to play its part in advancing the wellbeing of the total Earth. The ecological university is an *institutional citizen* of the universe.

Two other key concepts in Bhaskar's philosophy, those of emergence and absence, are pertinent here and a connection can be drawn between them. Emergence is the property of interacting entities in open systems to produce unexpected outcomes of an order different from the entities themselves. Matters could not have been predicted. The collapse of the Soviet Union was not widely anticipated and nor was the global economic crash of 2008 widely anticipated among economists. The ecosystems in which universities are necessarily implicated are open systems. In speaking of the university engaging with the world, therefore, we are speaking of complex institutions – that is, universities – engaging in complex ways (as we have charted in this chapter) with interacting complex and open systems. This is at once a recipe for and a facilitator of emergence. After all, we have here, a situation of: 'mechanisms operating at radically different levels of reality and orders of scale [which] presupposes that the systems in which the mechanisms act are open and that some of these mechanisms operate at levels which are emergent from others' (Bhaskar, 2010: 10).

In other words, the university can expect unforeseen happenings to appear as a result of its interventions in and engagements with its seven ecosystems and at its different levels.

Let us turn to that other key concept in Bhaskar's philosophy which is of help here, that of absence. For Bhaskar, absence is a necessary constituent of the world. Without it, the world would be inert, and non-functioning. 'Absence is not only necessary for being, but change, properly understood, presupposes absence, i.e. the coming into being of new properties or entities and the passing away from being of previously existing ones' (2010: 15). We see here a vivid link to emergence: *through absence, emergence is possible*. In other words, because the universe is a set of open systems, absent entities can provoke emergence. The absence of democracy can provoke both efforts to bring it about and, in the process, entirely new forms of democracy might emerge.

This is of great moment to the ecological university. The perceived absence of proper debate in society may induce a university to marshal its resources to help to bring about a more rational world and a learning world (cf. Habermas, 1972; 1987). Neither is with us at this moment. And the relevant systems are all the time in flux. So it is unclear just what might transpire. But something could transpire of fundamental significance for the whole world if, say, all 26,000 universities in the world were to bend their efforts towards such aims, those of assisting the generation of new societal learning systems and furthering democracy and global spaces of reasoning and communication.

Conclusions

The idea of the university engaging with the wider world has been given much mileage of late and it is not without its merit, so far as the ecological university is concerned. But it needs to be taken up carefully, with certain distinctions being made and its metaphorical content delineated. Some of its more instrumental nuances should be given a wide berth. Correspondingly, its more hermeneutical aspects – the need for it to understand the world and to listen to the world – may seem *prima facie* appealing, but care has to be taken not to overlook the resources that the university has which allow it to possess and to deploy its ecological possibilities; its *ecological agency*, indeed. The concept of entanglement helps to bring out the interactive connotations of engagement that are connected with the idea of engagement. But engagement has turned out to be something of a weasel term of our age. It can only be legitimate if it is taken to imply a reciprocity. The ecological university is simultaneously and – yes, the term can be used here without flinching – *dialectically*, a university *for*-the-world and a university *from*-the-world.

A distinction, too, should be made between a university being involved in civic engagement and in engaging with the public sphere. *Both* are important for the ecological university and neither is reducible to the other.

The university, as an ecological agent, has multiple possibilities in intervening in the ecosystems that enwrap it. But these possibilities cannot be simply read off from the world. Rather, they have to be discerned and even imagined, and worked at; and at all levels of the university, from small groups within departments – perhaps associated with particular programmes of study or scholarly or research programmes – through to the university as a whole. And since the university is manifestly a complex institution that is interweaving with ecosystems, the matter of the university being engaged is to open unforeseen potential for emergence, for absenting absence (in Bhaskar's terminology) and for new happenings and developments, and at all levels from the personal to the cosmological.

In the end, the matter of engagement raises issues about the way in which the university addresses the whole Earth, and uses its collective imagination to discern possibilities for transformation, both inwardly and outwardly.

Notes

1 Though see McIlrath and Mac Labhrainn (2007), which explores 'international perspectives' of civic engagement; and Hall et al. (2013), which contains numerous case studies of 'community-university research partnerships in global perspectives'. As Hall indicates, there are the makings of an international community concerned with promoting the civic engagement of higher education, a leading light in which was David Watson (as Hall mentions and who I mention also elsewhere) who, *inter alia*, strove to develop the 'civic and community engagement' mission of the University of Brighton (UK) while being its Vice-Chancellor (Watson, 2007; Watson et al., 2011).
2 For instance, Levin and Greenwood (2016) make a fascinating link between the university's public goods and democracy, but do not widen the argument to include consideration of the public sphere. Pusser's essay (2012) mentions Habermas and 'public sphere' (several times) but tries to tease out the idea of higher education as itself a public sphere rather than carrying forward the idea of public sphere in a Habermasian sense – as a space of public discourse – and analysing the potential of the university thereto. Closer to that quest are Nixon (2011) and Williams and Filippakou (2015). Nixon's beautiful and restrained text touches the argument here at several points and indicates the

intertwinedness of the facets of the university's functioning, such that public goods, the public sphere, mutual recognition and a 'republic of learning' may all be promoted simultaneously. (See especially pp. 124–125, but also throughout that book.) See also Rammell (2016) for a sketch of a programme aimed at 'protecting the public interest in higher education'.
3   Cf. Donati:

> The relational nature of engagement . . . concerns the relations between the subject and [the] environment . . . the subject's mental activity (internal conversations) . . . the elements of the reflexive process and agency [and] the outcomes of engagement in terms of structural elaboration.
>
> (Donati, 2013: 134)

If we substitute 'university' for 'subject', this set of observations is directly applicable to the present argument. However, I am going further in anticipating a mutuality between the subject/university and the environment.
4   See again Levin and Greenwood (2016) and the collection edited by Weber and Bergan (2006), perhaps especially the essay by Pavel Zgaga (pp. 107–116).
5   Ultimately, of course, such a philosophy leads to 'God', understood as 'the ultimate but ingredient categorial structure of the world; as its most basic truth and ground' constituting 'the unifying, totalising, liberating power of the universe' (Bhaskar, 2010: 40, 45).

PART III
Ecological audit

11
THE IDEA OF THE ECOLOGICAL UNIVERSITY

An audit

Introduction

In the twenty-first century, nothing can be left to chance or to fend for itself and simply prove its worth – or otherwise – in the world. Now, institutions, processes and even ideas have to be audited. And all too often the clamour for an audit is accompanied by the urging: 'give us your metric' or even worse, 'we will tell you by which metrics we shall judge you'. But what might constitute an appropriate form of audit in evaluating the very *idea* of the ecological university? Our method will be that old-fashioned ploy of using reason and judgement; in other words, an audit of an idea by means of ideas.[1]

Reason and judgement can only come into play in the company of features felt to be significant. Brought into service in this audit, such features constitute *criteria of adequacy* (Barnett, 2013) and I would pick out no fewer than nine such criteria of adequacy by which *any* idea of the university might be judged; namely, those of institutional grasp, scope and range, timefulness, locale, particularity and universality, emergence, wellbeing, criticality and feasibility. Collectively, these criteria amount to severe tests of the idea, but perhaps in this *conceptual* testing, the strength of the idea may become even more apparent.

1. Institutional grasp

The ecological university understands that it is institutionally implicated, being caught up in institutional structures beyond itself. This rather bald observation deserves to be amplified.

First, the ecological university has a concern towards social institutions and, thereby, towards society as such. Whereas the entrepreneurial university has a primary concern for the economy, the ecological university has a *primary* concern for the whole world. It looks to identify impairments in and across the world.

It notices the extreme and growing levels of inequality – both absolutely and in life chances – in many countries. It observes the pollution of the natural environment. It has a sensitivity towards poverty and it has a concern that many suffer disease. It has an empathy towards those whose freedoms are injured. It notices ways in which the public sphere is limited (dominated by a few large corporations). And such concerns are reflected both in the inner activities of the ecological university, in its teaching and research, and in its engagements with the wider society.

It follows that the ecological university will reach out across its whole ecosphere, engaging with all manner of institutions, both corporations – whether in the public or private or non-governmental sectors – and social institutions that are part of the fabric of society (families, the professions, the education system as a whole, religion and so forth). Its locus will be that of playing its part in strengthening such social institutions, particularly where there are manifest impairments that it can legitimately address. Judgements will need to be made. Under which conditions and for which reasons might it engage with governmental agencies (including those of the military) and powerful private sector organizations in, say, the pharmaceutical, agri-business, bioengineering or geo-petroleum industries? It would do so only if it judges that its own integrity is not going to be impaired (for instance, in the non-publication of research results) and if it can reasonably look to see some demonstrable improvement in the wider society. The ecological university, therefore, has to establish a *judgemental capacity* capable of taking the widest view of its engagements.

Second, as Alisdair MacIntyre observed, there is a fundamental difference between institutions and practices. Indeed, 'practices must not be confused with institutions' (1985: 194). For example, 'Chess, physics and medicine are practices; chess clubs, laboratories, universities and hospitals are institutions' (1985: 194). Institutions are essential for the maintenance of practices: 'no practices can survive for any length of time unsustained by institutions'. But this vote for institutions – which explicitly includes universities – is qualified, for

> institutions are characteristically . . . concerned with . . . external goods. They are involved in acquiring money and other material goods; they are structured in terms of power and status . . . [so] the ideals and the creativity of the practice are always vulnerable to the acquisitiveness of the institution.
> (MacIntyre, 1985: 194)

Practices, in contrast, are more identified through their internal goods and their associated virtues. Virtues, internal goods and practices are intertwined – albeit in 'a complex relationship' (p. 195) – and constitute living traditions.

A casual reading might suggest that MacIntyre accords the palm to practices while down-valuing institutions. But MacIntyre holds them beguilingly together:

> We shall be unable to write a true history of practices and institutions unless that history is also one of . . . virtues and vices. For *the ability of a practice to*

> *retain its integrity will depend on the way in which the virtues can be and are exercised in sustaining the institutional forms which are the social bearers of the practice.*
> (MacIntyre, 1985: 195; emphasis added)

This last move is crucial. Universities *qua* institutions can and should take on the virtues of the practices with which they are intimately associated. The ecological university does just this, with virtues of inquisitiveness, dialogue, authenticity, reasonableness, truthfulness and concern for persons characterizing its practices.

Third, the ecological university has a *deep* institutional grasp, delving beneath the surface of institutions. It understands that it is caught in a penumbra of social institutions which are imbued with power – often with political and economic orientations. But the ecological university does what it can to stand, and even advance, its ground. Carefully, diplomatically and even subversively, it looks to realize its own possibilities. This university attempts, if necessary, to outflank institutions – and their ideologies – that would limit its being. Such tactics are not to be understood just as forms of resistance, but at their most forthright, as instances of furthering the projects of the ecological university. We see this daily, right across the world, as universities seek variously to speak and act in the causes of freedom, social mobility, reason and a widening of the public sphere. The ecological university is, perforce, a political university.

The ecological university, then, is and has to be acutely aware of and sensitive to the deep 'generative mechanisms' (Bhaskar, 2008b: 48–49) that underlie the surface of the dominant institutions. It understands that there are layers of the world that constitute its 'real' features, and which hold the forces of power. The ecological university is a realist university.

The ecological university works to maintain its integrity and more constructively to find, imagine and to live out possibilities that advance the ecosystems in which it is implicated, even as powerful forces would suppress and limit its room for manoeuvre. *Such stratagems may not be available.* The state may be awakened to take action. It may close universities and imprison their institutional leaders and/or their academics and/or their students; or it may withdraw public funding; or it may put into senior management and leadership positions its own chosen appointees; or it may steer its research funding arrangements so as to meet its own short-term interests. Nevertheless, the ecological university does what it can to hold and even to advance its ground.

The ecological university, therefore, has an acute *institutional grasp* and is adept at working out possibilities for itself, amid its institutional environment. It maintains its own locus, giving neither the political nor the economic institutions simply what they call for. Its ambit and vision are much larger and extend over a long duration. At times, this institutional adeptness will cause it to be a fly in the ointment of the big battalions. Its institutional grasp does not straightforwardly bequeath institutional *power*. But it maintains its integrity, nonetheless. Only so can it do justice to its manifold ecological leanings.

2. Scope and range

'Scope' and 'range' refer not only to the range of activities in which the ecological university might be involved – which are assuredly infinite – but more especially to the range of ways in which the idea of the ecological university itself might be taken up. The ecological university, for instance, opens to institutional practices and policies, but it also opens to empirical inquiry (since its various incarnations in universities across the world could helpfully be examined), to conceptual exploration (including the evaluation of different interpretations of the very idea of the ecological university and the sighting of new concepts) and to theoretical insight (which conditions would favour the emergence of the ecological university?). The idea of the ecological university has considerable scope and range.

These applications of the idea of the ecological university can readily be extended. The ecological university is manifest in time and space. In its spatial manifestation, a university may be ecological in its immediate locale, in its host nation and across the world. In its temporal state, the ecological university can frame its projects both in the here-and-now and ahead, over a long time horizon. The idea of the ecological university could be suggestive of university policies, at both institutional and national levels. It could be taken up by teaching-intensive universities (for example, in exploring the idea of global citizenship among its students) or by research-intensive universities, in making available their research endeavours across society (for example, through their academics becoming public intellectuals or through posting their research findings and data on the internet for wide audiences).

In relation to its scope and range, therefore, the idea of the ecological university is conceptually fecund (opening to multiple and even contesting interpretations), theoretically provocative (posing questions as to its institutional realization), empirically intriguing, potent for policy development and significantly practical (opening to all manner of imaginative practices). Its scope and range are infinite.

3. Timefulness

The ecological university lives in multiple timeframes simultaneously. It lives in the here-and-now, not least in responding to the exigencies of the day, and it forges for itself longer-term horizons. Whether it has a thousand years of history behind it or is a newly formed institution, an ecological university deliberately situates its major tasks and commitments with a sense of their playing out over very long timespans. This is not a matter of the obvious points that an estates strategy or a major set of goals – perhaps trying to generate philanthropic funds on a large scale – can be achieved only over a long period of time, perhaps even over a generation. Or that, say, in working with local and regional authorities and organizations, a university has to be willing to commit itself over a very long timeframe, for such efforts can yield results only very gradually. Rather, this consideration conveys the dual sense that the university has longevity to it and that its activities in and for the world have a temporal significance without limit and should be playing their part against a horizon of the ever-continuing story of the university.[2]

The ecological university has the future in its collective bones. It lives in and for the very long term; which is to say it lives in never-ending time. But also, the ecological university, as stated, has to get through the day, bringing with it unbidden challenges. A funding stream may suddenly be reduced or a threat to its reputation may appear overnight. That such disturbances are part of the fabric of university life is one reason for the emergence of a more dirigiste management, for the university has to be managed amid such turmoil. And such temporal challenges may strike at the university's inner life, as when a government agency calls for a report – from research that it has funded – in an overly short timeframe, so impairing the study's methodological integrity.

Consequently, it is hardly surprising – as challenges appear regularly calling for more or less immediate responses from universities – that the longer-term horizons are forsaken and the resources required seriously to discern longer-term possibilities are neglected. Nevertheless, the ecological university has a duty to attend to its own sustainability over the longer term, making its short-term adjustments against the background of very long-term time horizons, of the larger possibilities that might be glimpsed for itself.

The ecological university, therefore, is *temporally adept*, understanding acutely that it has its being in time. This temporal consciousness is more than horizon-scanning for it understands that it has temporal movement, and in multiple timeframes. The ecological university works with time, and plays with time, as it seeks to amplify its possibilities. It moves deftly, alert to ways in which it might further its ecosystems – of knowledge, culture, social institutions and so forth – whether in the short or longer term. Those who bear particular responsibilities for taking the university forward understand that many of the timeframes extend beyond any association of individuals with a university. The ecological university, accordingly, takes on something of the character of a mediaeval cathedral, the stone-masons working diligently away in the service of a high calling, as the building is crafted and developed with care over centuries. Ultimately, nothing is ever finished.

4. Locale

The ecological university understands that it is located spatially, in its immediate region, its host nation and the world, but also looks actively to move in all of its spatial planes. It feels the world pressing in, as academic life becomes ever more subject to global dimensions. Publications, research, the movement of students and researchers, and information flows all move globally. Academic identities are distributed across the world, and judgements are formed cross-nationally. The academic has her or his bodily movements in a singular place at any one time, but her or his being is scattered across the world. These reflections hold for the university itself. The university is both held and moves in and across multiple spaces, even despite itself; and it is judged locally, nationally and across the world.

The ecological university understands all this very well – and puts effort into glimpsing spaces that are opening for it. It abhors parochialism of *any* kind. It manufactures its own re-territorialization and it reconstitutes itself spatially. Certainly, it has a concern for its reputation in different regions of the world, close to home and much further afield. But the ecological university wins its spurs by actively and deliberately stretching its limbs into new crevices of the world, physically and virtually, and not to strengthen its global position but to assist the world. The doom-mongers are quite wrong in espousing their dismal readings of the university, for the twenty-first century is opening new spaces.

The ecological university is always on the move, but with a practical and ethical intent, putting its epistemological, technological and symbolic resources to work across the world. A drama department might take its students to an African country to put on a Shakespeare play for local townships; a civil engineering department might link with another such department in a far-distant land and explore possibilities either in teaching or research or both; an education department might provide advisory services to a government in a developing country in developing its school system. The ecological university happily lives in open spaces.

It is a distributed university culturally and epistemologically. Of course, such global distribution brings problems of supply chains, of communication and translation systems, and of multiple identities and cross-cultural (mis)understandings. It is admittedly not always certain that the ecological university possesses the equipment to solve all such problems. The ecological university is always on the edge of linguistic and cultural (mis)recognition.

5. Particularity and universality

For centuries, universities have tried to ride both horses – particularity *and* universality.[3] Across the world, universities are understood through universal categories of truthfulness, disinterestedness, openness, fair-dealing, carefulness, sincerity and honesty. That universities fail to live up to this billing and are judged accordingly – with charges of corruption, nepotism, dogmatism, data manipulation, closed-mindedness, self-interest and so forth – is testimony to the *presence* of such universal categories. And this is a landscape that continues to widen as new universals – wellbeing, employability, impact, access and so on – are heaped on the university, *many of which conflict with each other*. There appears to be no end to the universals now arriving at this station. At the same time, any university lives with its own particularities. Its internal resources, materials and characteristics, and moreover, its external settings, are a complex of individual entities: its particulars *are* particular to it.[4]

This is of real moment to the ecological university. Its universal callings have to be interpreted and given form through its particulars – its members, its resources, its networks and its reputation. But – demanding as it is – this *is* trivial in a way and is not very ecological. The ecological university addresses larger challenges.

First, the ecological university is sensitive to the value choices posed by its landscape of universality. It understands that the universals contend with each other. Fairness is in tension with the cliché of excellence; disinterestedness is in tension with financial security (as opportunities arise to generate income from both the state and external parties that would impose conditions); employability stands in contrast to deep understanding and criticality; and truthfulness contends with competitiveness. The ecological university goes further, however, and weaves a path through these challenges, putting its particular resources into the service of its primary values. There is here an *ecological wisdom* (Mickey, 2016), as the ecological university places its options against the horizon of universals that serve the wellbeing of its ecosystems.

Second, it strives to advance its suite of particulars so that it is better placed to live up to its being as an ecological university. It keeps under review its disciplinary mix and looks for ways it can organically widen so as to follow its ecological openings. It encourages cross-disciplinary inquiry and debate within itself. It considers the extent to which its academics are sharing their interests, ideas and understandings with constituencies beyond the university. It monitors the workloads of its academic staff. It considers the ways in which its own campuses are open to the public. And it reflects on the extent to which it is active across the world, especially in developing North–South relationships.

And third, it plays its part in public debate by widening the universals that are constituting the discursive environment in which universities move. It does not shrink from playing up concepts such as criticality, fairness, openness, understanding and so forth, even to the extent of engaging with those on campus who would 'no platform' visiting speakers. It seeks to offer a *universal* discursive space, in which all comers can have their day. And it encourages the formation of citizen scientists and citizen scholars.[5]

The idea of the ecological university opens, then, a space in which *both* universality and particularity can be held together. However, the ecological university favours universals that allow it to assist in improving the whole Earth. Profit, impact, income, employability, skills and reputation may have become universal categories of higher education, but they are not such that will help the university to strengthen its ecosystems. But this is not to disparage, and still less to repudiate universals – say, as symptoms of globalization or neoliberalism or as mere constructions of the university. To the contrary, some universals – such as global wellbeing, criticality, fairness, public understanding, openness, generosity and even truthfulness – may point paths for the ecological university within a challenging world. The actual journey that any university might take, however, calls for hard work, vigilance and courage, so as to discern ways forward that fit its own particulars (its resources, networks, epistemic communities and its own value position). Within the ecological university, both particulars and universality are vividly present and in constant tension with each other.

6. Emergence

The idea of the ecological university, as noted, is intimately associated with emergence. Both as a general concept, and in particular forms as exemplified by different universities, emergence is a constituting feature. The ecological university gains its ecological laurels in part through its quality of emergence.

Emergence here refers to process *and* to powers. The ecological university is always emerging. New forms, new interventions, new interminglings with and in its ecosystems are always spawning, as it swims among those ecological formations. New forms of openness, new possibilities for students' development (their becoming), new arrangements for interdisciplinary inquiry, and new kinds of engagement with the wider society are always unfolding. These are signs of emergence in the strict sense of the concept. Emergence, after all, betokens *processes* in which new entities and new formations appear from existing entities and formations in open systems that could not have been predicted.

But the ecological university does not just exhibit general processes of emergence, for it also contains its own powers of emergence. The *processes* of emergence are characteristic of the ecological university in itself, while the *powers* of emergence refer to the relationships between the ecological university and its wider ecosystems. All universities have powers, which they do not always realize. But the ecological university both recognizes that it has powers and seeks to realize them. In doing so, it strengthens its various ecosystems. It can help to strengthen public discourse and the growth of understanding in society, and it can enhance social integration (by boosting, for example, social mobility).

The ecological university has *double* powers of emergence. First, it can act so as to open spaces for its *own* emergence. It can bring its disciplines together in unlikely combinations; it can encourage its members – both staff and students – to orient themselves with the wider world; it can encourage its students to widen the horizons through which they understand themselves; and it can speak with integrity to the institutions of the state and other centres of power. And these powers of emergence can be encouraged, not least in thought and imagination. Second, the ecological university can directly release its own emergent powers *into the wider world*. And, in so doing, it can – as indicated – impart power and strength to its ecosystems of knowledge, persons, social institutions, learning and so on. The ecological university is *pari passu* an emergent institution.

7. Wellbeing

If there is one driving concern in front of the ecological university, it is that of wellbeing; but, as in some of its other aspects, the concept has to be interpreted generously. Despite the considerable attention that it has been receiving of late, the concept of wellbeing surely deserves further consideration.[6]

Filling out the concept of wellbeing should acknowledge a point made at the outset of this inquiry; namely, that the ecosystems of the university are in a state of disrepair. To compose an oxymoron, there is a *necessary contingency* at work here.

The university is placed in a world riven by inequality, asymmetrical power structures, woefully insufficient usage of knowledge and understanding in public policy-making, narrow personhoods and an impoverished array of symbols in cultural life. In short, the university's ecosystems are impaired and could plausibly be said to be imperilled. The university cannot save the world single-handedly, but it can play a part in strengthening the ecosystems in which it is implicated. Its main aim in addressing such challenges must be that of bringing about a state of improved wellbeing in those ecosystems, putting its resources – technical, epistemological, human, intellectual and, indeed, economic – to work in that endeavour.

What, it may be pressed, would wellbeing look like? An answer may be essayed by discerning its opposite. What might a state of *dis*repair look like in each of the university's ecosystems? Indications have just been given in relation to the limited life chances, poverty of public understanding, and weaknesses in public policy-making; but others can be identified. The *knowledge ecosystem* is impaired when there are limitations over the access that members of society have to knowledge; and universities are in a position to address this situation by, for example, making publicly available the knowledge and epistemic frameworks that they create. The *culture ecosystem* is impaired when symbols circulating in society are limited in range and are devoid of critical commentary; and the ecological university will address this situation through its academics – across all disciplines – showing their willingness publicly to examine conventional tropes and so help to widen the symbols in society and, at the same time, advance the wellbeing of the culture industry. The *ecosystem of social institutions* may be impaired, one manifestation of which may be that local communities are run down. The ecological university can help to bring about a measure of wellbeing in such communities through its academics in social work, planning, architecture, sociology, economics and even archaeology coming together with local institutions to address directly such issues. In relation to the *ecosystems both of learning* and *of persons*, the university could directly orient its pedagogical efforts towards the wellbeing of students. And such an orientation on the part of the ecological university would eschew any talk of satisfying students, but would be stretching them into challenging spaces.

Such a programme is never-ending. There is always more that can be done: wellbeing is continually being put at risk and the very idea of wellbeing goes on continually being stretched – and, indeed, some severe stretching is being suggested here, right across the university's ecosystems. In the process, no less than a project of *global wellbeing* has opened (Naidoo, 2015), understood as the university advancing the wellbeing of its differentiated ecosystems. Certainly, the ecological university knows that controversy attends that idea – of global wellbeing – even as it tries to further it.

8. Criticality

It has long been an axiom of the university that it be a space for critical thought. Seldom spelt out, there are two lines of consideration here. First, what is to count as worthwhile and even valid thinking is thinking that is exposed to counter-views and has to come up to muster within such contestation. In the process, the thinking moves on, and is made more secure. There is a sense here, therefore, that what it is to be a university is intimately associated with a certain kind of institutional orientation, buttressed by, as Gouldner long ago (1979: 28–30) put it, a 'culture of critical discourse'; in other words, an institutional space for and of 'dissensus' (Readings, 1997: 187–188). But second, there is also a sense that such critical thought is valuable for the wider society. In particular, democracy requires that at least some of its major institutions be centres of societal critique. A further axiom arises, therefore, that universities need to be afforded space – institutional autonomy – and their academics intellectual room – academic freedom – in order to speak out on issues.

The ecological university is fully aware of these considerations, but goes further. The ecological university builds critique into its bones. It cannot hope to further the wellbeing of major ecosystems if it does not first identify impairments in those ecosystems, or even fundamental absences – whether in the natural environment, the economy, in being a person, in social institutions, in culture and so forth. And all this requires critical inquiry, research and commentary.[7] But the ecological university goes further still. Having identified impairments and absences in the ecosystems of the wider world, the ecological university will then strive to strengthen those ecosystems (even though any stance will be controversial).

Critical thinking is insufficient, therefore, for the ecological university. Even extending critical thinking into critique is insufficient. It is not even enough for the university to call attention to the limited frames of thought and understanding that are characteristic of society. And hence arises the concept of criticality (Barnett, 1997), for the idea of criticality goes much further than the idea of critical thinking. To critical thinking and critique, the ecological university couples critical action, a critical culture and critical dispositions in its stances towards the world.

Accordingly, the ecological university is not a university that plays safe. It does not just provide the world with services and solutions that the world is calling for. On the contrary, it is its own agent. It both stands off from the world and engages with the world, including the conflicting discourses of the world. More, it brings critique into the world, so advancing the *critical society*, but couples with it critical action and its critical dispositions. This will be at times disturbing for the wider world, and so there is much risk here. Through its criticality, the ecological university puts itself at risk. It lives permanently on the edge.

9. Feasibility

Feasibility may seem a strange criterion, in an audit of the idea of the ecological university. Has this inquiry not been a *philosophical* journey, focused on a concept (that of the ecological university)? Where does feasibility make its appearance? Indeed, has not the argument critiqued contemporary university formations and explicitly urged a kind of university not much in evidence? If this book has taken on the appearance of a castle-in-the-air, perhaps that is no bad thing: after all, even these castles could be said to possess astrength of their own. But still, it may be felt that the thesis advanced here is literally utopian, pointing to a university that is nowhere.

This line of thought has to be addressed. The idea of the ecological university is utopian, but it possesses a certain feasibility. It is no less than an example of a 'feasible utopia' (Barnett, 2013). *First*, as indicated, we can glimpse embryonic examples of what it might mean in practice to be an ecological university. We can see instances of universities expanding the public sphere (and attending to the ecosystems of knowledge and social institutions); we can observe universities that hold out against narrow pedagogical conceptions of student satisfaction or trigger warnings and attempt, instead, to draw students out of themselves into difficult spaces (and so advance the ecosystems of persons and learning); we can observe a widening of professionalism within professional education; and we can see universities working constructively to address problems of the natural environment. Often, it is a department or a research team or a particular programme of study that has taken on such ecological characteristics and is somewhat hidden from view.

Second, what it is to be an ecological university can be, and has to be, imagined for each university. The idea of the ecological university is no 'blueprint philosophy' (cf. Jacoby, 2005: 32–33), but requires hard imaginative work to realize its possibilities in different contexts. The ecological university is both real and imaginary.[8]

Third, there are both leadership and managerial implications in universities becoming ecological. Challenges will open pedagogically, epistemologically, organizationally, politically and financially. But these are challenges that are being addressed by some universities. Leadership is necessary imaginatively to broaden a university's sense of its possibilities; management is necessary to help the university realize those possibilities. But this would amount to a new concept of leadership. Not even just a matter of handling complexity, but of foraging for possibilities in the university's total ecological terrain, of bringing those possibilities into view and of marshalling the university's resources in realizing those possibilities. This, of course, points to a distributed leadership (Bolden, 2011; Jones and Harvey, 2017), such capabilities being developed throughout the university.

Feasibility, accordingly, is a crucial part of the idea of the ecological university. To be clear, feasibility does not entail realization, but rather the *possibility* of realization. The idea of the ecological university amounts to a social philosophy of the university with a practical intent and an empirical warrant. The ecological university has many difficulties ahead of it, but there are also indications that its time has come. The world is calling it forward, albeit hesitantly. The ecological university is needed by the world, and spaces are opening for it.

Conclusion

Any idea of the university should be subjected to the severest tests. And just such an interrogation has been attempted here for the ecological university. The idea has withstood – and indeed fares well against – the nine criteria of adequacy that have just been pitched against it.

The idea of the ecological university possesses *institutional grasp* (it is alert to the university itself as a complex social institution necessarily connected to other social institutions); it has *scope and range* (opening itself to theoretical, conceptual, policy and practical possibilities); it has a *timefulness* (sensitive to its past, aware of its present, and concerned for the short- and much longer-term futures); it has a rich *locale* (being both of its immediate vicinity and of the world); it exhibits both *particularity and universality* (as its particular moments take on their character partly in virtue of its associated universals); it has considerable qualities of *emergence*, both of emergent processes and of powers of emergence; it is acutely concerned to advance the *wellbeing* of the world (especially in advancing the wellbeing of its ecosphere); and it is marked by its *criticality* (exhibited internally and externally, in thought, action and its dispositions). However, being an ecological university is fraught with conceptual and practical controversy. The ecological university is always on the edge. It is a liminal institution.

This interrogation has also assessed the feasibility of the ecological university. It has turned out to be – to put the matter formally – an *onto-conceptual* entity, at once an institution and an idea with real aspects, with both of those moments being in dialectical interaction. It is an idea and it can be realized.

The idea of the ecological university is, therefore, an optimistic concept. This is not to say that it will be realized, but it is to say that there are good grounds for believing that the world is opening spaces for its emergence and that, in due course, the world is likely – if hesitantly – to beckon it forward. Indeed, there are embryonic signs of the ecological university already manifest. (All of the examples in this book can be witnessed in the first quarter of the twenty-first century.) The doom-mongers are wrong: the university is severely damaged, but it is not in ruins; not yet at any rate. The entrepreneurial university is not the end-point of the evolution of the university, being but a mere stage in its history. Spaces are already opening for a new kind of university; and for it to enter a new stage in its long history. The ecological university is presaging itself, with its actual arrival much dependent on its being willed into being, and not only by the wider world but also from within the university itself.

Notes

1 Judgemental rationalism formed, for Bhaskar (2002b: 12) one element of the 'Holy Trinity' of his Critical Realism, through which 'at any one moment of time there will be better or worse grounds for preferring one rather to another theory'. Bhaskar was essentially talking about the way in which theories relate to the external world and ways of evaluating those theories, whereas I am suggesting that there may be criteria through which our *concepts* may be judged. There is overlap here, in that both forms of judgement take into account the relationship of those theories or concepts to reality. To put it formally – in Bhaskarian language – the process of judgement suggested here sustains 'both ontological realism and judgmental rationality' (p. 211).

2   Perhaps the best, if not the only, serious examination of the temporal character of universities is that of Gibbs et al. (2015).
3   Certainly, there is an 'unresolvable tension between attention to the particular and commitment to the universal' (Williams, 2007, ch. 4: 64), even though 'we cannot . . . think particulars as particulars' (ch. 3: 35).
4   'To regard, as do deep ecologists, the sheer diversity of beings as itself something to be respected, valued and defended is to have a sense of the significance of each form of life in its own particularity' (Benton, 2007: 246).

By the way, there are clear connections between the argument here – about the ecological university being closely attentive to the particulars that it encases and touches – with the philosophy of Henri Lefebvre, for whom the philosopher 'sees everyday life as the repository of mysteries and wonders' (2016/1971: 15). In fact, that book, *Everyday Life in the Modern World*, resonates with the approach taken here at several points, including the remark that 'our undertaking must be both polemical and theoretical' (p. 23) and the statement (p. 64) that '*we are all utopians*, so soon as we wish for something different' (emphasis in original). Indeed, 'it is not excessive to claim that [Lefebvre] is the eco-philosopher of the twenty-first century' (Aronowitz, 2015: 73).

5   There is a 20-year-long literature on the idea of citizen scientists, which includes practical guides. On the idea of citizen scholars, see the recent volumes by Ackerman and Coogan (2013) and Arvanitakis and Hornsby (2016).
6   The publisher, Wiley, has produced a massive six-volume set on *Wellbeing: A Complete Reference Guide*. For an accessible account of wellbeing, see Vernon (2008).
7   There is also 'the question of whether sustainable development can in the long run co-exist with uncriticised, unchallenged, transnational organizations' (Rowan Williams in Foster and Newell [2005: 83]).
8   Pertinent here is a paper by Christoforus Bouzanis (2016: 569) which argues that 'social structures are existentially dependent upon ideational elaboration', pointing to 'the ontological pervasiveness of the culturally shared imaginary schemata'.

12
A UNIVERSITY FOR THE WHOLE EARTH

Overview

In this final chapter, I shall draw out some of the main strands of the argument here, and under six headings: three planes; deep ecology; a liquid world; sensuousness; and revisit the matters of a feasible utopia and criticality. This set of reflections will enable us to place my thesis – about the university as 'ecological' – in yet wider debates. Ultimately, to speak of the ecological university is to speak of concerns in relation to the whole Earth.

Three planes

This book was preceded by a trilogy of books. That trilogy was relatively abstract, being an inquiry into what it is to understand the university and constituted, therefore, a meta-inquiry. The trilogy did not seek – to any great extent – to offer a definite idea of the university, but offered a set of foundations for any such endeavour. This book has been just such an attempt to build on that groundwork, in offering a specific idea of the university, and a positive idea at that.

Each book in that trilogy had its own thesis. *First*, the thesis of *Being a University*: the entrepreneurial university is not the end-point of the university. Both as an idea and as an institution, the university will continue to develop. It has options in front of it. The entrepreneurial university is not the only game in town. *Second*, the thesis of *Imagining the University*: there is much work for the imagination to do in the unfolding of the university. However, quite different imaginings of the university can be discerned, and that book offered a *typology* of imaginings of the university that can come into play. It argued that in short supply are imaginative ideas of the university that are at once *critical*, *optimistic* and *realistic*.

Third, the thesis of *Understanding the University* identified three planes, namely:

1   *The university as institution – the university as idea.* These two poles stand on the same plane, interacting with each other. Ideas of the university have sometimes taken their bearings from the form that the university as an institution has assumed at different times and places; and, in turn, ideas of the university have influenced the university in its development as an institution.
2   *The/a university in its here-and-now form – its future possibilities.* Again, these two poles interact. Future possibilities that may be envisaged for a particular university have to take account of its contemporary form. For any one university, its possibilities are both infinite *and* bounded. A small local and teaching-oriented university cannot plausibly expect soon to become a global research-dominated university (even if it wished to do so) but its possibilities are still infinite, for all that. Correspondingly, the future possibilities that might be glimpsed for it will colour ways in which its present resources and features are viewed. So there is an interaction between the two poles of this plane too.
3   *The particulars of a university – the universals of the university.* Any university may be understood as a collection of particulars – its people, its resources, its entities, its disciplines and so forth. Any university has also to be understood through an array of universal categories. And those universal categories are far from fixed. Categories such as knowledge, truth, critical dialogue, freedom and autonomy are being overlaid by categories of economy, employability, skills, knowledge transfer and so forth.

    Particulars and universals are intertwined. The universals of the university affect the marshalling of the particulars of the university – the organization of the university and its direction – *and* the particular location of a university influences the universals that loom into view in its self-understanding *and* in the perceptions held of it in the wider milieu. (Compare the categories through which a new technological university is viewed with those of an avowedly multi-faculty university that still protects spaces for scholarly work in the humanities.)

The thesis here can be understood very much as a particular working out of those theses of that trilogy. In keeping with the thesis of *Being a University*, the idea of the ecological university can be seen as a contender with that of the entrepreneurial university. In relation to the thesis of *Imagining the University*, the idea of the ecological university can be seen to exhibit an imagination that is at once optimistic, realist and critical.[1] It is grounded in a sense of the large forces that are destabilizing the university and steering it in certain pernicious directions and so is realist and critical. But it has, too, a measure of optimism in that it glimpses embryonic examples of the ecological university already present, and there are grounds for believing that the world will call it forward still further.

So far as the three planes of *Understanding the University* are concerned (the third book in that trilogy), the idea of the ecological university can inform the development of the university both as *idea* and as an *institution* (plane 1). It can also help to glimpse practical possibilities for any particular university in its own time and space (plane 2). And it helps to open new concepts of the university (plane 3), not only of ecology itself but of wellbeing, absence, entanglement, the university as an agent and so on. The discernment of such concepts helps not merely to contend against the universals that have come globally to *limit* understandings of the university, but can also lay the ground for a new conception of the university and can offer a panoply of ideas through which each university can discern its ecological possibilities. The ecological university, quietly and determinedly, sets itself out to play its part (even if modest) in transforming the whole Earth.

A feasible utopia

The idea of a feasible utopia opens a space for imagining the university and *both* terms in that phrase – 'feasible utopia' – matter.

'Feasibility' was on view in Chapter 11, constituting one criterion – of several criteria – through which the idea of the ecological university was interrogated. That examination suggested that, indeed, the ecological university could be said to be feasible. Its feasibility emerges as a result of a conjunction of circumstances. *First*, despite the many pernicious forces at work, spaces are nevertheless opening in which the ecological university might emerge. *Second*, such spaces, we may hazard, are likely to grow since it is probable that, in a world of increasing turmoil and massive challenges, governments – singly and collectively – are likely to come to expect far more from universities than merely their economic productivity. *Third*, as exemplified throughout this book, we can already glimpse instances of university happenings that can fairly be said to be indicative of stirrings in the direction of the ecological university. And the university possesses agentic powers to pursue an ecological journey.

With those *aides-mémoire* on the matter of feasibility, let us turn more fully to that of utopia (the other term in a 'feasible utopia'). The idea of the ecological university constitutes a *utopia* in that it is unlikely fully to be realized, given the deep structures that are at work, within and beyond the university. The university is buffeted by global forces including neoliberalism, marketization, the growth of a performative culture, digital reason, cross-university competition (fuelled by global rankings), the down-valuing of truthfulness, and managerialism in public services (including the use of data analytics and performance management). These forces have energized instrumental reason such that it has perniciously affected both the university's activities and also how academics and students are perceived and even how they have come to understand themselves. Given the weight of such massive forces, the idea of the ecological university will clearly struggle to gain a purchase. After all, this idea presents an assault on the values, implicit epistemology and very being of the entrepreneurial university.

So far as *values* are concerned, the entrepreneurial university is characteristically a care-less institution in that its value position is that of a university-for-itself. It does not have a care as such for the wider world. The ecological university, in contrast, has pre-eminently a concern for the world; for the whole Earth.[2] Indeed, it is this concern that drives the ecological university forward; that imparts an *élan vital* to it.³ So far as its *implicit epistemology* is concerned, as stated, that of the entrepreneurial university is that of instrumental reason. It deploys reason to further its own self, its own projects, its financial situation and its own administrative functioning – which in turn contribute to the growth of worldly cognitive capital (Boutang, 2011). The ecological university, by contrast, has an implicit knowledge foundation in ecological reason. It uses reason to advance its concerns for the world (which include itself).

The ecological university, then, is a feasible utopia. It could emerge in the best of *possible* worlds, and there are good grounds for believing that it just may yet emerge. The idea is an optimistic idea. This is not to say that it is likely to appear, given the circumstances of the world. But, realistically, it could appear. It is already with us, in some respects and it will grow still further. It may not be long before we can point and say, '*There* is an example of the ecological university'.

This is not to pretend that feasibly we shall see lots of examples of universities exhibiting their ecological credentials *tout court*. But it is quite possible that we might find a significant presence of ecological leanings within universities in all their hybridity. Universities, after all, are supremely layered institutions. Still now, we can see layers of earlier metaphysical and scholarly callings, even if overlain by successive strata of internet flows, systematized knowledge and entrepreneurialism and corporate-like behaviours. The ecological university, therefore, represents one more layer to be added to the genealogy *within a single university*. And for those universities that may be properly called examples of the ecological university, it will be their ecological leanings that stand out within their admixture of stances. We may even see in such universities residual – if fading – elements of the entrepreneurial university. Already, we are witnessing universities proclaiming and heralding their public mission. The ecological university would represent a further stratum in the evolution of the university.

Practising criticality

The ecological university does not simply give to the world that which the world is calling for. Rather, it is an inherently critical institution.

Criticality springs from the ecological university's concern for the world. In being concerned about the world, the ecological university forms views about the world. 'Concern' here, therefore, is a term that deliberately equivocates. The ecological university acknowledges the world *and* considers that the world is significant. In particular, this consideration is deepened in that the ecological university recognizes that it is implicated in at least seven major ecosystems of the world and so the ecological university's general concern for the world takes on substantial form. It has concerns for knowledge, social institutions, persons, the economy, learning, culture and the natural environment. The ecological university is deeply aware of these features of the whole Earth, acknowledges them, and considers itself to be in significant relationships with these ecosystems – which it is.

But this general concern does not end there. It deepens into an active stance in which the ecological university *takes a look* at these features of the world. It inquires into them *and* it has a concern about their wellbeing. Being a university, this looking is not a trivial matter but takes the form of investigations. It systematically inquires into the world. And, being concerned about the wellbeing of those ecosystems, its concerns are heightened when it becomes aware of any shortcomings or lacunae in those ecosystems.

The ecological university understands that it is placed in the world; it is not apart from the world, but the world is in the university. Here arises that equivocation in the term 'concern'; and it opens the way to an account of the ecological university as a critical institution. The ecological university has a general concern towards the world. For the ecological university, the world – indeed, the whole Earth – is understood as a significant part of its whole being. It acknowledges its entanglements with the world. And those entanglements come to constitute a major element in its self-understanding and its identity. But then, having that generalized concern for the world, it is led to form evaluations of the world. It cannot do other, for it has concerns for the wellbeing of the Earth.

The ecological university is, therefore, an inherently critical institution. Its concerns for the world lead it to inquire into the world, and to take up an evaluative stance; a critical stance. On occasions, it will find the ecosystems of the world to be falling short of their potential and even to be impaired. Its critical stance will open out to critique. It will survey the world through frameworks that stand outside given understandings. It will create new understandings of the world and reveal the world in strange ways. It may even glimpse new possibilities for and in the world.

And the university now has spaces opening to it that allow it to carry its critical stance into the world. Its criticality as an epistemological stance can now be accompanied by its criticality in practice. The internet, the university's close company with the political sphere, its globality with its activities around the world, so-called 'third stream' activities in which it is engaged by external parties, the interest taken in it by local communities, and its possibilities for itself as a space for public debate: developments such as these are inviting the university to become much more an actor in the world. As stated (in Chapter 11), critical thought, critical action and critical being: the university can now exemplify all these three moments of criticality. Theory and practice can be united in the university's critical endeavours.[4]

A liquid world

The university is buffeted hither and thither, to accept a particular funding model, to play the games of global rankings, to seek private funders for its research, to treat students as customers in a market-place, and is encouraged to adopt managerial disciplines of performance management that severely diminish the space of individual academics. At the same time, knowledge swirls crazily across the internet, with concepts and theories born in one discipline being picked up and mischievously transported into an alien discipline, and so it spurts off in a new direction, to be tested in an unequal market-place of ideas.

These are less lines of flight than they are *lines of disturbance*. It is precisely a milieu in which the entrepreneurial university can have its day, as it seeks out the main chance and delights in seizing opportunities that come its way to further its own interests. But what of the ecological university? How can it gain *its* bearings in this maelstrom?

The ecological university gains its bearings severally. The knowledge society continually craves new frameworks of understanding the world. This is easily – and not uncommonly – derided as an interest in instrumental reason.[5] It is that, but it is more. It betokens an interest in cognitive innovation as such. Doubtless the world is hoping and even expecting that any such innovation will have demonstrable impact in and on the world. But this very demand necessitates the opening of cognitive spaces to the university. And so room opens too for ecological interests, in the broad sense in which we have sketched them here.

It is also in the interests of the wider world to grant the university some autonomy, since the wider world needs some assurance that the university's interpretations contain some degree of disinterestedness. Departments of humanities may close, staff on longer terms of appointment may be replaced by those on short or part-time appointments, letters to the press may be vetted by a university's press and publicity office and external speakers may be no-platformed, but large portions of cognitive freedom will remain, over the scope of the university's inquiries, its topics, the methods of inquiry and the means of their ensuing publications. A regulated autonomy it may be,[6] but at least pools of autonomy remain to it and even, in an internet age, open yet further to it.

It is important to understand why this is necessarily the case. The infringements on the university's autonomy work on the level of its *complexity*. It is the *systems* in which the university moves that are affected by state and corporate promptings. Funding, evaluation, contracts, staffing arrangements and so forth are all matters of systems maintenance.

It is, in contrast, at the level of *supercomplexity* (Barnett, 2000), that the university enjoys its greater freedoms. It is in the realm of ideas, representations of the world, that the university can realize its ecological aspirations in the first place.[7] The university is an active player in the creative and inchoate swirl of concepts, theories and frameworks that form the larger cognitive world. It is here that the world's representations of itself are critiqued and are held up to scrutiny and new imaginative representations brought forward.[8] This is a world of supercomplexity because it is here that the dominant representations of the world and the forms of complexity that they intimate – money, finance, impact, control, systems, management, power and so on – can be interrogated. *In the world of supercomplexity, complexity is itself examined*. And whereas it might be assumed that in the world of complexity, problems of its systems *could* yield secure answers, in the realm of supercomplexity, there can be no secure answers, but only contest and even critique, and possibly startling new representations of the world.

This significance that attaches to the possibilities of universities as centres of critical discourse is why authoritarian regimes often act with a heavy hand towards their universities and academics. It is the power of ideas that is so threatening. But it is also why newly emerging nations turn often to their universities and their academics to help in national reconstruction. We have witnessed this in Africa, South America and in Eastern Europe.

The ecological university seizes on this thesis. It takes up understandings of the world, critiques them and unfolds new worldly representations. And it does so with an ecological intent to play its part in improving the world. In turn, its new representations of the world, coupled with its concern for the world, lead it on to do what it can practically to be involved in the world. And 'world' here includes, it will be recalled, itself as well as the external world. It attends to its curricula, to its construals of what it is to be a student, to its research ethics, to the manner and character of its publications and to all the conditions of its many interactions with the wider world. Its ecological leanings stretch into its own reflexivity.

And so, in this liquid world, the ecological university does what it can to hold to a set of principles or maxims for itself (Chapter 5). Even as its autonomy is challenged, and even as the worlds in which it moves – of systems and of cognitions – become ever more inchoate, still the ecological university does what it can to steer itself. It steers away from the rocks of both self-interest and sheer instrumental reason. It flies its ecological colours not as indicators of any sure end-point, but as signs of its momentum and its value structures, as it strives towards a better world.

Deep ecology

'Deep ecology' has two aspects. First, matters of ecology are not just out there in the world, but inhere in human beings, in their thoughts and in their social institutions, and so there cannot seriously be felt to be a sharp separation of Nature and the social world. But this is a facile point. The very idea of ecology drawn out in this inquiry goes much wider than the natural world, to embrace the whole of the world. Actually, we do not have an adequate word for this sense of the whole world – the term 'the Earth' comes with its own baggage. However, the idea of ecology can illuminate the large systems that constitute the world; hence 'ecosystems' and 'ecosphere'. And every university is implicated in large ecosystems, whether it realizes it or not and whether it acknowledges the fact or not.

And so we can legitimately say that the ecological university is *deeply* ecological. The seven ecosystems – of knowledge, social institutions, persons, the economy, learning, culture and the natural environment – have so found their way into the university that they have come in large part to constitute the university. Accordingly, the university of the twenty-first century has come to be ecologically implicated and even ecologically hooked. It cannot evade its ecological positioning. That being the case, the impairments of the seven ecosystems are simultaneously impairments of the Earth, and of the university.

These reflections constitute but the brute facts of the matter, as it were. The other aspect of deep ecology that is characteristically picked out in the literature is the suggestion that there is an inescapable value element in the idea of ecology.[9] The term 'ecology' has come to acquire not just factual elements – that a system hangs together in some way, that it has self-sustaining powers, that it characteristically exhibits diversity, that it may be impaired and that humanity has been often responsible for that impairment – but it also has come to indicate that systems to which the idea of ecology has application have their own inherent value.

We can extend this suggestion to the seven ecosystems in which the university is implicated. The natural world is of value in itself, the economy is valuable as a means of allocating scarce resources, knowledge is of value in aiding an understanding of the world, learning is of value in furthering the wellbeing of individuals and society itself, social institutions are of value in providing purpose and identity, culture is of value in furnishing symbols and meaning structures by which society might anchor itself in a changing world, and persons are of value as ends in themselves.

If we put these two aspects of 'deep ecology' together – of fact and value – a third aspect emerges, that of responsibility. The matter as to whether the university can be associated with the idea of responsibility was one raised by Derrida (1992) but, hardly surprisingly, he was unable from within his philosophy of deconstruction to offer a serious answer. The idea of responsibility, after all, relies on just the kind of firm foundations that his philosophy had repudiated. Now, however, we can give an answer to the question, through the idea of 'deep ecology'. The university does indeed have a responsibility; namely, that of responding to the implicit claims of the ecosystems in its midst, inherently valuable as they are. Their limited internal diversity, their impairments and fragility, and their being valuable in themselves, usher in an injunction upon the university to use its resources to attend to those ecosystems, and to play its part in the repair of those ecosystems and, wherever possible, in their development.

This is a responsibility that the ecological university cannot evade. It has a responsibility to see how it can play its part – for example – in bringing about a fairer economy, an open circulation of ideas, enlivening cultural symbols (not least in its use of language), a more emancipatory learning experience, more effective social institutions, an understanding of persons as ends and not merely units of consumption, shaping a science more oriented to 'what is of value in life' (Maxwell, 2007; 2008: 2) and a natural environment that can go on sustaining and opening possibilities for all life on this small planet. Each of these suggestions will be contested; but that contest can be played out in the university itself. And such a rivalrous debate would constitute but an example of the university working to strengthen several of its ecosystems, especially those of knowledge, social institutions (especially if the wider society can be drawn into those debates) and learning.

The ecological university, therefore, does not merely acknowledge that it is ecologically implicated in profound ways, but also that it has responsibilities to work out for itself its ecological possibilities. This is a far from easy task and is never-ending as each university struggles to find political, financial and epistemological ways through. Fact and value, and theory and action are all present in the deep ecology of this university.

The claims of sensuousness

To speak of the ecological university is to do much more than to draw in rather cold and abstract themes. Yes, it involves consideration of ecosystems, networks, the world, globalization, assemblages and even implicatedness and entanglements. Even to speak of the responsibilities of the ecological university could be felt to continue a rather cool, if not icy, approach to the matter, to invoke ideas of reason, concern, judgement, duty and so forth. But the idea of the ecological university, in its essence, is full of spirit and imbued with sensuousness.

There is much warrant for drawing in considerations of sensuousness. Hegel, at least in his commentary on Kant, was keen to draw attention to 'the *a priori* fact of sensuous existence' (1837: n.p.). Marx and Feuerbach both explicitly pointed up the sensuous nature of humanity, in their visions of a different world order. Sensuousness was not a luxurious add-on, but was in the world: 'sensuous reality' was 'its own subject' possessing 'absolutely independent, divine, and primary significance' (Feuerbach, 1972/1843: n.p.). Subsequently, the first generation of Critical Theorists paid much attention to *culture* as a site of human emancipation. Horkheimer, Adorno and Marcuse all looked to the sensuous realm as offering a space in which humanity could find itself, and a mode of being in contrast to the instrumental reason that had come to so dominate the world. Separately, of course, it was central to Romanticism that humanity could find a kind of salvation in sensuous delight in the natural world, epitomized – in England – by poets such as Wordsworth, Coleridge and Keats and by painters such as Constable and Turner. More recently still, the theme of sensuousness has been explicit in the ecological movement, notably in the important book on *The Spell of the Sensuous* (1996) by David Abram, for whom the natural world offers an 'ecology of magic'.

There is, therefore, a certain legitimacy in putting the idea of the ecological university together with the theme of sensuousness. The ecological university, after all, is a university that listens to and seeks a better world, repudiates the instrumental reason characteristic of the dominant cognitive frameworks, and looks to alternative ways of understanding the world. It has a care towards the wider world and that care naturally extends to a concern with what it is to be human. And so, in turn, avenues open to the sensuous.

Feuerbach (1972/1843: n.p.) suggested that 'the reality of the Idea is sensuousness, but reality is also the truth of the Idea – hence sensuousness is the Truth of the Idea'. In other words, there is an intimate relationship between truth, ideas and sensuousness. Do we not see this over and over again in the autobiographies of or biographies on scientists and others who peer into the fabric of the world? Einstein, Feyerabend, Feynman, Russell, Hawking – and very many others – have explicitly remarked upon the awe or beauty that they found in the patterns of the world as revealed to them in their studies. Some – and not only theologians – have glimpsed something of the divine in such patterns. The ecological university is sensitive to such aesthetic impulses, for such impulses are bound up in a sensitivity to the world.

This sensitivity towards the whole world and the impulse to inquire into it help to impart energy and spirit. This care for the world and this wish to see deeply into the world animate the ecological university. These impulses *in*-spire the ecological university. We see this in the laboratory, in the classroom, on field trips, and in the clinical situation, as students and researchers struggle to understand the world, but do so fascinated by the patterns they observe.

But in the ecological university, this sensuousness finds additional sources, as it is energized by the impulse to carry the world forward in some way. Whether in opening its grounds with displays of public art, in adding new insights to the world in the research literature, in advancing medicine, in seeing students transform themselves (and animatedly saying at the graduation ceremony to their parents in front of a tutor that 'being here has changed my life'), in being involved in community projects and enabling local groups to a new stage of empowerment (in social housing, in health or in education), or in helping a city to understand itself so that its aesthetic appearance may be improved, there are opportunities aplenty for the sensuous to show itself in the ecological university. The ecological university finds delight in such endeavours. I mentioned earlier the interest in moments of personal disclosure evinced by the theologian, I T Ramsay (marked by simple phrases such as 'the penny dropped'); and here we may speak of *institutional disclosure*.

The sensuous may be found, too, in the interstices of the ecological university. The smile in the corridor, the fleeting expression of humour in the committee room, the form of a university building and its spaces, the play of – and a playfulness in – ideas, the delicacy of a comment on an essay, the crafting of a text (even of a set of committee minutes) and the evident delight in collectively celebrating a colleague's success as part of an informal end-of-week gathering: the ecological university harbours its sensuous side. And if it is said that *some* of this may be seen, too, in the entrepreneurial university, that reflection adds to the argument here about spaces arising for the ecological university to emerge.

This sensuousness is not a gloss on the serious business of the ecological university addressing the whole world, but is integral to it. This sensuousness, this spirit, is *pari passu* with the determination of the ecological university to break with instrumental reason in all of its forms (which the university has so come to express right across the world). Through such sensuousness, the ecological university becomes itself and dissolves instrumental thought and action. The ecological university is a joyful place in which to study and to work and to be.

Conclusion

The ecological university lives for the whole Earth. It has a care towards the world in all its reaches and plays a part in helping to take it forward. But the ecological university is part *of* the world and recognizes this situation. The major ecosystems of the world – knowledge, social institutions, persons, the economy, learning, culture and the natural world – find their way into the university. And so the university is ecologically implicated. The ecological university understands that this is the case and two consequences arise. *First*, the ecological university understands itself as having responsibilities towards the whole Earth; namely, that of using its resources – and these vary considerably, university to university – to aid, to strengthen, to develop and even on occasions, to transform those ecosystems.

Second, since the ecological university understands that it is implicated in the ecosystems of the world, it has to concern itself with itself. This is not a matter of leadership, or knowledge management or institutional research, important though they are, for questions arise as to the value background behind such features. Rather, this is a matter of the concern that the ecological university has towards the whole world extending inwards to the university itself, to its concerns for the persons who participate in it, to its knowledges and their orchestration in the world, and to its own values. Just as the ecological situation of the whole world continues to unfold, so the ecological university will continue to unfold as it critically keeps itself in view, in realizing its hopes for the world.

Notes

1 Cf. 'The institution of society is in each case the institution of a magma of social imaginary significations, which we can and must call a world of significations.' (Castoriadis, 1997/1975: 359). He continues, 'Society brings into being a world of significations and itself exists in reference to such a world' (p. 359). This book perhaps may be seen in just that vein – as a set of significations encouraged into being by society and so existing in reference to the world, and so – it is hoped – contributing to the institution of a new world.
2 A tantalizing little book – and one which resonates with the general argument here – is Juha Varto's (2008/1991) *Song of the Earth*. For instance, he observes (p. 59) that 'Imagination . . . feeds on knowledge and speech that also capture and thus allow it to be represented again'.
3 I take the phrase *'élan vital'* from Bergson's (1998/1911) *Creative Evolution* – although in the English it is variously translated as 'vital impulse' (p. 126), 'vital impulsion' (p. 135) and 'vital activity' (p. 248). Despite the objections it has received over the past hundred years, the idea seems to me to have value here. Many of the passages of that book speak directly to the argument here, for instance: 'the force which is evolving throughout the . . . world is . . . always seeking to transcend itself and always remains inadequate to the work it would fain produce' (p. 126). The evolution of the university – to its present 'entrepreneurial' state *and onwards* – can be seen in just this light.

Also hugely pertinent here is Deleuze's (2006) book, *Bergsonism*. Deleuze poses the question directly: 'What does Bergson mean when he talks about *élan vital*?' And he answers: 'It is always . . . a totality in the process of dividing up'. But the totality is not thereby prejudiced: 'differentiation . . . presupposes unity' (pp. 94–95). Again, this is in keeping with the present argument, in which is posited the prospect of an infinite variety of the ecological university emerging; that is, differentiation within a unity.
4 There are all manner of connections, and tensions, with the Frankfurt School of Critical Theory both here and throughout – albeit beyond the scope of – this book. For instance, the programme being urged here seeks not to unite humanity and Nature (a theme in that School's work) but to work towards a new relationship, in which humanity assists

continuously in taking forward 'Nature' in its fullest sense. Just one of the very helpful recent critical commentaries is that of Masquelier (2015). He notes that 'Frankfurt school critical theorists, with the possible exception of Habermas, have refrained from exploring the institutional arrangement potentiality capable of yielding emancipatory practices' (p. 125). I would like to think that the present work might be seen in something of that light.

5 A classic critique – possibly the classic critique of instrumental reason is that mounted by Horkheimer, in his (2004) *Eclipse of Reason*, in which he contrasts instrumental – or 'subjective' – reason with objective reason, from which derived a universal rationality which posited a rationality consisting of a 'harmony' with the totality of the objective world. Again, that much in the present book chimes with that work is hardly surprising, since the idea of the ecological university is set off against the idea of instrumental reason and the recent turning of the university towards that form of reason. It is important here to note that while Horkheimer is hostile to instrumental reason, he neither comes down on the side of objective reason nor posits an alternative, and so leaves matters rather hanging.

6 Relevant here is the long-lasting debate over the idea of 'the evaluative state', inspired by Guy Neave. See the special issue of the *European Journal of Education*, 33(3), September 1998, which includes a paper by Neave himself.

7 Admittedly, there are all manner of dangers here, both intellectual and practical, of which Lysenkoism (Wikipedia: 'Lysenkoism') remains perhaps the most egregious example – the biological and agricultural programme sparked by the ideas of Lysenko in the Soviet Union, in which a set of ideas about inheritance in plants issued in a total(itarian) state ideology. Perhaps we are now seeing the beginnings of a parallel in the contemporary 'post-truth' world (Wikipedia: 'Post-truth politics').

8 Imagination, as I have insisted throughout (and also in my [2013] book) certainly needs to be kept under some kind of control: it cannot be a case of 'anything goes', a phrase with which Paul Feyerabend was notoriously associated (see his [1975] *Against Method*). Gellner is characteristically, splendidly and shamelessly ascerbic here, seeing in Feyerabend's work 'the poetry of irrationalist nostrums' (Gellner, 1992: 105).

9 The concept of deep ecology is especially associated with Petter Naess – see his essay (2012), but see also, for instance, Plumwood (2002, especially ch. 8: 196–217), Moog (2009), Lehman (2015, especially ch. 10: 133–144), Riggio (2015), Mickey (2016: 91), and Hourdequin (2015: 79–80). A key issue in this debate is the relationship of humanity to nature. I am wanting to have my cake and eat it; namely, that the university is deeply implicated in ecosystems, but it has agentic possibilities and, indeed, has a responsibility to realize its ecological possibilities.

CODA: A REVOLUTION IN THE OFFING?

A global academic ecosystem

A matter has been glimpsed from time to time in this inquiry but we may dwell on it in this final reflection. This is the matter of the 25,000 or more universities worldwide as constituting an ecosystem in themselves. Admittedly, there is a fly-in-the-ointment. Global groupings of universities are forming, with *layered* flows of cognitive capital. Researchers collaborate across the elite universities, and universities sign memoranda of understanding characteristically with other universities where an affinity is felt. World rankings, the distribution of monies by cross-national research agencies, flows of international students are additional factors in the stratification of universities. But more subtle features are also to be observed in the evolution of North–South academic relationships, leading to a marginalization of indigenous and traditional cultures of knowledge (which has even been termed an 'epistemicide' [de Sousa Santos, 2016]).

It may be tempting to see in these phenomena an ineradicable intensifying of university stratification on a global scale. Academic birds of a feather will increasingly flock together, not least in a situation of heightened worldwide university competition. But the situation is far from straightforward.

A geopolitics of the academic world is playing out, one which has yet to be fully understood. It cuts across universities, not least because the different disciplines possess different degrees of autonomy, have their own spaces and flows and possess their own levels of *epistemic generosity*, as cognitive strangers are welcomed with hospitality (or not, as the case may be). Universities in the North and the South are engaging with each other, both on a bilateral basis and via formalized associations. Teachers and scholars in quite different kinds of university collaborate, in pedagogical ventures and in the writing of research papers.

To pick up some of the terminology of this inquiry, we are witnessing a re-territorialization of the global knowledge economy, a reconfiguring of the geopolitical assemblages across universities (Moisio and Kangas, 2016). The idea, therefore, of universities worldwide as constituting a *global academic ecosystem* can plausibly be entertained. As observed here, every university is to some extent global, in participating – even as recipient – in academic conversations that span the world, and in discursive flows that encircle the globe. Public or private, multi-faculty or specialist, face-to-face or digital: every university is a player in this worldly academic community. And many universities feel it and act on it with some deliberation. But just perhaps a new stage in this worldly community may be in sight.

Ideas and revolutions

In the opening passages of this inquiry, I noted that Umberto Eco had explicitly addressed the matter of the book. In an internet age, and in an era of the internet 'book', are its days now numbered? Eco was 'not convinced'. 'The book is like the spoon, scissors, the hammer, the wheel. Once invented, it cannot be improved' (Eco and Carriere, 2012: 4). And so I would like to honour an old-fashioned idea of the book, that – like Brighton rock – it should have a connecting thread running through it. In the initial pages of this book's Introduction, I referred to the work of Félix Guattari, and his work (sometimes alone and sometimes in his partnership with Gilles Deleuze) has provided a continuing thread here. I should like, *en finale*, to return to Guattari, specifically to his posthumous (2016) book *Lines of Flight*.

It is surely evident that the future of the university is at once a political and a global matter. The issue is the extent to which and the ways in which universities, collectively across the world, can go on forging themselves as a unified entity, expressive of the kinds of values and orientation embodied in the ecological university. Even if they are persuaded by the idea as *an idea*, many will be pessimistic about the political possibilities (and there is much to be pessimistic about). But, as Guattari remarked, '[o]ne can never say about a particular situation of oppression that it offers no possibility for struggle' (p. 104). And, as observed, universities possess considerable powers that are not being fully realized, powers that extend across the seven ecosystems in sight here.

There is, therefore, a politics – and a geopolitics at that – opening before the ecological university. Guattari (p. 75) distinguishes two kinds of politics: a 'politics of potential', which echoes the idea here of the possibilities of the university as an *idea* (how might it be imagined?); and a 'politics of power', which here links to the university as an *institution* in the world (which powers does it possess and how might they be harnessed?). But *can* this dual potential be harnessed? Guattari is adamant: 'Collective equipment on the large scale, like universities . . . ha[s] started to function in the . . . struggles of desire and ha[s] served as a support' for new ways of thinking, understanding and communication (p. 67). How might we understand this process (an emergent process if ever there was one)? Such shoots, such new happenings 'break something in the collective routine [and] sometimes succeed in catalysing . . . a chain of entirely unforeseen phenomena of disinhibition' (p. 55).

It is evident, then, that *the university as an institution and the university as an idea have to be understood together*. If it is to hold water, any vision of 'institutional reformism without any revolutionary horizon and revolutionary movements without any immediate praxis of everyday life must be questioned altogether' (p. 55). Only in this way can one seriously conceive that 'one day, other relations will succeed in establishing themselves between the State, institutions, collective equipment and users' (p. 51).

This inquiry into and this advocacy of the ecological university, have been an imaginative quest for just such an idea of the university, one that is at once realist, critical and optimistic. The stance here is not that the ecological university *will* come about, but that it realistically *could* come about. It is an imagining of the university that is utopian but also feasible.

Imagine, then, what it would be if the universities of the world built on their connections already in view and came increasingly to understand themselves to be part of a world community of ecological universities. Imagine what kind of impact there might be on the world's society, on culture, communication, human understanding and planetary prospects if this worldwide university ecosystem came to act increasingly together. Why might it not be said: 'Universities of the world unite!'? The whole Earth may be slumbering just now but may yet awake to being receptive to such a calling.

BIBLIOGRAPHY

Abram, D (1996) *The Spell of the Sensuous.* New York: Vintage.
Ackerman, J M and Coogan, J (eds) (2013) *The Public Work of Rhetoric: Citizen-Scholars and Civic Engagement.* Columbia, SC: University of South Carolina.
Adorno, T (2014/1966) *Negative Dialectics.* New York and London: Bloomsbury.
Adorno, T and Horkheimer, M (1989/1944) *Dialectic of Enlightenment.* London and New York: Verso.
Albrow, M (1996) *The Global Age: State and Society Beyond Modernity.* Cambridge: Polity Press.
Annette, J and McLaughlin, T (2005) 'Citizenship and Higher Education in the UK', in J Arthur (ed.), *Citizenship and Higher Education: The Role of Universities in Communities and Society.* London and New York: RoutledgeFalmer.
Archer, M A and Outhwaite, W (eds) (2004) *Defending Objectivity: Essays in Honour of Andrew Collier.* London and New York: Routledge.
Archer, M S (2003) *Structure, Agency and the Internal Conversation.* Cambridge: Cambridge University Press.
Archer, M S and Maccarini, A M (eds) (2013) *Engaging with the World: Agency, Institutions, Historical Formations.* London and New York: Routledge.
Aronowitz, S (2015) 'Henry Lefebvre: The Ignored Philosopher and Social Theorist', in S Aronowitz, *Against Orthodoxy: Social Theory and its Discontents* (chapter 5). New York: Palgrave Macmillan.
Arvanitakis, J and Hornsby, D (eds) (2016) *Universities, the Citizen Scholar and the Future of Higher Education.* Basingstoke, UK and New York: Palgrave Macmillan.
Assiter, A (2004) 'The Objectivity of Value', in M S Archer and W Outhwaite (eds), *Defending Objectivity: Essays in Honour of Andrew Collier.* London and New York: Routledge.
Astley, J, Francis, L, Sullivan, J and Walker, A (eds) (2004) *The Idea of a Christian University: Essays on Theology and Higher Education.* Milton Keynes, UK: Paternoster.
Bachelard, G (1994) *The Poetics of Space.* Boston, MA: Beacon.
Badiou, A. (2007/1988) *Being and Event.* London: Continuum.
Badiou, A and Žižek, S (2009) *Philosophy in the Present.* Cambridge: Polity Press.
Bagnall, R G (2016) 'A Critique of Peter Jarvis's Conceptualisation of the Lifelong Learner in the Contemporary Cultural Context', *International Journal of Lifelong Education*: http://dx.doi.org/10.1080/02601370.2017.1268838

Bibliography

Bakhurst, D (2011) *The Formation of Reason*. Chichester, UK: Wiley–Blackwell.
Bakken, T and Hernes, T (eds) (2003) *Autopoietic Organization Theory: Drawing on Niklas Luhmann's Social Systems Perspective*. Copenhagen: Copenhagen Business School.
Barber, M, Donnelly, K and Rizvi, S (2013) *An Avalanche Is Coming: Higher Education and the Revolution Ahead*. London: IPPR.
Barnett, R (1990) *The Idea of Higher Education*. Stony Stratford, UK: Open University Press.
Barnett, R (1997) *Higher Education: A Critical Business*. Buckingham, UK: Open University Press/SRHE.
Barnett, R (2000) *Realizing the University in an Age of Supercomplexity*. Buckingham, UK: Open University Press/SRHE.
Barnett, R (2003) *Beyond All Reason: Living with Ideology in the University*. Buckingham, UK: Open University Press/SRHE.
Barnett, R (2007) *A Will to Learn: Being a Student in an Age of Uncertainty*. Maidenhead, UK and New York: McGraw-Hill/Open University Press.
Barnett, R (2010) 'Life-Wide Education: A New and Transformative Concept for Higher Education?', in N Jackson and R Law (eds), *Enabling a More Complete Education: Encouraging, Recognizing and Valuing Life-Wide Learning in Higher Education*, conference proceedings, University of Surrey, Guildford, 13–14 April 2010: http://lifewidelearningconference.pbworks.com/f/Lifewide+learning+Conference+E-Proceedings+version+April+09+2010.pdf
Barnett, R (2011) *Being a University*. London and New York: Routledge.
Barnett, R (ed.) (2012) *The Future University: Ideas and Possibilities*. London and New York: Routledge.
Barnett, R (2013) *Imagining the University*. London and New York: Routledge.
Barnett, R (2015) 'In Search of a Public: Higher Education in a Global Age', in G Williams and O Filippakou (eds), *Higher Education as a Public Good: Critical Perspectives on Theory, Policy and Practice*. New York: Peter Lang.
Barnett, R (2016) *Understanding the University: Institution, Idea, Possibilities*. London and New York: Routledge.
Barnett, R (2017) 'Foreword: Energising an Institution', in D Fung, *A Connected Curriculum for Higher Education*. London: UCL Press.
Barnett, R and Bengtsen, S (2017) 'Universities and Epistemology: From a Dissolution of Knowledge to the Emergence of a New Thinking', *Education Sciences*, 7(38): www.mdpi.com/2227-7102/7/1/38
Barnett, R and Coate, K (2005) *Engaging the Curriculum in Higher Education*. Maidenhead, UK and New York: Open University Press/McGraw-Hill/SRHE.
Barnett, R and Di Napoli, R (eds) (2009) *Changing Identities in Higher Education*. London and New York: Routledge.
Barnett, R. and Guzmán-Valenzuela, C (2016) 'Sighting Horizons of Teaching in Higher Education', *Higher Education*, 73(1): 113–126.
Barnett, R and Peters, M A (eds) (2018) *The Idea of the University: Volume 2 – Contemporary Perspectives*. New York: Peter Lang.
Barnett, R, Temple, P and Scott, P (eds) (2016) *Valuing Higher Education: An Appreciation of the Work of Gareth Williams*. London: UCL IOE Press.
Bartelson, J (2009) *Visions of World Community*. Cambridge: Cambridge University Press.
Bartlett, P F and Chase, G W (eds) (2013) *Sustainability in Higher Education: Stories and Strategies for Transformation*. Cambridge, MA: The MIT Press.
Batchelor, D (2006) 'Vulnerable Voices: An Examination of the Concept of Vulnerability in Relation to Student Voice', *Educational Philosophy and Theory*, 38(6): 787–800.
Bauman, Z (2000) *Liquid Modernity*. Cambridge: Polity Press.

Bekhradnia, B (2016) *International University Rankings: For Good or Ill?* Report 89. Oxford: Higher Education Policy Institute.

Beloff, M (1968) *The Plateglass Universities*. London: Secker and Warburg.

Bendik-Keymer, J (2006) *The Ecological Life: Discovering Citizenship and a Sense of Humanity*. Lanham, MD: Rowman & Littlefield.

Bengtsen, S and Barnett, R (2016) 'Confronting the Dark Side of Higher Education', *Journal of Philosophy of Education*: http://onlinelibrary.wiley.com/wol1/doi/10.1111/1467-9752.12190/full

Bennett, J (2010) *Vibrant Matter: A Political Ecology of Things*. Durham, NC and London: Duke University Press.

Benton, T (2007) ' "Realism about the Value of Nature?": Andrew Collier's Environmental Philosophy', in M S Archer and W Outhwaite, *Defending Objectivity: Essays in Honour of Andrew Collier*. London and New York: Routledge.

Bergson, H (1998/1911) *Creative Evolution*. New York: Mineola.

Bernstein, B (1996) *Pedagogy, Symbolic Control and Identity*. London and Bristol, PA: Taylor & Francis.

Bhaskar, R (2002a) *Reflections on Meta-Reality: Transcendence, Emancipation and Everyday Life*. New Delhi: Sage.

Bhaskar, R (2002b) *From Science to Emancipation: Alienation and the Actuality of Enlightenment*. New Delhi, Thousand Oaks, CA and London: Sage.

Bhaskar, R (2008a) *Dialectic: The Pulse of Freedom*. London and New York: Routledge.

Bhaskar, R (2008b) *A Realist Theory of Science*. London and New York: Verso.

Bhaskar, R (2010) *From East to West: Odyssey of a Soul*. London and New York: Routledge.

Bhaskar, R (2012) 'Contexts of Interdisciplinarity: Interdisciplinarity and Climate Change', in R Bhaskar, C Frank, K G Hoyer, P Naess, and J Parker (eds), *Interdisciplinarity and Climate Change: Transforming Knowledge and Practice for our Global Futures*. London and New York: Routledge.

Bhaskar, R (2013) 'Prolegomenon: The Consequences of the Revindication of Philosophical Ontology for Philosophy and Social Theory', in M Archer and A Maccarini (eds), *Engaging with the World: Agency, Institutions, Historical Formations*. London and New York: Routledge.

Bhaskar, R with Hartwig, M (2010) *The Formation of Critical Realism: A Personal Perspective*. London and New York: Routledge.

Bhaskar, R, Frank, C, Hoyer, K G, Naess, P and Parker, J (eds) (2012) *Interdisciplinarity and Climate Change: Transforming Knowledge and Practice for our Global Futures*. London and New York: Routledge.

Bhaskar, R, Hoyer K G and Naess, P (eds) (2012) *Ecophilosophy in a World of Crisis: Critical Realism and the Nordic Contributions*. London and New York: Routledge.

Bird, S E (2011) 'Surviving through Engagement: The Faculty Responsibility to Defend Liberal Education', in B Zelizer (ed.), *Making the University Matter*. London and New York: Routledge.

Bleiklie, I and Henkel, M (eds) (2005) *Governing Knowledge: A Study of Continuity and Change in Higher Education*. Dordrecht: Springer.

Bloom, A (1987) *The Closing of the American Mind: How Higher Education Has Failed Democracy and Impoverished the Souls of Today's Students*. London: Penguin.

Bok, D (2003) *Universities in the Marketplace: The Commercialization of Higher Education*. Princeton, NJ and Woodstock, UK: Princeton University Press.

Bolden, R (2011) 'Distributed Leadership in Organizations: A Review of Theory and Research', *International Journal of Management Reviews*, 13(3): 251–269.

Bonnett, M (2004) 'Retrieving Nature: Education for a Post-Humanist Age', Special Issue, *Journal of Philosophy of Education*. Malden, MA and Oxford: Blackwell.
Bonnett, M (2012) 'Environmental Concern, Moral Education and our Place in Nature', *Journal of Moral Education*, 41(3): 285–300.
Bookchin, M (1980) *Toward an Ecological Society*. Montreal, Que.: Black Rose Books.
Bookchin, M (1996) *The Philosophy of Social Ecology: Essays on Dialectical Naturalism*. Montreal, Que., New York and London: Black Rose Books.
Bourdieu, P (2000) *Pascalian Meditations*. Cambridge: Polity Press.
Bourner, T (2008) 'The Fully Functioning University', *Higher Education Review*, 40(2): 26–45.
Boutang, Y M (2011) *Cognitive Capitalism*. Cambridge: Polity Press.
Bouzanis, C (2016) 'Ontogenesis versus Morphogenesis: Towards an Anti-Realist Model of the Constitution of Society', *Human Studies*, 39(4): 569–599.
Brady, M and Pritchard, D (eds) (2003) *Moral and Epistemic Virtues*. Oxford: Blackwell.
Bragg, E A (1996) 'Towards Ecological Self: Deep Ecology Meets Constructionist Self-Theory', *Journal of Environmental Psychology*, 16: 93–108.
Briggs, A (1964) 'Drawing a New Map of Learning', in D Daiches (ed.), *The Idea of a New University: An Experiment in Sussex*. London: Deutsch.
Brown, R (ed.) (2011) *Higher Education and the Market*. New York and London: Routledge.
Brubacher, J S (1977) *On the Philosophy of Higher Education*. San Francisco, CA and London: Jossey-Bass.
Buber, M (2002/1947) *Between Man and Man*. London: Routledge.
Butler, J, Laclau, E and Žižek, S (2000) *Contingency, Hegemony, Universality: Contemporary Dialogues on the Left*. London and New York: Verso.
Calhoun, C (2011) 'Civil Society and the Public Sphere', in M Edwards (ed.), *The Oxford Handbook of Civil Society*. New York: Oxford University Press.
Carlin, M (2016) 'Amputating the State: Autonomy and La Universidad de la Tierra', in M Carlin and J Wallin, *Deleuze and Guattari, Politics and Education: For a People-Yet-To-Come*. New York and London: Bloomsbury.
Carlin, M and Wallin, J (eds) (2016) *Deleuze and Guattari, Politics and Education: For a People-Yet-To-Come*. New York and London: Bloomsbury.
Castells, M (1996) *The Rise of the Network Society*. Malden, MA and Oxford: Blackwell.
Castoriadis, C (1997/1975) *The Imaginary Institution of Society*. Cambridge: Polity Press.
Chiosa, S (2017) 'As Students Move Away from the Humanities, Universities Adapt', *The Globe and Mail*, Canada, 3 March.
Christian Wells, E (2013) 'Metabolism and Resiliency: Key Concepts for Catalyzing Transformational Change', in P F Bartlett and G W Chase, *Sustainability in Higher Education: Stories and Strategies for Transformation*. Cambridge, MA: The MIT Press.
Clark, B R (1983) *The Higher Education System: Academic Organization in Cross-National Perspective*. Berkeley, Los Angeles and London: University of California Press.
Clark, B R (1998) *Creating Entrepreneurial Universities: Organizational Pathways of Transformation*. Oxford: Pergamon and IAU Press.
Clayton, P (2003) 'God and World', in K J Vanhoozer (ed.), *The Cambridge Companion to Postmodern Theology*. Cambridge: Cambridge University Press.
Cohen, T (ed.) (2001) *Jacques Derrida and the Humanities: A Critical Reader*. Cambridge: Cambridge University Press.
Cole, D R (2016) 'Inter-Collapse . . . Educational Nomadology for a Future Generation', in M Carlin and J Wallin (eds), *Deleuze and Guattari, Politics and Education: For a People-Yet-To-Come*. New York and London: Bloomsbury.
Colhoun, C (2011) 'Civil Society and the Public Sphere', in M Edwards (ed.), *The Oxford Handbook of Civil Society* (chapter 25). New York and Oxford: Oxford University Press.

Comte-Sponville, A (2007) *The Book of Atheist Spirituality: An Elegant Argument for Spirituality without God*. London: Bantam.
Connell, R (2007) *Southern Theory: The Global Dynamics of Knowledge in Social Science*. Cambridge: Polity Press.
Cooper, D (2002) *The Measure of Things: Humanism, Humility, and Mystery*. Oxford: Clarendon Press.
Cranfield, S (2016) *F R Leavis: The Creative University*. Dordrecht: Springer.
Critchley, S (2008) *Infinitely Demanding: Ethics of Commitment, Politics of Resistance*. London and New York: Verso.
Crosling, G, Nair, M and Vaithilingam, S (2015) 'A Creative Learning Ecosystem, Quality of Education and Innovative Capacity', *Studies in Higher Education*, 40(7): 1147–1163.
Dall'Alba, G and Barnacle, R (2005) 'Embodied Knowing in Online Environments', *Educational Philosophy and Theory*, 37(5): 719–744. doi:10.1111/j.1469-5812.2005.00153.x
DeLanda, M (2013/2006) *A New Philosophy of Society: Assemblage Theory and Social Complexity*. London and New York: Bloomsbury.
DeLanda, M (2015) *Philosophy and Simulation: The Emergence of Synthetic Reason*. London and New York: Bloomsbury.
Deleuze, G (1994) *Difference and Repetition*. London: Continuum.
Deleuze, G (2006) *Bergsonism*. New York: Zone Books.
Deleuze, G (2012) *Pure Immanence: Essays on a Life*. New York: Zone Books.
Deleuze, G and Guattari, F (2007/1980) *A Thousand Plateaus: Capitalism and Schizophrenia*. London: Continuum.
Deleuze, G and Guattari, F (2013/1991) *What Is Philosophy?* London: Verso.
Deneulin, S and Townsend, N (2007) 'Public Goods, Global Public Goods and the Common Good', *International Journal of Social Economics*, 34 (1–2) 19–36
Derrida, J (1992) 'Mochlos; or, The Conflict of the Faculties', in R Rand (ed.), *Logomachia: The Conflict of the Faculties* (pp. 1–34). Lincoln and London: University of Nebraska.
Derrida, J (2001) 'The Future of the Profession or the University without Condition (Thanks to the "Humanities", What *Could Take Place* Tomorrow)', in T Cohen (ed.), *Jacques Derrida and the Humanities: A Critical Reader*. Cambridge: Cambridge University Press.
Derrida, J (2006) *Deconstruction Engaged: The Sydney Seminars*. Sydney: Power Publications.
de Sousa Santos, B (2016) *Epistemologies of the South: Justice against Epistemicide*. London and New York: Routledge.
Dienstag, J F (2006) *Pessimism: Philosophy, Ethic, Spirit*. Princeton, NJ and Oxford: Princeton University.
Dill, D (2016) 'Managerialism, Garbage Cans, and Collegial Governance: Reflections on an Economic Perspective of University Governance', in R Barnett, P Temple and P Scott (eds), *Valuing Higher Education: An Appreciation of the Work of Gareth Williams*. London: UCL IOE Press.
Donati, P (2013) 'Engagement as a Social Relation: A Leap into Trans-Modernity', in M Archer and A Maccarini (eds), *Engaging with the World: Agency, Institutions, Historical Formations*. London and New York: Routledge.
Douglas, J A (ed.) (2016) *The New Flagship University: Changing the Paradigm from Global Ranking to National Relevancy*. Basingstoke, UK and New York: Palgrave Macmillan.
Duke, C (1992) *The Learning University: Towards a New Paradigm?* Buckingham, UK: Open University Press.
Dunne, J (1993) *Back to the Rough Ground: 'Phronesis' and 'Techne' in Modern Philosophy and in Aristotle*. Notre Dame, IN and London: University of Notre Dame.
Eagleton, T (2009) *Trouble with Strangers: A Study of Ethics*. Chichester, UK: Wiley-Blackwell.

Ecclestone, K and Hayes, D (2009) *The Dangerous Rise of Therapeutic Education*. London and New York: Routledge.

Eco, U and Carriere, J-C (2012) *This Is Not the End of the Book;*. London: Vintage.

Englund, T (2008) 'The University as an Encounter for Deliberative Communication: Creating Cultural Citizenship and Professional Responsibility', *Utbildning & Demokrati*, 17(2): 97–114.

Etxkowitz, H and Leysdesdoff, L (2000) 'The Dynamics of Innovation: From National Systems and "Mode 2" to a Triple Helix of University–Industry –Government Relations', *Research Policy*, 29(2): 109–123.

Fanghanel, J and Cousin, G (2012) '"Worldly" Pedagogy: A Way of Conceptualizing Teaching Towards Global Citizenship', *Teaching in Higher Education*, 17(1): 39–50.

Ferry, V (2012) 'What Is Habermas's "Better Argument" Good For?', *Argumentation and Advocacy*, 49(2): www.questia.com/library/journal/1G1–332892402/what-is-habermas-s-better-argument-good-for

Feuerbach, L (1972/1843) 'Principles of the New Philosophy', 31, *Principles of Philosophy of the Future*: www.marxists.org/reference/archive/feuerbach/works/future/

Feyerabend, P (1975) *Against Method*. London and New York: New Left Books.

Feyerabend, P (2001) *Conquest of Abundance: A Tale of Abstraction versus the Richness of Being*. Chicago, IL and London: University of Chicago.

Finnegan, R (ed.) (2005) *Participating in the Knowledge Society: Researchers beyond the University Walls*. Basingstoke, UK and New York: Palgrave Macmillan.

Fleming, T (2010) 'Condemned to Learn: Habermas, University and Learning Society', in M Murphy and T Fleming (eds), *Habermas, Critical Theory and Education* (chapter 8). London and New York: Routledge.

Foster, C and Newell, E (2005) *The Worlds we Live in: Dialogues with Rowan Williams on Global Economics and Politics*. London: Darton, Longman and Todd.

Fox, C (2016) *'I Find that Offensive'*. London: Biteback Publishing.

Fransman, J (forthcoming) 'Understanding "Research Engagement" in the UK-Context: Navigating the Conceptual Landscape', *Research for All: Universities and Society*.

Freidson, E (2001) *Professionalism: The Third Logic*. Cambridge: Polity Press.

Fuchs, C and Hofkirchner, W (2009) 'Autopoiesis and Critical Social Systems Theory', in R Magalhaes and R Sanchez (eds), *Autopoiesis in Organization Theory and Practice* (pp. 111–129). Bingley, UK: Emerald.

Fung, D (2017) *A Connected Curriculum for Higher Education*. London: UCL Press.

Furedi, F (2016) *What's Happened to the University?* London and New York: Routledge.

Gadamer, H-G (1985/1965) *Truth and Method*. London: Sheed and Ward.

Gadamer, H-G (2001) *Gadamer in Conversation*. New Haven, CT and London: Yale University Press.

Gallie, W B (1956) 'Essentially Contested Concepts', *Proceedings of the Aristotelian Society*, 56(1): 167–198.

Gallie, W B (1960) *A New University: A D Lindsay and the Keele Experiment*. London: Chatto and Windus.

Gellner, E (1974) *The Legitimation of Knowledge*. London: Cambridge University Press.

Gellner, E (1991) *Plough, Sword and Book: The Structure of Human History*. Paladin: London.

Gellner, E (1992) *Reason and Culture: The Historic Role of Rationality and Rationalism*. Oxford: Blackwell.

Gibbons, M, Limoges, C, Nowotny, H, Schwartman, S, Scott, P and Trow, M (1994) *The New Production of Knowledge: The Dynamics of Science and Research in Contemporary Societies*. London: Sage.

Gibbs, P T (2004) *Trusting in the University: The Contribution of Temporality and Trust to a Praxis of Higher Learning*. Dordrecht: Kluwer.
Gibbs, P, Ylijoki, O-H, Guzmán-Valenzuela, C and Barnett, R (eds) (2015) *Universities in the Flux of Time: An Exploration of Time and Temporality in University Life*. London and New York: Routledge.
Giddens, A (1995) *Modernity and Self-Identity: Self and Society in the Late Modern Age*. Cambridge: Polity Press.
Gomes Zuin, V and Lopes de Almeida Pacca, J (2012) 'Formation of Teachers in Chemistry and Curricular Environmentalization: A Case Study in a Tertiary Education Institution in Brazil', *Ensenanza de las Ciencias*, 31(1): 79–93.
Gordon, P and White, J (1979) *Philosophers as Educational Reformers: The Influence of Idealism on British Educational Thought and Practice*. London: Routledge & Kegan Paul.
Gouldner, A (1976) *The Dialectic of Ideology and Technology: The Origins, Grammar and Future of Ideology*. Basingstoke, UK: Macmillan.
Gouldner, A (1979) *The Future of Intellectuals and the Rise of the New Class*. Basingstoke, UK: Macmillan.
Grun, M (2005) 'Gadamer and the Otherness of Nature: Elements for an Environmental Education', *Human Studies*, 28(2): 157–171.
Guattari, F (2005/1989) *The Three Ecologies*. London and New York: Continuum.
Guattari, F (2016) *Lines of Flight: For Another World of Possibilities*. London and New York: Bloomsbury.
Guzmán-Valenzuela, C (2016a) 'Neoliberal Discourses and the Emergence of an Agentic Field: The Chilean Student Movement', in R Brooks (ed.), *Student Politics and Protest* (pp. 47–62). London: Routledge and SRHE.
Guzmán-Valenzuela, C (2016b) 'Unfolding the Meaning of Public(s) in Universities: Toward the Transformative University', *Higher Education*, 71(5): 667–679.
Habermas, J (1972) *Towards a Rational Society: Student Protest, Science and Politics*. London: Heinemann.
Habermas, J (1978) *Knowledge and Human Interests*. London: Heinemann.
Habermas, J (1984) *The Theory of Communicative Action: Reason and the Rationalization of Society*. Volume One. Cambridge: Polity Press.
Habermas, J (1987) 'The Idea of the University: Learning Processes', *New German Critique*, 41(Spring–Summer).
Habermas, J (1989) *The Theory of Communicative Action: The Critique of Functionalist Reason*. Volume Two. Cambridge: Polity Press.
Habermas, J (2001) *The Liberating Power of Symbols: Philosophical Essays*. Cambridge: Polity Press.
Habermas, J (2003) *The Future of Human Nature*. Cambridge: Polity Press.
Habermas, J (2005/1962) *The Structural Transformation of the Public Sphere*. Cambridge: Polity Press.
Habermas, J (2010a) *An Awareness of What Is Missing: Faith and Reason in a Post-Secular Age*. Cambridge: Polity Press.
Habermas, J (2010b) *Between Naturalism and Religion: Philosophical Essays*. Cambridge: Polity Press.
Hall, B and Tandon, R (2017) 'Decolonization of Knowledge, Epistemicide, Participatory Research and Higher Education', *Research for All*, 1(1): 6–19.
Hall, B, Jackson, E, Tandon, R, Fontan, J-M and Lall, N (eds) (2013) *Knowledge, Democracy and Action: Community–University Research Partnerships in Global Perspectives*. Manchester and New York: Manchester University Press.

Hards, L, Vaughan, S and Williams, J (2014) 'Place-Making and Other Purposes: Public Art on Campus', in P Temple (ed.), *The Physical University: Contours of Space and Place in Higher Education*. London and New York: Routledge.

Harman, G (2010) *Towards Speculative Reason: Essays and Lectures*. Winchester, UK: Zero Books.

Hartwig, M (2010) 'Introduction', in R Bhaskar with M Hartwig, *The Formation of Critical Realism: A Personal Perspective*. London and New York: Routledge.

Hartwig, M and Morgan, J (eds) (2014) *Critical Realism and Spirituality*. London and New York: Routledge.

Hassan, R (2003) *The Chronoscopic Society: Globalization, Time and Knowledge in the Network Economy*. New York: Peter Lang.

Hawkins, J N (2016) 'The Predicament of the Quest for WCU Status and Seeking an Asian Flagship University', in J A Douglas (ed.), *The New Flagship University: Changing the Paradigm from Global Ranking to National Relevancy*. Basingstoke, UK and New York: Palgrave Macmillan.

Heap, S (ed.) (2017) *The Universities We Need: Theological Perspectives*. London and New York: Routledge.

Hegel, G W F (1837) 'Kant: Critique of Pure Reason', in *Lectures on the History of Philosophy*: www.marxists.org/reference/archive/hegel/works/hp/hpkant1.htm

Heidegger, M (1998/1962) *Being and Time*. Oxford: Blackwell.

Heidegger, M (2000) *Metaphysics*. New Haven, CT and London: Yale University Press.

Heidegger, M (2004/1954) *What Is Called Thinking?* New York: HarperCollins.

Heidegger, M (2007/1978) *Basic Writings*. Edited by D F Krell. London and New York: Routledge.

Hier, S P and Greenberg, J (eds) (2007) *The Surveillance Studies Reader*. Maidenhead, UK: McGraw-Hill/Open University Press.

Higton, M (2013) *A Theology of Higher Education*. Oxford: Oxford University Press.

Hillman, N (ed.) (2015) *It's the Finance, Stupid! The Decline in Part-Time Higher Education and What to Do About It*. Oxford: HEPI.

Hillman, N (2017) *Keeping Schtum? What Students Think of Free Speech*. HEPI Report 85. Oxford: HEPI.

Hoffman, A J (ed.) (2015) *Academic Engagement in Public and Political Discourse*. Ann Arbor, MI: University of Michigan.

Hopkinson, P and James, P (2013) 'Whole Institutional Change Towards Sustainable Universities', in S Sterling, L Maxey and H Luna (eds), *The Sustainable University: Progress and Prospects*. London and New York: Routledge.

Horkheimer, M (2004) *Eclipse of Reason*. London and New York: Continuum.

Hourdequin, M (2015) *Environmental Ethics: From Theory to Practice*. London and New York: Bloomsbury.

Hroch, P (2016) 'Deleuze, Guattari, and Environmental Pedagogy and Politics: Ritournelles for a Planet-Yet-To-Come', in M Carlin and J Wallin (eds), *Deleuze and Guattari, Politics and Education: For a People-Yet-To-Come*. New York and London: Bloomsbury.

Hung, R. (2008) 'Educating for and Through Nature: A Merleau-Pontian Approach', *Studies in the Philosophy of Education*, 27(5): 355–367.

Hutchins, R (1936) *The Higher Learning in America*. New Haven, CT: Yale.

Ignatieff, M (1984) *The Needs of Strangers*. London: Vintage.

Ingold, T (2000) *The Perception of the Environment: Essays in Livelihood, Dwelling and Skill*. London and New York: Routledge.

Innerarity, D (2015) *The Democracy of Knowledge*. New York and London: Bloomsbury.

Irwin, A and Michael, M (2003) *Science, Social Theory and Public Knowledge*. Maidenhead, UK: McGraw-Hill/Open University Press.
Jackson, N (2016) *Exploring Learning Ecologies*. Dorking, UK: Chalk Mountain.
Jacoby, R (2005) *Picture Imperfect: Utopian Thought for an Anti-Utopian Age*. New York and Chichester, UK: Columbia University Press.
Jarvis, P (1992) *Paradoxes of Learning: On Becoming an Individual in Society*. San Francisco, CA: Jossey-Bass.
Jarvis, P (2010) *Adult Education and Lifelong Learning: Theory and Practice*. 4th edition. London and New York: Routledge.
Jones, S and Harvey, M (eds) (2017) 'Leading the Academy: Building Capacity through Distributed Leadership', Special Issue, *Journal of Higher Education Policy and Management*, 39(2).
Judson, G (2010) 'Imaginative Ecological Education', in T W Nielsen, R Fitzgerald and M Fettes (eds), *Imagination in Educational Theory and Practice: A Many-Sided Vision*. Newcastle upon Tyne, UK: Cambridge Scholars.
Kant, I (1992) *The Conflict of the Faculties*. Lincoln and London: University of Nebraska.
Kemmis, S, Wilkinson, J, Hardy, I and Edwards-Groves, C (2012) 'Leading and Learning: Developing Ecologies of Educational Practice', in P Hager, A Lee and A Reich (eds), *Practice, Learning and Change* (pp. 33–40). Dordrecht: Springer.
Kennedy, M D (2015) *Globalizing Knowledge: Intellectuals, Universities and Publics in Transformation*. Stanford, CA: Stanford University.
Kjaer, P (2006) 'Systems in Context: On the Outcome of the Habermas/Luhmann_Debate', *Ancilla Iuris*, 1: 66–77: www.anci.ch/_media/beitrag/ancilla2006_66_kjaer_systems.pdf
Kreber, C (2013) *Authenticity in and through Teaching in Higher Education: The Transformative Potential of the Scholarship of Teaching*. London and New York: Routledge.
Kress, G (2010) *Multimodality: A Social Semiotic Approach to Contemporary Communication*. London and New York: Routledge.
Kweik, M (2006) *The Classical German Idea of the University Revisited, or on The Nationalization of the Modern Institution*. Centre for Public Policy Research Papers Volume 1. Poznan University, Poland.
Langley, C (2009) 'Commercialised Universities: The Influence of the Military', in J Satterwaite, H Piper and P Sikes (eds), *Power in the Academy*. Oakhill, UK and Sterling, VA: Trentham.
Law, P and Law, A (2014) 'Digital Badging at The Open University: Recognition for Informal Learning', in *The Open and Flexible Higher Education Conference 2014: 'New Technologies and the Future of Teaching and Learning'*, 23–24 October, Krakow, Poland.
Leavis, F R (1969) *English Literature in our Time and the University*. London: Chatto and Windus.
Lefebvre, H (2004/1992) *Rhythmanalysis*. London and New York: Continuum.
Lefebvre, H (2016/1971) *Everyday Life in the Modern World*. London and New York: Bloomsbury.
Lehman, G (2015) *Charles Taylor's Ecological Conversations: Politics, Commonalities and the Natural Environment*. Basingstoke, UK and New York: Palgrave Macmillan.
Levin, M and Greenwood, D J (2016) *Creating a New Public University and Reviving Democracy: Action Research in Higher Education*. New York and Oxford: Berghahn.
Levinas, E (2005/1969) *Totality and Infinity: An Essay on Exteriority*. Pittsburgh, PA: Duquesne University Press.
Levitas, R (2013) *Utopia as Method: The Imaginary Reconstitution of Society*. Basingstoke and New York: Palgrave Macmillan.
Lipovetsky, G (2005) *Hypermodern Times*. Cambridge: Polity Press.

List, C and Pettit, P (2011) *Group Agency: The Possibility, Design, and Status of Corporate Agents*. Oxford: Oxford University Press.
Loftus, S (2015) 'Embodiment in the Practice and Education of Health Professionals', in B Green and N Hopwood (eds), *The Body in Professional Practice, Learning and Education* (chapter 9). Dordrecht: Springer.
Luhmann, N (2003) 'Organization', in T Bakken and T Hernes (eds), *Autopoietic Organization Theory: Drawing on Niklas Luhmann's Social Systems Perspective*. Copenhagen: Copenhagen Business School.
Luhmann, N (2013) *Introduction to Systems Theory*. Cambridge: Polity Press.
Luna, H and Maxey, L (2013) 'Towards a Green Academy', in S Sterling, L Maxey and H Luna (eds), *The Sustainable University: Progress and Prospects*. London and New York: Routledge.
Lyotard, J-F (1984) *The Postmodern Condition: A Report on Knowledge*. Manchester: University of Manchester Press.
Maccarini, A M (2013) 'A Morphogenetic-Relational Account of Social Emergence: Processes and Forms', in M Archer and A Maccarini (eds), *Engaging with the World: Agency, Institutions, Historical Formations*. London and New York: Routledge.
Macfarlane, B (2004) *Teaching with Integrity: The Ethics of Higher Education Practice*. London and New York: RoutledgeFalmer.
Macfarlane, B (2007) *The Academic Citizen: The Virtue of Service in University Life*. London and New York: Routledge.
Macfarlane, B (2012) *Intellectual Leadership in Higher Education: Renewing the Role of the University Professor*. London and New York: Routledge.
Macfarlane, B (2017) *Freedom to Learn: The Threat to Student Academic Freedom and Why It Needs to Be Reclaimed*. London and New York: Routledge.
MacIntyre, A (1985) *After Virtue: A Study in Moral Theory*. London: Duckworth.
MacIntyre, A (2011) *God, Philosophy, Universities: A Selective History of the Catholic Philosophical Tradition*. Lanham, MD: Rowman & Littlefield.
Marginson, S (2017) 'Higher Education – The key to greater freedom', *University World News*, 8 March, issue 499.
Marginson, S and Rhoades, G (2002) 'Beyond National States, Markets, and Systems of Higher Education: A Glonacal Agency Heuristic', *Higher Education*, 43(3): 281–309.
Markham, I S (2004) 'The Idea of a Christian University', in J Astley, L Francis, J Sullivan and A Walker (eds), *The Idea of a Christian University: Essays on Theology and Higher Education*. Milton Keynes, UK: Paternoster.
Marques Pereira, G da, Jabbour, C, Borges de Oliveira, S V W and Alves Teixeira, A (2014) 'Greening the Campus of a Brazilian University: Cultural Challenges', *International Journal of Sustainability*, 15(1): 34–47.
Masquelier, C (2015) *Critical Theory and Libertarian Socialism: Realizing the Political Potential of Critical Social Theory*. New York and London: Bloomsbury.
Maxwell, N (2007) *From Knowledge to Wisdom: A Revolution for Science and Humanities*. 2nd edition. London: Pentire.
Maxwell, N (2008) 'Wisdom in the University', in R Barnett and N Maxwell (eds), *Wisdom in the University*. London and New York: Routledge.
McAfee, N (2009) *Civil Society or the Public Sphere?* Personal blog: https://gonepublic.net/2009/07/24/civil-society-or-the-public-sphere
McArthur, J (2014) *Rethinking Knowledge within Higher Education: Adorno and Social Justice*. London: Bloomsbury.
McIlrath, L and Mac Labhrainn, I (eds) (2007) *Higher Education and Civic Engagement: International Perspectives*. Aldershot, UK and Burlington, VT: Ashgate.

Mckenzie, H, Tolley, H, Croft, T, Grove, M and Lawson, D (2016) 'Senior Management Perspectives of Mathematics and Statistics Support in Higher Education: Moving to an "Ecological" Approach', *Journal of Higher Education and Management*, 38(5): 551–561.

Meillassoux, Q (2008) *After Finitude: An Essay on the Necessity of Contingency*. New York: Bloomsbury.

Mendieta, E and Vanantwerpen, J (eds) (2011) *The Power of Religion in the Public Sphere*. New York and Chichester, UK: Columbia University Press.

Merleau-Ponty, M (1994) *Phenomenology of Perception*. London: Routledge.

Meyer, J H F and Land, R (2005) 'Threshold Concepts and Troublesome Knowledge: Epistemological Considerations and a Conceptual Framework for Teaching and Learning', *Higher Education*, 49(3): 373–388.

Mickey, S (2016) *Whole Earth Thinking and Planetary Coexistence: Ecological Wisdom at the Intersection of Religion, Ecology, and Philosophy*. London and New York: Routledge.

Minogue, K (1973) *The Concept of a University*. London: Weidenfeld & Nicolson.

Mitchell, C (2017) 'Transforming the Economics Curriculum around the World', *University World News*, 27 May: www.universityworldnews.com/article.php?story=20160527081049981

Moisio, S and Kangas, S (2016) 'Reterritorializing the Global Knowledge Economy: An Analysis of Geopolitical Assemblages of Higher Education', *Global Networks*, 16(3): 268–287.

Monk, N, Chillington Rutter, C, Neelands, J and Heron, J (2011) *Open Space Learning: A Study in Transdisciplinary Pedagogy*. London and New York: Bloomsbury.

Montefiore, A (ed.) (1975) *Neutrality and Impartiality: The University and Political Commitment*. London: Cambridge University Press.

Moog, S (2009) 'Ecological Politics for the Twenty-First Century: Where Does "Nature" Fit In?', in S Moog and R Stones (eds), *Nature, Social Relations and Human Needs: Essays in Honour of Ted Benton*. Basingstoke, UK: Palgrave Macmillan.

Moog, S and Stones, R (eds) (2009) *Nature, Social Relations and Human Needs: Essays in Honour of Ted Benton*. Basingstoke, UK: Palgrave Macmillan.

Morton, T (2010) *The Ecological Thought*. Cambridge, MA: Harvard University Press.

Mullins, P and Jacobs, S (2006) 'T S Eliot's Idea of the Clerisy, and its Discussion by Karl Mannheim and Michael Polanyi in the Context of J H Oldham's Moot', *Journal of Classical Sociology*, 6(2): 147–176.

Naess, A (2012) 'The Deep Ecological Movement: Some Philosophical Aspects', in R Bhaskar, K G Hoyer and P Naess (eds), *Ecophilosophy in a World of Crisis: Critical Realism and the Nordic Contributions*. London and New York: Routledge.

Naidoo, R (2015) 'Transnational Perspectives on Higher Education and Global Well-Being', Seminar, Society for Research into Higher Education: https://srheblog.com/2015/10/14/transnational-perspectives-on-higher-education-and-global-well-being/

Naruse, M and Iba, T (2008) 'Ecosystem as an Autopoietic System: Considering Relationship between Ecology and Society based on Luhmann's Theory': http://web.sfc.keio.ac.jp/~iba/papers/2008JJNAMS08-ecosystem.pdf

NCIHE (National Committee of Inquiry into Higher Education) (1997) *Higher Education for a Learning Society*. London: HMSO.

Neave, G (1998) 'The Evaluative State Reconsidered', *European Journal of Education*, 33(3): 265–284.

Newman, J H (1976) *The Idea of a University*. Edited by I T Ker. Oxford: Clarendon Press.

Nielson, T W, Fitzgerald, R and Fettes, M (eds) (2010) *Imagination in Educational Theory and Practice: A Many-Sided Vision*. Newcastle upon Tyne, UK: Cambridge Scholars.

Nietzsche, F (2003/1889) *Twilight of the Idols and The Anti-Christ*. Trans. R J Hollingdale. London: Penguin.
Nisbet, R (1970) *The Degradation of the Academic Dogma*. London: Heinemann.
Nixon, J (2008) *Towards the Virtuous University: The Moral Bases of Academic Practice*. New York and London: Continuum.
Nixon, J (2011) *Higher Education and the Public Good: Imagining the University*. London and New York: Continuum.
Nowotny, H (1996) *Time: The Modern and the Postmodern Experience*. Cambridge: Polity Press.
Nowotny, H, Scott, P and Gibbons, M (2001) *Re-Thinking Science: Knowledge and the Public in an Age of Uncertainty*. Cambridge: Polity Press.
Nussbaum, M C (2010) *Not for Profit: Why Democracy Needs the Humanities*. Princeton, NJ and Oxford: Princeton University Press.
Oakeshott, M (1989) *The Voice of Liberal Learning*. Edited by Timothy Fuller. New Haven, CT and London: Yale University Press.
Ortega y Gasset, J (1946) *Mission of the University*. London: Kegan Paul, Trench, Trubner and Co.
Ostrom, E (2012) *The Future of the Commons: Beyond Market Failure and Government Regulations*. London: London Publishing Partnership: IEA.
Palardy, G J (2014) 'High School Socioeconomic Composition and College Choice: Multilevel Mediation via Organizational Habitus, School Practices, Peer and Staff Attitudes', *School Effectiveness and School Improvement*: http://dx.doi.org/10.1080/09243453.2014.965182
Papaioannou, T, Wield, D and Chataway, J (2009) 'Knowledge Ecologies and Ecosystems? An Empirically Grounded Reflection on Recent Developments in Innovation Systems Theory', *Environment and Planning C: Government and Policy*, 27(2): 319–339.
Parameswaran, R (2011) 'Producing Cosmopolitan Global Citizens in the US Academy', in B Zelizer (ed.), *Making the University Matter*. London and New York: Routledge.
Pata, K (2009) 'Revising the Framework of Knowledge Ecologies: How Activity Patterns Define Learning Spaces', in N Lambropoulos and M Romero (eds), *Educational Social Software for Context-Aware Learning: Collaborative Methods and Human Interaction* (pp. 241–267). New York: Hershey.
Peters, M A (2009) 'Degrees of Freedom and the Virtues of Openness: The Internet, the Academy and Digital Rights', in J Satterwaite, H Piper and P Sikes (eds), *Power in the Academy*. Oakhill, UK and Sterling, VA: Trentham.
Peters, M A (2013) *Education, Science and Knowledge Capitalism: Creativity and the Promise of Openness*. New York: Peter Lang.
Peters, M A (2015) 'The University in the Epoch of Digital Reason: Fast Knowledge in the Circuits of Cybernetic Capitalism', in P Gibbs, O-H Ylijoki, C Guzmán-Valenzuela and R Barnett (eds), *Universities in the Flux of Time: An Exploration of Time and Temporality in University Life*. London and New York: Routledge.
Peters, M A (2018) 'Renewing the Idea of the University: The Cosmopolitan and Postcolonial Projects', in R Barnett and M A Peters (eds), *The Idea of the University: Volume 2 – Contemporary Perspectives*. New York: Peter Lang.
Peters, M A and Araya, D (2009) 'Network Logic: An Ecological Approach to Knowledge and Learning', in M McKenzie, P Hart, H Bai and B Jickling (eds), *Fields of Green: Restorying Culture, Environment, and Education*. New York: Hampton Press.
Peters, M A and Barnett, R (eds) (2018) *The Idea of the University: Volume 1 – A Reader*. New York: Peter Lang.
Peters, M A and Gietzen, G (2012) 'Knowledge Socialism and Universities: Intellectual Commons and Opportunities for "Openness" in the 21st Century', in M A Peters,

T-G Liu and D J Ondercin (eds) *The Pedagogy of the Open Society: Knowledge and the Governance of Higher Education*. Rotterdam: Sense.

Peters, M A, Gietzen, G and Ondercin, D J (2012) 'Knowledge Socialism: Intellectual Commons and Openness in the University', in R Barnett (ed.), *The Future University: Ideas and Possibilities*. London and New York: Routledge.

Peters, R S (1966) *Ethics and Education*. London: George Allen & Unwin.

Piketty, T (2014) *Capital in the Twenty-First Century*. Cambridge, MA: Harvard University Press.

Pillay, S and Lavern, S (2016) 'Collaborative Online International Learning (COIL) at Durban University of Technology', paper given at Durban University of Technology, 5th Learning, Teaching and Assessment Symposium, Coastlands, 9–11 November: http://er.dut.ac.za/handle/123456789/208

Pleyers, G (2010) *Alter-Globalization: Becoming Actors in the Global Age*. Cambridge: Polity Press.

Plumwood, V (2002) *Environmental Culture: The Ecological Crisis of Reason*. London and New York: Routledge.

Porpora, D V (2013) 'The New World Order: What Role for Critical Realism?', in M Archer and A Maccarini (eds), *Engaging with the World: Agency, Institutions, Historical Formations*. London and New York: Routledge.

Pringle, J and Naidoo, R (2016) 'Branding and the Commodification of Academic Labour', in R Barnett, P Temple and P Scott, *Valuing Higher Education: An Appreciation of the Work of Gareth Williams*. London: UCL IOE Press.

Proctor, J D and Larson, B M H (2005) 'Ecology, Complexity, and Metaphor', *BioScience*, 55(12): 1065–1068.

Pusser, B (2012) 'Power and Authority in the Creation of a Public Sphere through Higher Education', in B Pusser, K Kempner, S Marginson and I Ordorika (eds), *Universities and the Public Sphere: Knowledge Creation and State Building in the Era of Globalization*. New York and London: Routledge.

Putnam, R (2001) *Bowling Alone: The Collapse and Revival of American Community*. New York: Touchstone/Simon & Schuster.

Rammell, B (2016) *Protecting the Public Interest in Higher Education*. Occasional Paper 15. Oxford: Higher Education Policy Institute.

Ramsey, I T (1957) *Religious Language: An Empirical Placing of Theological Phrases*. London: SCM Press.

Readings, B (1997) *The University in Ruins*. Cambridge, MA and London: Harvard University Press.

Rhoten, D and Calhoun, C (eds) (2011) *Knowledge Matters: The Public Mission of the Research University*. New York and Chichester, UK: Columbia University Press.

Rieff, P (1987) *The Triumph of the Therapeutic: Uses of Faith after Freud*. Chicago, IL and London: University of Chicago.

Riggio, A (2015) *Ecology, Ethics, and the Future of Humanity*. Basingstoke, UK and New York: Palgrave Macmillan.

Robbins, L (1963) *Higher Education: Report of the Committee Appointed by the Prime Minister Under the Chairmanship of Lord Robbins 1961–63*. Cmnd. 2154. London: HMSO.

Robinson, D (2004) 'Sedes Sapientiae: Newman, Truth and the Christian University', in J Astley, L Francis, J Sullivan and A Walker (eds), *The Idea of a Christian University: Essays on Theology and Higher Education*. Milton Keynes, UK: Paternoster.

Robinson, S and Katulushi, C (eds) (2005) *Values in Higher Education*. St Bride's Major, Glamorgan, UK: Aureus/University of Leeds.

Bibliography

Rolfe, G (2013) *The University in Dissent*. London and New York: Routledge/SRHE.

Roszak, T (2001/1996) *The Voice of the Earth: An Explanation of Ecopsychology*. Grand Rapids, MI: Phanes Press.

Rothblatt, S (1997) *The Modern University and its Discontents: The Fate of Newman's Legacies in Britain and America*. Cambridge: Cambridge University Press.

Russell, B (1967/1912) *The Problems of Philosophy*. London: Oxford University Press.

Russell, B (1968) *The Autobiography of Bertrand Russell: 1914–44*. Volume II. London: George Allen & Unwin.

Rustin, M (2013) 'A Relational Society', *Soundings*, July: 23–36.

Sabri, D (2010) 'Absence of the Academic from Higher Education Policy', *Journal of Educational Policy*, 25(2): 191–205.

Sargisson, L (2001) 'Green Utopias of Self and Other', in B Goodwin (ed.), *The Philosophy of Utopia*. Ilford, UK and Portland, OR: Frank Cass.

Satterwaite, J, Piper, H and Sikes, P (eds) (2009) *Power in the Academy*. Oakhill, UK and Sterling, VA: Trentham.

Savin-Baden, M. (2008) *Learning Spaces: Creating Opportunities for Knowledge Creation in Academic Life*. Maidenhead, UK: McGraw-Hill/Open University Press.

Savin-Baden, M (2015) *Rethinking Learning in an Age of Digital Fluency*. London and New York: Routledge.

Sayce, S, Farren Bradley, J, Ritson, J and Quinn, F (2013) 'Well-Being: What Does It Mean for the Sustainable University?', in S Sterling, L Maxey and H Luna (eds), *The Sustainable University: Progress and Prospects*. London and New York: Routledge.

Schön, D (1971) *Beyond the Stable State*. London: Temple Smith.

Schudson, M (2011) 'The Problem of General Education in the Research University', in B Zelizer (ed.), *Making the University Matter*. London and New York: Routledge.

Schuller, T and Watson, D (2009) *Learning through Life: Inquiry into the Future for Lifelong Learning*. Leicester: NIACE.

Searle, J (1995) *The Construction of Social Reality*. London: Allen Lane/Penguin.

Searle, J (1999) *Mind, Language and Society: Doing Philosophy in the Real World*. London: Weidenfeld & Nicolson.

Searle, J (2010) *Making the Social World: The Structure of Human Civilization*. Oxford and New York: Oxford University Press.

Seidl, D (2004) 'Luhmann's Theory of Autopoietic Social Systems', Ludwig-Maximilians Universität München, Munich School of Management: /www.researchgate.net/profile/David_Seidl2/publication/277293382_Luhman'stheory of autopoietic social systems/links/564db64b08aefe619b0e109f.pdf

Skolverket (2000) *Lifelong Learning and Lifewide Learning*. Report for Swedish National Agency for Education. Stockholm: Liber Distribution.

Slaughter, S and Cantwell, B (2018) 'Academic Capitalism: Reflections on Higher Education in the United States and European Union', in R Barnett and M Peters (eds), *The Idea of the University: Volume 2 – Contemporary Perspectives*. New York: Peter Lang.

Slaughter, S and Rhoades, G (2010) *Academic Capitalism and the New Economy: Markets, State, and Higher Education*. Baltimore, MD: Johns Hopkins University.

Sloman, A E (1964) 'A University in the Making'. BBC Reith Lectures. London: BBC.

Small, H (2013) *The Value of the Humanities*. Oxford: Oxford University Press.

Smith, B and Searle, J (2003) 'The Construction of Social Reality: An Exchange', in D Koepsell and L S Moss (eds), *John Searle's Ideas about Social Reality: Extensions, Criticisms and Reconstructions*. Malden, MA and Oxford: Blackwell.

Smith, J and Jenks, C (2007) *Qualitative Complexity: Ecology, Cognitive Processes and the Re-Emergence of Structures in Post-Humanist Social Theory*. London and New York: Routledge.
Sorlin, S (2002) 'Cultivating the Places of Knowledge', *Studies in Philosophy and Education*, 21(4–5): 377–388.
Standeart, N (2018) 'Displaced Towards a Networked University', in R Barnett and M A Peters (eds), *The Idea of the University: Volume 2 – Contemporary Perspectives*. New York: Peter Lang.
Stehr, N (1994) *Knowledge Societies*. London and Thousand Oaks, CA: Sage.
Sterling, S (2013) 'The Sustainable University: Challenge and Response', in S Sterling, L Maxey and H Luna (eds), *The Sustainable University: Progress and Prospects*. London and New York: Routledge.
Sterling, S, Maxey, L and Luna, H (eds) (2013) *The Sustainable University: Progress and Prospects*. London and New York: Routledge.
Stiegler, B (2014) *The Re-Enchantment of the World: The Value of Spirit Against Industrial Populism*. London and New York: Bloomsbury.
Stiglitz, J E (2013) *The Price of Inequality*. London: Penguin.
Stratford, R (2015) 'What Is the Ecological University and Why Is it a Significant Challenge for Higher Education Policy and Practice?', *Educational Philosophy and Theory*: www.academia.edu/19661131/What_is_the_ecological_university_and_why_is_it_a_significant_challenge_for_higher_education_policy_and_practice
Tallis, R (1999) *Enemies of Hope: A Critique of Contemporary Pessimism*. Basingstoke, UK and New York: Macmillan and St Martin's Press.
Taylor, C (1969) 'Neutrality in Political Science', in P Laslett and W G Runciman (eds), *Philosophy, Politics and Society: Third Series*. Oxford: Blackwell.
Taylor, C (1991) *The Ethics of Authenticity*. Cambridge, MA: Harvard University Press.
Taylor, C (1992) *Sources of the Self: The Making of the Modern Identity*. Cambridge: Cambridge University Press.
Taylor, C (2007) *Modern Social Imaginaries*. Durham, NC and London: Duke University Press.
Taylor, R (2013) 'Bottoms Up for Sustainability', in in S Sterling, L Maxey and H Luna (eds), *The Sustainable University: Progress and Prospects*. London and New York: Routledge.
Temple, P (2014a) *The Hallmark University: Distinctiveness in Higher Education Management*. London: IOE Press.
Temple, P (ed.) (2014b) *The Physical University: Contours of Space and Place in Higher Education*. Abingdon and New York: Routledge.
Temple, P (2016) 'David Watson 1949–2015: A Life in Higher Education', *London Review of Education*, 14(1): 143–155.
Thevenot, L (2013) 'The Human Being Invested in Social Forms: Four Extensions of the Notion of Engagement', in M Archer and A Maccarini (eds), *Engaging with the World: Agency, Institutions, Historical Formations*. London and New York: Routledge.
Thompson, C (2015) 'The Philosophy of Education as the Economy and Ecology of Pedagogical Knowledge', *Studies in the Philosophy of Education*, 34(6): 651–664.
Tilbury, D (2013) 'Another World Is Desirable: A Global Rebooting of Higher Education for Sustainable Development', in S Sterling, L Maxey and H Luna (eds), *The Sustainable University: Progress and Prospects*. London and New York: Routledge.
Urry, J (2003) *Global Complexity*. Cambridge: Polity Press.
Varto, J (2008/1991) *Song of the Earth*. Helsinki, Finland: Aalto University.
Vernon, M (2008) *Wellbeing*. Stocksfield: Acumen.

Virilio, P (2005/1984) *Negative Horizon*. London: Continuum.
Virilio, P (2008/1995) *Open Sky*. London and New York: Verso.
Virilio, P (2010) *University of Disaster*. Cambridge: Polity Press.
Wals, A E J (2016) 'Beyond Unreasonable Doubt: Education and Learning for Socio-Ecological Sustainability in the Anthropocene', Inaugural address. Wageningen University, Wageningen, the Netherlands.
Ward, S C (2014) *Neoliberalism and the Global Restructuring of Knowledge and Education*. New York and London: Routledge.
Watermeyer, R (2016) 'Public Intellectuals vs. New Public Management: The Defeat of Public Engagement in Higher Education', *Studies in Higher Education*, 41(12): 2271–2285.
Watson, D (2007) *Managing Civic and Community Engagement*. Maidenhead, UK: McGraw-Hill/Open University Press.
Watson, D, Hollister, R M, Stroud, S E and Babcock, E (2011) *The Engaged University: International Perspectives on Civic Engagement*. New York and London: Routledge.
Weaver-Hightower, M B (2008) 'An Ecology Metaphor for Educational Policy Analysis: A Call to Complexity', *Educational Researcher*, 37(3): 153–167.
Weber, L and Bergan, S (eds) (2006) *The Public Responsibility for Higher Education and Research*. Strasbourg: Council of Europe.
Weber, M (1991) 'Science as a Vocation', in H H Gerth and C Wright Mills (eds), *From Max Weber: Essays in Sociology*. London: Routledge.
Welikala, T and Watkins, C (2008) *Improving Intercultural Learning: Experiences in Higher Education*. London: Institute of Education.
White, R (2013) *The Heart of Wisdom: A Philosophy of Spiritual Life*. Lanham, MD: Rowman & Littlefield.
White, R M (2013) 'Sustainable Research: A Novel Mode of Knowledge Generation to Explore Alternative Ways for People and Planet', in S Sterling, L Maxey and H Luna (eds), *The Sustainable University: Progress and Prospects*. London and New York: Routledge.
Williams, B (2002) *Truthfulness: An Essay in Genealogy*. Princeton, NJ and Oxford: Princeton University.
Williams, B (2008/1985) *Ethics and the Limits of Philosophy*. London: Routledge.
Williams, G and Filippakou, R (eds) (2015) *Higher Education as a Public Good: Critical Perspectives on Theory, Policy and Practice*. New York: Peter Lang.
Williams, R (2003) *Silence and Honey Cakes: The Wisdom of the Desert*. Oxford: Lion Hudson.
Williams, R (2007) *Wrestling with Angels: Conversations in Modern Theology*. Edited by Mike Higton. London: SCM Press.
Wilson, A (2016) 'The Science of Cities', *Prospect*, May. (UK magazine)
Wittgenstein, L (1978/1953) *Philosophical Investigations*. Oxford: Blackwell.
Wright, D (2010) 'Imaginative Education: Nurturing our Social Ecology', in T W Nielsen, R Fitzgerald and M Fettes (eds), *Imagination in Educational Theory and Practice: A Many-Sided Vision*. Newcastle upon Tyne, UK: Cambridge Scholars.
Yilmaz, D and Stockhammer, E (2015) 'Alternative Economics: A New Student Movement', *Radical Philosophy*, 189(Jan./Feb.): www.radicalphilosophy.com/commentary/alternative-economics
Zelizer, B (ed.) (2011) *Making the University Matter*. London and New York: Routledge.
Zgaga, P (2006) 'Higher Education for a Democratic Culture: The Public Responsibility', in L Weber and S Bergan (eds), *The Public Responsibility for Higher Education and Research*. Strasbourg: Council of Europe.
Žižek, S (1993) *Tarrying with the Negative: Kant, Hegel, and the Critique of Ideology*. Durham, NC: Duke University Press.
Žižek, S (2016) *Disparities*. New York and London: Bloomsbury.

Other documents

Arts and Humanities in Higher Education (2015) Special Issue on 'Civic Engagement in the Arts and Humanities', 14(3).
European Journal of Education (1998) Special Issue on 'The Evaluative State Revisited', 33(3).
Global University Network for Innovation (GUNI) (2017) *Towards a Socially Responsible University: Balancing the Global with the Local.* Higher Education in the World, Report 6. Girona: www.guninetwork.org/files/download_full_report.pdf
PCES (University of Manchester Post-Crash Economics Society) (2014) *Economics, Education and Unlearning: Economics Education at the University of Manchester.* Manchester: PCES: www.post-crasheconomics.com/economics-education-and-unlearning/

Websites not listed above

Aristotle on civil society: https://en.wikipedia.org/wiki/Civil_society
Terry Eagleton–Roger Scruton debate about 'culture': www.youtube.com/watch?v=qOdMBDOj4ec
'Engagement' in fencing: https://en.wikipedia.org/wiki/Outline_of_fencing
'Entanglement': https://en.wikipedia.org/wiki/Quantum_entanglement
'Impact', as defined by the UK's Higher Education Funding Council for England: www.hefce.ac.uk/rsrch/REFimpact/
Kant rarely leaving Königsberg: www.kant-online.ru/en/?p=265
Knowledge Ecology International: attending and mending the knowledge ecosystem:www.keionline.org/about
'Knowledge ecosystem': https://en.wikipedia.org/wiki/Knowledge_ecosystem
'Lysenkoism': https://en.wikipedia.org/wiki/Lysenkoism
Médecins sans Frontières: www.msf.org.uk/
Elinor Ostrom – economics for 'the commons': www.onthecommons.org/magazine/elinor-ostroms-8-principles-managing-commmons
Plymouth University – Centre for Sustainable Futures: www.plymouth.ac.uk/your-university/sustainability/sustainability-education
'Post-truth world': https://en.wikipedia.org/wiki/Post-truth_politics
Republican Party of Texas (2012) Report of Platform Committee: www.texasgop.org/wp-content/themes/rpt/images/2012Platform_Final.pdf
Donald Schön's 1970 BBC Reith Lectures, 'Beyond the Stable State': www.bbc.co.uk/programmes/p00h3xfh
Peter Scott – public lecture, University of Toronto OISE, Worldviews Lecture on Media and Higher Education, 'Populism – Is the Academy on the Wrong Side of History?': www.universityworldnews.com/article.php?story=20170321131230967
Roger Scruton on Deleuze and Guattari's *A Thousand Plateaus*: www.spiked-online.com/spiked-review/article/interview-roger-scruton/17689#.WJdNdX8QQdU
Student as 'producer': http://studentasproducer.lincoln.ac.uk/
Talloires Network declaration: http://talloiresnetwork.tufts.edu/who-we-are/talloires-declaration/
United Nations Sustainable Development Goals: https://sustainabledevelopment.un.org/post2015/transformingourworld
World of Learning (2014), which carries a set of introductory essays on the theme of 'The University in Turbulent Political Times'. Abingdon, UK: Routledge: www.worldoflearning.com

SUBJECT INDEX

Major references are emboldened; references to footnotes are italicised; quotation marks indicate a phrase especially associated with a scholar or group of scholars.

25,000+ universities worldwide 12, 59, 151, 182

Absence 51–52, 70, 151–52, 172
Academic autonomy 88, 182
'Academic capitalism' 7, 62
Academic freedom 20, **118–19**, 166
Academic identity 61, 78, 92, 161
Access to higher education 52, 162
Accountancy 81
Agency 27, 48, 60, 70, 128, 172, 142, 181; see also ecological agency
Anthropocene 49, *54*, 86
Anthropocentricism 76
Anthropology 130, 149
Archaeology 165
Architecture 50, 165
Art 87, 149, 179
Asia 4, 145
Assemblages 11, 29, 40–41, *85*, 106, 113–15, 117, 121, 127, 178, 183
'*A Thousand Plateaus*' 20, 115
Audit 7, *40*, 119, **157–169**
Australasia 4
Authenticity 104, 108, 116, 131–33, 139, 159
Autonomy 94, 104, 166, 171, 175
Autopoiesis 11, **44–46**, 48–49

Being 12, 110, 116, 126, 133–34, 150; see also human being; institutional being
'*Being a University*' 170–71
Buddhism 23, 41
Bildung 12
Biochemistry 50, 142
Bioengineering 58, 147, 158
Book, the 5, 183
Branding 82
Brighton rock 183

Canada *68*
Cake 181
Care 22, 37, 48, 65–66, 70, 74, 76, 101, 110, *112*, 130–31, 137, 162, 172; university 19, 58, 88, 161, 178–79
Castle-in-the-air 167
Cathedrals 161
Change 49, 151
Chemistry 114
Cities 83
Citizen scholars 163, *169*
Citizen scientists 63, 163, *169*
Citizenship 68, 112, *125*, *139*, 160
Civic engagement 141, 145–48, *152*; see also engagement
Civil society 146
Clinical relationship 136

Clouds 70, 75
'Cognitive capitalism' 51, 93, 173, 182
'Cognitive justice' 142
'Cognitive perspective' 149
Collectivity 26, 74, 183
Colonisation 57
Communication 7, 53, 95, 151
Communities of practice 127
Competition 51
Complexity 19, 23, *28*, 32, 61, 75, 100, 111, 114, 120, 137, 167, 175
Computer science 58
Connectedness 48, 121
Concepts 7–8; *see also* threshold concepts
Concern 6, 8, 36, 65, 78, 110, 157, 159, 172–74, 178
Contestability 31
Continents: Africa 4, 35, 145, 162, 176; Eastern Europe 176; South America 176
Contingency 32, 164
Conversations 53, 90, 97, 136
Corporate strategy, university 9, 79
Countries: England 12, 31, 61, 144, 178; Japan 68; Scandinavia 13; Scotland 12, 31; Singapore *68*; South Africa 92, 145; Soviet Union 151; United Kingdom 4, 96, 139; United States of America 4, 12, *28*, 31, 102, *139*, 148; *see also* North-South; United Nations
Courage 91, 101, 117, 135, 163
Creativity 87, 135, 139
Criteria of adequacy 157
Criticality 12, 52, 163, 165–66, 168, **173–74**
Critical dialogue 44, 73, 80, 171
Critical dispositions 166
Critical Realism 5, *12–13*, *28*, 34, 51, *168*
Critical reason 81
Critical society 166
Critical thinking *54*, 57, 61, 83, 166
Critical Theory 5, 23, *125*, 178
Critique 3, 166, 174
Cultural capital 120
Cultural scripts 21, 32
Culture 22, 57, 64–66, 109, *112*, 120, 138, 165, 177–78; common 65, *68*; ecosystem of 21, **64–66**, 77, 149, 161, 165; *see also* ecosystems, seven
Culture of concern 65–66
'Culture of critical discourse' 65, 166
Cultures 106, 120, 137

Culture wars 65
Curricula 4, 8, 51, 66, 75, 91, 104, 111, 120–21, 137–38, 176
Curriculum as an ecosystem **113–125**
Cybernetic world 21

Deep ecology: *see* ecology, deep
Democracy 6, 20, 124, 151
De-territorialization 21, 49, 118
Development Goals 43–44
Dialectic *13*
Digital revolution 6, 34, 104, 172
Disciplines 18, 23, 26, 36–38, 53, 65, *68*, 81, 163, 174–75; STEM 58
Disembeddedness 100; *see also* embeddedness
Dispositions 12, 100–01, 104, 110, 123, 135; *see also* ecological dispositions
'Dissensus' 3, 166
Diversity 10, 17–18, 121, 177
Divine, the 179
Doctors 127, 129, 134, 136, *139*; *see also* medicine
Drama 162

Earth 2, 6, 9, 12, 23–24, 34, 39–40, 43, 47, 49–51, *54*, 67, 69, 74–76, 78, 87, 90, 94, 112, 123–24, *139*, 150–52, 163, 170, 172–74, 176, 179–80, 184
Ecological agency 12, 68, 151
Ecological authenticity 131
Ecological capital 27
Ecological crisis 18–19
Ecological differentiation 150
Ecological disposition 36, 47, 74, 84
Ecological environment 11
Ecological epistemology 11
'Ecological ethics' 39
Ecological ethos 11, 77
Ecological feeling 39
Ecological footprint 48, 148
Ecological health 46, 57
Ecological hinterland 73
Ecological implicatedness 180
Ecological inquiry 11, **86–98**
'Ecological intelligence' 124
Ecological interests 89, 93
Ecological journey 172
Ecological learner: *see* learner, ecological
Ecological leanings 59, 77, 114, 173, 176
Ecological learning 86

Ecological movement 42
Ecological orientation 37
Ecological otherness 11
Ecological pattern 67
Ecological philosophy 23
Ecological positioning 176
Ecological potential 57, 79
Ecological professionalism 11, **126–140**
Ecological profile 10, 37, 67
Ecological perspective 10
Ecological possibilities: *see* possibilities
Ecological registers 130, 173
Ecological signature 37
Ecological situation 77, 180
Ecological spirit 37, 39, 77
Ecological thinking 27, 148
Ecological university: *see* university, the ecological
'Ecological wisdom' 37, 70, 163
'Ecologies of practice' 36
Ecology 4–6, 8, 11, 17, 38, *41*, 73–74, 172
Ecology, concept of 1, 8, 10, 18–19, 23, 27, 36, 44–45, 49, 74, 87, 129, *139*, 177
Ecology, deep 12, 18, 66, 129, *169*, 176–77, *181*
Ecology, discursive 132
Ecology, global 37
Ecology, human *28*
Ecology, narrative of 38–39
'Ecology of higher education' 145
'Ecology of magic' 178
Ecology, shallow 66
Ecology, social 11, 67, **69–70**
Economics 2, *68*, 90, 130, 165
Economy 7–8, 21–22, 51, 76, 171, 177; economy as ecosystem 21, 61–63, 137, 149–50; *see* ecosystems, seven
Eco-philosophy 5–6, *13*, 18, 23, 27, 38, 49
Ecosphere 11, 68, 113, 158, 176
Ecosophy 10–11, 18, 27, 133, 135
Ecosystem 5, 10, 18, 50, 55, 70, 126
Ecosystems 9–10, 17–18, 20–21, 24, 26–27, 32, 34, 37–38, 45–46, 51, 53, 55, 69–70, 78–79, 83, 94, 99, 109, 111, 114–15, 118–121, 123, 129, 134, 137, 144, 163, 165, 174, 176–78
Ecosystems, seven 4, 9, 11, **19**, 22–23, 39–40, 42, 46–47, 50, 56, 63, 67, 74, 76–77, 81, 90, 92, 106, 109, 113, 116, 137, 148, 161, 173, 176–77; *see also* Knowledge; Social Institutions; Persons; Economy; Learning; Culture; Environment, natural
Eco-university 11, 75, 84, *85*
Education 81, 104, 162, 179
Emancipation 87, 91, 94, 177
Embeddedness 121
Embodiment 57, 92, 97
Emergence 10, *12*, 24, 34–35, 48, 115, 151, 164, 168
Empirical warrant 12, 167
Empiricism, radical *12*
Employability 162–63, 171
Empty signifier 78
Engagement 34–35, 48, 131, 134, **141–44**, 158; asymmetrical engagement 142; 'regimes of' 37
Engineering 36, 40, 67, 81, 121, 162
Entanglement 12, 33–34, **143–45**, 152, 172, 174
Environment, natural 43, 47–8, 66, 74–75, 92, 109, 114, *125*, 138, 158, 167; *see also* Ecosystems, seven
Epistemic generosity 182
'Epistemicide' 182
Epistemic legitimacy 89
Epistemic mélange 56
Epistemic orientation 89
Epistemic responsibility 133
Epistemic struggle 88
'Epistemic virtues' 101
Epistemological abundance 97
Epistemological buoyancy 47
Epistemological contamination 88, 90
Epistemological footprint 46, 78–79, 93
Epistemological habitus 46
Epistemological health 57
Epistemological interest 97
Epistemological openness 78–79
Epistemological otherness 98
Epistemological profit 97
Epistemological stance 88, 98, 174
Epistemological surplus 98
Epistemological trajectories 79
Epistemology 18–19, 66, 89, 94; North-South 57
Equity 36, 52, 91
Ethics 11, 27, 40, 48, 63, 114, 130, *139*
'Ethno-epistemic assemblages' 56, 97
Ethos 11, 53, 65, 75, 77

Subject index

Expressive elements 11, 32, 126; *see also* material elements
Europe 4, 96, 139
Excellence 3, 40, 163
Exploration 116

Fearlessness 9, 73, **80–82**
Feasibility 3, 12, **166–68**, 172
Feminism 23
Flourishing 65
Flows 53
Fluidity 20, **114**
Fragility 106, 177
Frameworks 79, 136, 165, 175
Frankfurt School *125*, *180–81*; *see also* Critical Theory
Freedom 7, 11, 52, 83, 91, 124, 159, 171, 175

General education 119–122
Generosity 65
Geology 108, 114
Geo-philosophy 49
Germany 31, 86
Global citizens, students as 37–38, 51, 99, 109, 123, 160
Globality 145–46, 174
Globalization 6, 34, 60, 77, 106, 163, 178
Glue 31
God 61, *153*
Goods 158
Graduate attributes 120

'Habitus' 77
Hermeneutics 57, 77, 143–44
Higher education 1, 26, 31, 47, 52, 68, 110, 119, 124; idea of 3–4; philosophy of 4
History 149
Homelessness 38, 96
Hope 3
Hopelessness 3
Horizons 36, 48, 50–51, 76, 103–04, 131, 136–37, 139, 160–61
Human being 120, 129, 178
Humanities 2, 57, 59, *68*, 116–17, 171, 175
Humanity 2, 6, *13*, 17–19, 27, 42–43, 49, *54*, 66, 70, 74–76, 86–88, 129, *139*, 178, *180*
Humour 133, 135, 138, 179

'Ideal speech situation' 81, 95, 138–39
Ideas 20, 30–31, 36, *40*, 81, 84, 136, 177
Ideology 1, 4, 35, 84, 88, 94, 103, 159
Identity 127, 133, 161–62
Imaginary 27
Imagination 9, 12, 27, 70, 79–80, 84, 91, 114, 135, 139, 141, 170–71, *181*, 184
'*Imagining the University*' 170–71
Impact 17, 24, 62, 144, 162, 175
Impairment 10, 17–18, 35, 50, 69–70, 87, 158, 165, 176–77
Imprisonment of academics 6, 20, 35, 159
Improvement 50, 74–76, 94
Inequality 52, 92, 165
Infinity 96
Inquiry 11; *see also* ecological inquiry; knowledge inquiry
Institutional being 150
Institutional grasp 68, **157–59**, 168
Instrumentalism 75–76, 79, 93, 100, 113, 115, 143–44
Integrity 101, 158–59
Intellectual property 86
Interconnectedness 1, 9, 17, 19, 27, 33, 38, 46, 65, 100, 106, 120, 129–30; *see also* connectedness
Interdisciplinarity 36, *41*
Interests 69, 89, 94; *see also* knowledge interests
'Internal conversations 60
Internationalisation 21
Internet 111, 174
Intersectionality 32

Judgement 135–36, 157–58, 161, *168*
Justice 91, 124

Kaleidoscopes 32
Knowledge 27, 36, 63, 78–79, 87–88, 92, 97, 101, 113, 165, 171, 173–74; democratic 98; hermeneutic 87; indigenous 57, 77; 'Mode 2' 97; professional 97, 130; 'socialist' 98
Knowledges 132, 134; North-South 163
Knowledge activities 93
Knowledge as ecosystem 19, 21, 32, 44, 50, 56–58, 77, **86–98**, 130, 137, 161, 164–65, 177; *see also* ecosystems, seven

Knowledge capitalism 63, 99, 182
Knowledge for-its-own-sake 87–88
Knowledge inquiry 95
Knowledge interests 57–58, **87–89**, **92–94**, 95, 97
Knowledge policy 98
Knowledge production 56, 87
Knowledge resources 86
Knowledge society 34, 56
Knowledge structures 130
Knowledge systems 58, 86

Languages 51, 77, 122, 136, 149
Leadership 33, *53*, 167, 180
Learner, ecological 11, 99, 106, 107–08, **109–111**; lifewide 101–02; liquid 99–101, 110
Learning 4, 8, 63, 86, 103, **107**, 113, **116**, 117–18, 137, 149; digital 104, 111; extra-mural 77, 103, 105; informal *111*; lifewide 77, 99, 102, 107, 109, 111; liquid 100–102; problem-based 104; service 102, 104; virtual 104; work-based 104
Learning analytics 7
Learning as ecosystem 21, 50, 63–64, 77–78, **99–112**, 149–50, 164–66, 177; *see also* ecosystems, seven
Learning biography 103, 108
Learning communities 63
Learning encounters 107
Learning ecologies *112*, 114
Learning experiences 104–05, 115, 117
Learning horizons: *see* horizons
Learning organizations 63
Learning outcomes 37, 119
Learning self 105
Learning processes 63, 95–96
Learning repertoire 121
Learning society 63
Learning systems 108, 151
Legal studies 37, 81, 138
Liberal arts 120
Life chances 43
Lifespan 77
Lifeworld 50, 77, 94, 100, 102, 105, 110
Liquid world 20, 100, 110, **174**; *see also* learner, liquid
Liminality 38
'Lines of flight' 19, 22, *28*, 114, *125*, 175, 183

Machines 68
Management 75, 167
Markets 6, *28*, 38, 119, 146, 172
Material elements 11, 32, 126; *see also* expressive elements
Medicine 37, 81, 114, 127, 158, 179
Memoranda of understanding 38, 142
Middle Ages 2, 33
Modernity 3
Multiculturality 122, 145
Multimodality 57
Music 102

Nanotechnology 34
Narrative: *see* ecology, narrative of
Nature *12*, 66, *70*, 121, 176–77, *180–81*
Neoliberalism 163, 172
Networking 33, 112, 128–29
Networks 97, 108–09, **128–29**, 132, 162, 178
New public management 134
No-platforming speakers 84
Nomadic spaces 11, 100, **115–18**, 133
Nomadic learners 105–107
North-South 77, 163, 182
Nursing studies 59, 114

Ontology *12*, 18, *28*, *40*, 79, 94, 133, *169*; *see also* social ontology
Openness 6–7, *28*, 31, 36–37, 48, 50–51, 55, 65, 75, 81, 84, 88, 91, 104, 118, **124**, 162–64; ontological 30
Open society 6
Optimism 171, 173, 184

Particularity 12, 123, 162–63, 167–68, 171
Pedagogical discomforting 78
Pedagogical relationships 53, 75, 78, 104, 138
Performance management 7, *13*
Pedagogical uncertainty 115, 117; *see also* risk, pedagogy of; strangeness, pedagogy of
Performativity 3, 7, 83, 139, 172
Performing arts 57
Persons, ecosystem of 21, 61, 149, 164–66, 177; *see also* ecosystems, seven
Pessimism 7, 96
Pharmaceutical companies 50, 128, 142, 158

Physics 144,, 158
Pharmacy 40, 50, 81
Philosophy 7, 36–37, 91, 114, 130; social 167
Planes of university 12, 63
Planning 50, 165
Poets 134
Political sphere 37, 183
Policy 92, 160, 165
Possibilities 1–2, 22, 24, 35–36, 76, 78, 119, 147, 167, 170, 172, 174, 176–77; paths of 27, 35, 70, 114; ecological 10, 26, 39, 114, 152, 159, 177, *181*; knowledge 58
Post-truth 65, 88, *98*, *181*
Poverty 92, 158
Power 40, 51, 57–58, 84, 142–43, 159, 164, 175, 183; cognitive 59
Powers 164
Practices 158, 160
Practising epistemologists 134
Practising ontologists 134
Problems 83
Professional being 126–27, 134–35
Professional courses 52
Professional ecosophy 133, 135
Professional identity 127
Professional life 126, 129, 134–35
Professional, networked 128
Professional practices 130
Professional registers **132**, 133–36
Professional self 130
Professional sustainability 131
Professionalism 11, 57, **126–140**, 129–30, 136–37, 167; authentic 128; ecological 131, 136–38; liquid 129; nomadic 133; 'Soul of' 131
Prosthetics 58
Psychology 104
Public art 21
Public domain 147
Public goods 62, *153*
Public intellectuals 91, 147
Public realm 2, 95
Publics 2, 96
Public sphere 2, 7, 12, 27, 63, 91, 95, 146, *152*, 158–59
Public understanding 37, 52, 58, 63, 97–98, 144, 146, 163, 165

Qualities 12, 100–01, 110, 123, 135

Rankings, world 1, 7, 26, 39, 59, 143, 172, 174, 182
Range 12, 160, 168
Rationality 13, 64
Rational society, the 95
Real, the 20
Realism 6, 8–10, 29–30, *40*, 159, 171, 173, 184
Reason 3, 7, 30–31, 65, 81, 139, 157, 159; critical 81–82; ecological 10, 113, 124; economic 113; instrumental 10, 18, 57, 75, 93, 113, *125*, 172–73, 175, 178–79, *181*; see also Instrumentalism; practical 90; public 147, 159; 'scholastic' 90; space of 65, 81, 147, 151; 'synthetic' 124; technical 28
'Recontextualisations' 119
Relationality 82, 119, *153*
Religion 50
Repetition *54*
Research 7–8, 34–35, 66, 75, 87, 91–92, 100, 119, 144, 149, 158–59, 161, 171, 176; participatory 92
Responsibilities 8, 19, 23–24, 46, 128; university 1, 19, 27, 55, 69, 84, 180
Responsibility 6, 8, 17–19, 40, 61, 82, 102, 104, 116, 132–33, 137, 148, 177, *181*; pedagogical 103; professional 11, 131, **133**; social 145
Restoration 17–18
Re-territorialization 21, 162, 182
Revolution 2, 24, 26, 79, 184
'Rhizome' 20, 56, 121
Rightness 83–84
Risk 116, 138, 166; pedagogy of 117, 149
Robbins Report *68*, 120
Ruins: *see* 'University in ruins'

Satisfaction, student 1, 35, 37, 61, 65, 80, 148, 165, 167
Scariness 116
Scholasticism 49, 90
Science 50, *54*, 59, 89, 91, 117
Scope 12, 160, 168
Self-belief 117
Self-organization 45, 47, 69, 110
Self-reproduction 45, 47, 69–70
Self-sustaining students 105, 110–111
Sensuousness 12, **178–79**
Service 62, 148; *see also* learning, service

Subject index

Singularity 26, 40
'Singularization' 25, 101, *111*
Skills 63, 101, 113, 120, 171
Social ecology **69–70**, 109, 121
Social institutions 48, 59, 137, 158, 177; as ecosystem 21, 50, 58–60, 109, 149, 161, 164–65; *see also* ecosystems, seven
Social media 147
Social mobility 159
Social ontology 9; *see also* ontology
Social science 91, 116–17
Social work 81, 133, 165
Society, the therapeutic 60
Sociology 36, 40, 165
Space 9, 20, 87, 160, 171; educational 124; universal 123
Space of university 2, 6, 52, 63, *68*
'Space of flows' 67, 105
Spaces 126, 135, 138, 161; clinical 127; cognitive 175; curriculum 117; hermeneutic 152; learning 99, 101–02, 104–05, 110–111; smooth 115–16, 118; striated 115–16, 118; *see also* nomadic spaces; reason, space of
Spirit 9, *85*, 133, 179; ecological spirit 9, 93
Sports studies 37
Squid 121, 125; *see also* university as
Standards 103
State, the 60, 159, 175; 'The evaluative state' *181*
Stickiness 31–32, 35–36
Strangeness 82, 115–16; pedagogy of 149
Student 4, 110, 110, 117–18, 138
Student as producer 33, *41*
Student experience 21, 37
Student radical movements 108
Students 7–8, 25–26, 52, 66, 77, 91, 99, 101–02, 104–05, 107, 116, 121, 138, 149, 161
Students, international 2, 32, 34, 182
Subjectivity 60
Subversion 85, 159
Supercomplexity 19, 33, 100–01, **135–137**, 175
Surveillance 6, 58, 60, 127
Sustainability 11, **42–54**, 73–74, 76, 108, *112*, 117, 131, 161
Systems 32, 45; open 151

Talloires Declaration 145–47
Teaching 7–8, 35, 75, 80, 119, 158, 171; research-led 40
Territorialization 21; *see also* de-territorialization; re-territorialization
Theology 36, 90, 130
Theory and practice 90–91, 174
Thinking 82–84, 166
'Threshold concepts' 116
Time 9, 20, 110, 126–27, *139*, 160, 169, 171
Timeframes 110, 127, 135, 137–38, 160
Timefulness 160–61, 167–68
Time-space complexes 127
Totality 95
Tradition, Great 3–4
Transcendentalism 75–76
Transgressivity *28*, **36–38**, *41*, 137
Trigger warnings 119, 167
'Triple helix' 57
Trojan horses 55, 82
Trust 54, 77, 106, 130
Truth 3, 7, *68*, 81, **88**, *98,* 171; *see also* post-truth
Truthfulness 31, 81, 159, 163, 172

Uncertainty 137
Undermining of the university 2–4, 6, *12*
Understanding 63, 87, 120, 137
Understanding the University 170–71
United Nations 43–44; *see also* development goals
Universality 12, 18, 36, 39–40, 100–01, 120, 123–24, 162–63, 168
Universities 5, 19, 21, 37, 51, 57–59, 61–62, 70, 107, 142, 145, 160; Berlin (*Germany*) *31;* Birkbeck College (UK) *31;* Bradford (UK) 85; Brighton (UK) *152;* Durham (UK) 25; Essex (UK) 31; Keele (UK) 31; Lancaster (UK) 85; Lincoln (UK) *41;* Manchester (UK) *68;* Open (UK) 31; Princeton (USA) 25; Sussex (UK) 31; Third Age (UK) 63; Warwick (UK) 25; University College London 25, 31; York (UK) 31; world community of 12
University as corporate agent 35, 172
University as critical institution 174
University as idea 30, 54, 86, 171, 184
University as institution 8–9, 159, 171, 183–84

University as squid 20, *125*; *see also* squid
University as worldly 36
University, being a 19, 26
University, distributed 162
University, forms of: the corporate 53; the differentiated 150; the digital 53; the entrepreneurial 7, 22, 24, 53, 76, 157, 168, 170–73, 179; the ethical 9; the exploring 78; the fearless 84; the intolerant 52; the principled 84; the research 80, 87; the revolutionary 53; the stretched 38; 'the sustainable university' 42, 53, 66, 75; the thinking 73, 82–84
University-for-the-world 148, 152
University-from-the-world 148, 152
University-in-the-world 148
University in crisis 1
'*University in ruins*' 1, 3, 6, 168
University of life 104
University, the 2–3, 7, 22, 24, 33–34, 36, 64, 67, 79, 87–88, 95, 148, 160, 171, 176
University, the ecological 1–3, 5, 8–12, 20, 24, 26–27, 30, 33, 36–40, 46–47, 50–53, 59, 62, **67**, 69–70, 73–75, 77, 79–80, 82–83, 86, 88–91, 93, 95, 97, 111, **113**, 123, 141, 143–44, **157–68**, *169*, 171, 173–77, 179–81, 183

Unpluggability 30
Utility *68*
Utopia 10, 79, 167, 172; feasible 10, 12, 80, 167, **172–173**, 184

Validity claims 81
Values 5, 58–59, 70, 78, 87, 89–90, 106, 110, 113, 119, *125*, 127, 138, *139*, 142, 172, 183
Virtues *125*, 158–59
Viscosity 32
Vocation 89

Wellbeing 7, 9, 12, 17, 24, 42, 46, 48, 52, 60, 62, 74, 78, 81, 83–84, *85*, 108, 136–37, 162, 164–65, 168, 172, 177; global *54*, 165; individual 99, 108, 149
Wisdom 6, *68*
Wisdom, ecological 6
World 2, 44–46, 69, 74–75, 79, 100, 137, 139, 157, 164, 174–76, 178–80; *see also* being, worldly
'World-class' universities 3, 40
World community 51, *125*, 146, 183–84; *see also* community, global
Work 102, 109
Work-life balance 135

Zones 8, 37, 56; ecological 22, **56–66**

NAME INDEX

Abram, D *85*, 178
Adorno, T 60, 83, 178
Annette, J *125*
Albrow, M 68
Araha, D 64
Archer, M 60, 136
Aristotle 145
Aronowitz, S *169*
Assister, A 51
Araya, D *112*
Arvanitakis, J *169*
Astley, J *125*

Bachelard, G 39
Bakken, T 45
Badiou, A *13*, 106
Bakhurst, D 65, 81
Barber, M 122
Barnacle, R 57
Barnett, R *12*, 19, 31, 61, 64, 70, 79–80, 83, *85*, 88, 95, 100, 102–03, 115, *125*, 136, 146, 157, 167
Bartlett, P *53*
Batchelor, D 115
Bateson, G 112
Bauman, Z 100
Bekhradnia, B 7
Beloff, M *41*
Bendik-Keymer, J *139*
Bengtsen, S 83
Bennett, J 66

Benton, T *169*
Bergan, S 153
Bergson, H *180*
Bernstein, B 47, 119
Bhaskar, R 5–6, *12–13*, 24, *28*, 34, *40–41*, 51–52, *54, 85*, 151, *153*, 159, *168*
Bird, S 148
Bleiklie, I *68*
Bloom, A 120
Bok, D *28*
Bolden, R 167
Bonhoeffer, D 122
Bonnett, M 66
Bookchin, M *70*
Bourdieu, P 49, 77, 88–90
Bourner, T 148
Boutang, M 51, *68*, 93, 173
Bouzanis, C *169*
Brady, M 101
Bragg, E 110
Briggs, A *41*
Brown, R *28*
Brubacher, J S 3
Buber, M 82

Calhoun, C 87, 146
Cantwell, B 7, 62
Carlin, M *54*
Carriere, J-C 5, 183
Castells, M 53, 67, 105, 128
Castoriadis, C *180*

Chase, G *53*
Chataway, J 86
Chiosa, S *68*
Christian Wells, E *53*
Clark, B R *13, 98*
Clayton, P 85
Coate, K 115
Cohen, T *68*
Cole, D *54*
Comte-Sponville, A 85
Connell, R 44
Cooper, D 131
Cornell, S *41*
Cousin, G 123
Cranfield, S 125
Critchley, S 2
Crosling, G *111*

Dall'Alba, G 57
DeLanda, M 5, 21, 29, 32, *40–41, 68*, 124
Deleuze, G 5–7, *12–13*, 19, 21–23, 27, *28*, 29, 34, 44, 50, *54*, 100, 107, 115, 118, 121, 125, *180*, 183
Deneulin, S 62
Derrida, J 3, *68, 98*, 107, 177
Descartes, R 64
de Sousa Santos, B 44, 57, 142
Dienstag, J 96
Dill, D 92
Di Napoli, R 61
Donati, P *153*
Donnelly, K 122
Duke, C 63
Dunne, J *28*

Eagleton, T 64, 107
Ecclestone, K 7
Eco, U 5, 183
Einstein, A 178
Etxkowitz, H 57

Fanghanel, J 123
Feuerbach, L 178
Ferry, V 140
Feyerabend, P 98, 178, *181*
Feyman, R 178
Fichte, J *125*
Filippakou, O *152*
Finnegan, R 38, 95
Fleming, T 68
Foster, C *169*

Fox, C 6
Fransman, J 79, 141
Freidson, E 131
Freud, S 60
Fuchs, C *54*
Fulford, A *12*
Fung, D 35, *85*
Funtowicz, S *41*
Furedi, F 61, 65

Gadamer, H-G 7, *85,* 103
Gallie, W 31, 142
Gansmo Jacobsen *13*
Gellner, E 62, 65, 97, *181*
Gibbons, M *28, 41, 68*
Gibbs, P *12, 54, 169*
Giddens, A 100
Gietzen, G 57, 98, 148
Gomes Zuin, V 114
Gordon, P 95
Gouldner, A 88, 166
Gramsci, A 122
Greenberg, J 60
Greenwood, D *153*
Grimm, S *13*
Grun, M *125*
Guattari, F 5–7, *12*, 18–19, 21–27, *28*, 29, 34, 39, *41*, 50, *54, 68*, 87, 100, 107, *111*, 115, 118, 121, 125, 133, 183–84
Guzmán-Valenzuela *40, 54*, 103

Habermas, J 3, 5, *13, 28*, 45, 50, 57, 63–64, *68*, 81, *85*, 87–89, 92, 94–95, *98*, 100, 108, *125, 139*, 146, 148, 151, *152, 181*
Hall, B 92
Hards, L 21
Harman, G *40–41*
Hartwig, M *54*, 150
Harvey, M 167
Hassan, R 57, 60
Hawking, S 178
Hawkins, J 145
Hayes, D 7
Heap, S 125
Hegel, G W *13, 85*, 178
Heidegger, M 5, 65, 82–83, *85*, 103, 106, 109–10, 116, 131, 133
Henkel, M *68*
Heraclitus 44
Hernes, T 45

Name index

Hier, S 60
Hillman, N 65, *68*
Hofkirchner, W *54*
Hopkinson, P 75
Horkheimer, M 60, *125*, 178, *181*
Hornsby, D *169*
Hoyer, K G 6, *13*
Hourdequin, M 66, *181*
Hroch, P *54, 85*
Hung, R 66
Husserl, E *85*
Hutchins, R 120

Iba, T 44
Ignatieff, M 10
Ingold, T 23
Innerarity, D *68*, 98
Irwin, A 56, *68*, 95

Jackson, N 64, 102, 108
Jacobs, S 62
James, P 75
Jarvis, P 104
Jaspers, K 3
Jones, S 167
Jenks, C *28, 40*
Judson, G 121

Kangas, S 183
Kant, I 2, 4, 31, *68*, 122, *125*, 178
Katulushi, C *125*
Kemmis, S 36
Kjaer, P 45, *54*
Kreber, C 104
Kress, G 57
Kweik, M 3

Laclau, E *85*
Land, R 116
Langley, C 57
Lavern, S 121
Law, A 111
Law, P 111
Leavis, F R 4, 117, *125*
Larson, B *28*
Lefebvre, H *28*, 102, *169*
Lehman, G *139, 181*
Levin, M *153*
Levinas, E 96
Leysdedorff, L 57
Lindsay, A D 31

List, C 35
Loftus, S 92, 135
Lopes de Almeida Pacca, J 114
Luhmann, N 45, *54*
Luna, H 42, *53*, 66, 75
Lyotard, J-F 3, 33, 120

Maccarini, A *41*
Macfarlane, B 7, *54*, 119
MacIntyre, A 3–4, 63, 80, 158–59
Mac Labhrainn, I *152*
Marcuse, H 60, 178
Markham, I *125*
Marques Pereira, G da 47
Marginson, S 2, 67, 91
Masquelier, C *181*
Marx, K 60, 178
Maturana, H 45
Maxey, L 42, *53*, 66, 75
Maxwell, N 177
McAfee, N 146
McArthur, J 92
McIlrath, L *152*
McLaughlin, T *125*
Meillassoux, Q *40*
Merleau-Ponty, M 57, *85*, 103
Meyer, J 116
Michael, M 56, *68*, 97
Mickey, S 5–6, 23, 37, 39, 51, 77, 163, *181*
Minogue, K *54*
Mitchell, C *68*
Moisio, S 183
Monk, N 121
Montefiore, A 89
Moog, S *181*
Morton, T 27
Mullins, P 62

Naess, A 5–6, *13, 41*, 66, *181*
Naidoo, R 25, *54*, 165
Nair, M *111*
Naruse, M 44
Neave, G *181*
Neary, M *41*
Newman, J H 3–4, *28*, 61, 87, 121
Newell, E *169*
Niblett, W R 4
Nietzsche, F vi, 131
Nisbet, R 88
Nixon, J *152*

Name index

Nowotny, H *28, 41*, 60, *68*, 127
Nussbaum, M *68*

Oakeshott, M 33
Ondercin, D 57, 98, 148
Ostrum, E 62

Palardy, G 77
Papaioannou, T 86
Parameswaran, R *125*
Parker, J *41*
Pata, K 86
Peters, M A *12*, 21, 31, 50–51, 57, 62–64, *68*, 98, *112*, 122, 148
Peters, R S 122, 149
Pettit, P 35
Petrovic, J *12*
Piketty, T *28*
Pillay, S 121
Pleyers, G 147
Plumwood, V 5, 66, *181*
Popora, D 24, *28*
Pringle, J 25
Pritchard, D 101
Proctor, J *28*
Pusser, B *152*
Putnam, R 111

Rammell, B *153*
Ramsey, I T 123, 179
Readings, B 3, 6, 22, 65, 166
Rhoades, G 7, 62, 67, *68*, 91
Rhoten, D 87
Riggio, A *181*
Rizvi, S 122
Robbins, Lord L *68*, 120
Robinson, D 119
Robinson, S *125*
Rolfe, G *85*
Rommetveit, K *41*
Roszak, T *112*
Rothblatt, S 62
Rustin, M 82
Russell, B 122, 124, 178

Sabri, D 80
Sartre, J-P 60, *85,* 103
Savin-Baden, M 102, *125*
Sayce, S *53*
Schon, D 54
Schopenhauer, A *85*

Schudson, M 120
Schuller, T 63
Scott, P 2, *28, 41, 68*
Scruton, R *28*, 64
Searle, J *40*
Seidl, D 45
Slaughter, S 7, 62, *68*
Sloman, A *41*
Small, H *68*
Smith, B *40*
Smith, J *28, 40*
Sorlin, S 66
Sterling, S 42, *53*, 66
Stiegler, B *111*
Stiglitz, J *28*
Stockhammer, D *68*
Strand, R *41*
Stratford, R 124

Tallis, R 96
Tandon, B 92
Taylor, C 5, 31, 131, *139*
Taylor, R *53*
Temple, P 26, 36
Thevenot, L 37
Thompson, C 109
Tilbury, D *53*
Townsend, N 62

Urry, J 20, 31

Vaithilingam, S 111
Varela, F 45
Varto, J *180*
Vaughan, S 21
Vernon, M *169*
Virilio, P 57, 102
von Humboldt, W 31

Wallin, J *54*
Wals, A 112
Ward, S *68*
Watkins, C 21
Watson, D 26, 63, 79, *152*
Weaver-Hightower, M *28*
Weber, L *153*
Weber, M 89
Wield, D 86
Welikala, T 21
White, J 95
White, R *41*

White, R M *53*
Williams, G 152
Williams, B 88
Williams, J 21
Williams, R 77, 85, *169*
Wilson, A 83
Wittgenstein, L 21, *28*, 124
Wright, S 121

y Gasset, Ortega 3–4, 23, 64
Yilmaz, D *68*
Young, M 31

Zgaga, P *153*
Zizek, S *13, 85*, 117, *125*